THE OCCULTIST®

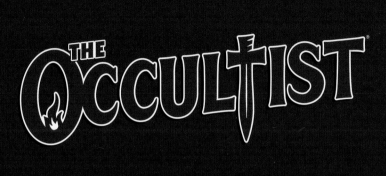

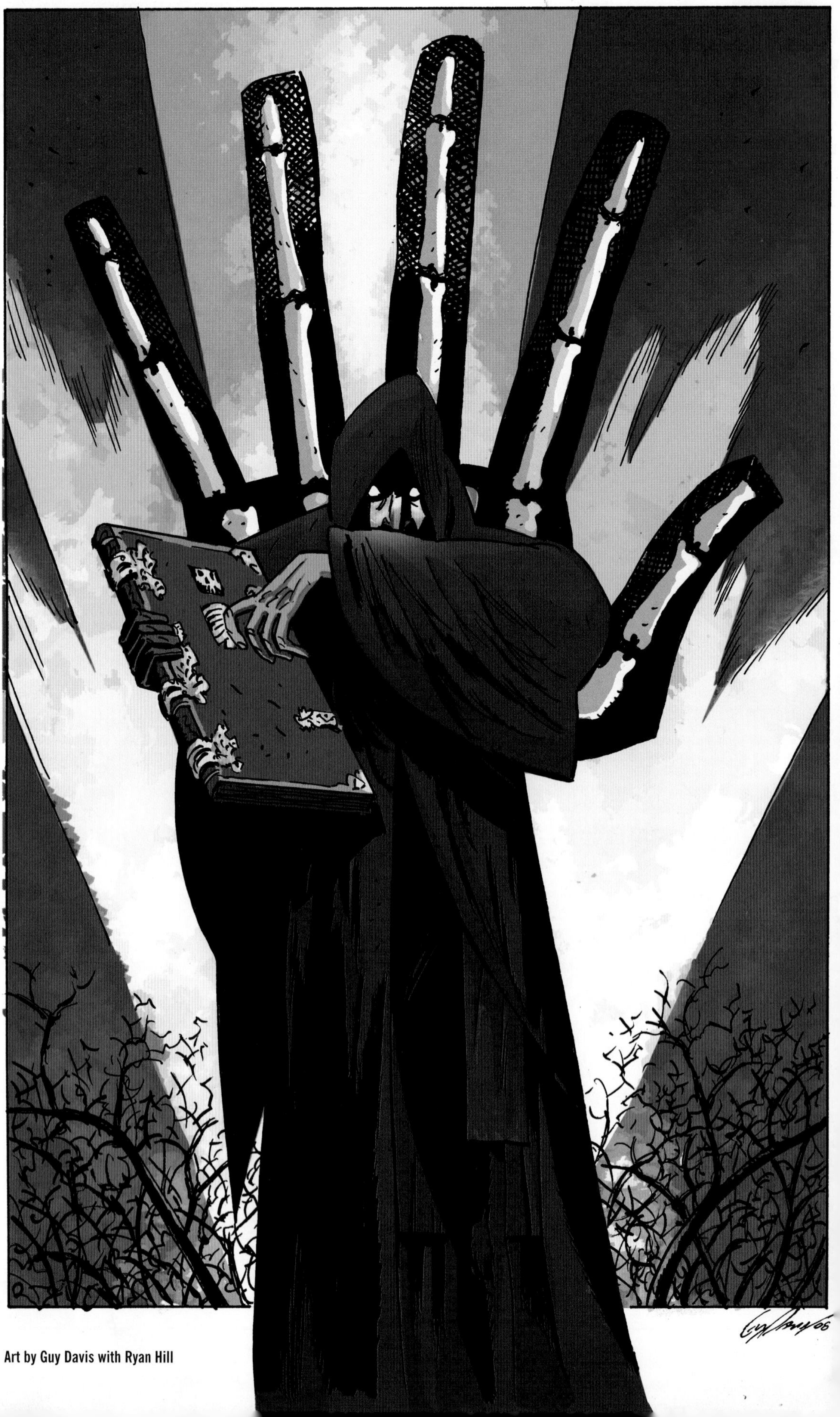

Art by Guy Davis with Ryan Hill

THE OCCULTIST

The Occultist created
and published by Mike Richardson

Story	**MIKE RICHARDSON** and **TIM SEELEY**
Script	**TIM SEELEY**
Art	**VICTOR DRUJINIU**
Chapter 1 inks	**JASON GORDER**
Colors	**ANDREW DALHOUSE**
Letters	**NATE PIEKOS** of Blambot®
Cover art and chapter breaks	**STEVE MORRIS**
The Occultist design	**GUY DAVIS**
Editor	**SCOTT ALLIE**
Assistant editors	**DANIEL CHABON** and **BRENDAN WRIGHT**
Collection designer	**JUSTIN COUCH**

DARK HORSE BOOKS

Published by Dark Horse Books
A division of Dark Horse Comics, Inc.
10956 SE Main Street
Milwaukie, OR 97222

First edition: July 2012

ISBN 978-1-59582-745-6

10 9 8 7 6 5 4 3 2 1

MIKE RICHARDSON President and Publisher • NEIL HANKERSON Executive Vice President • TOM WEDDLE
Chief Financial Officer • RANDY STRADLEY Vice President of Publishing • MICHAEL MARTENS Vice President
of Book Trade Sales • ANITA NELSON Vice President of Business Affairs • DAVID SCROGGY Vice President
of Product Development • DALE LAFOUNTAIN Vice President of Information Technology • DARLENE VOGEL
Senior Director of Print, Design, and Production • KEN LIZZI General Counsel • MATT PARKINSON Senior
Director of Marketing • DAVEY ESTRADA Editorial Director • SCOTT ALLIE Senior Managing Editor • CHRIS
WARNER Senior Books Editor • DIANA SCHUTZ Executive Editor • CARY GRAZZINI Director of Print and Devel-
opment • LIA RIBACCHI Art Director • CARA NIECE Director of Scheduling

This book collects the one-shot *The Occultist*, the series *The Occultist* #1–#3, and "The Occultist" from
Dark Horse Presents #11–#13.

CHAPTER ONE

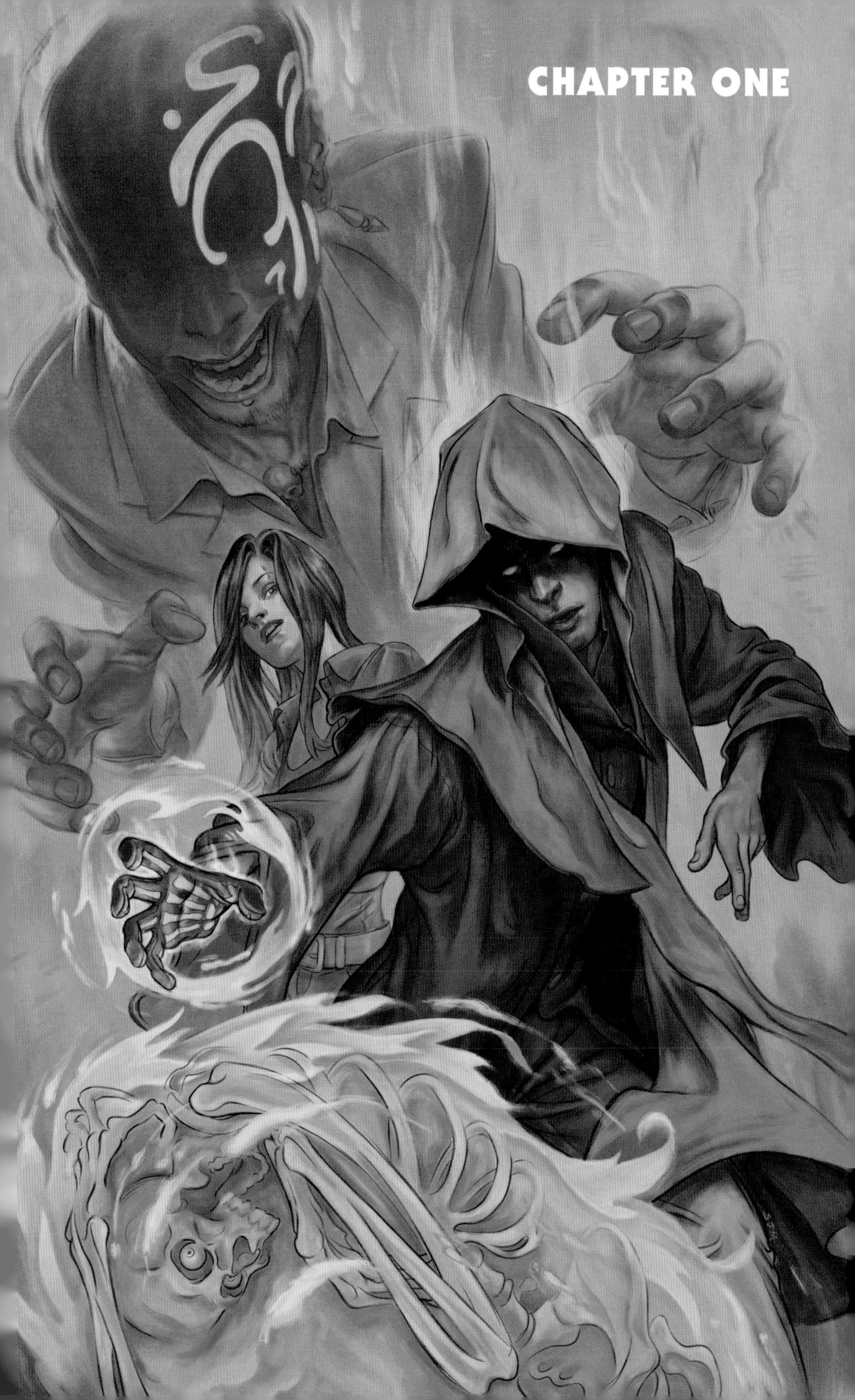

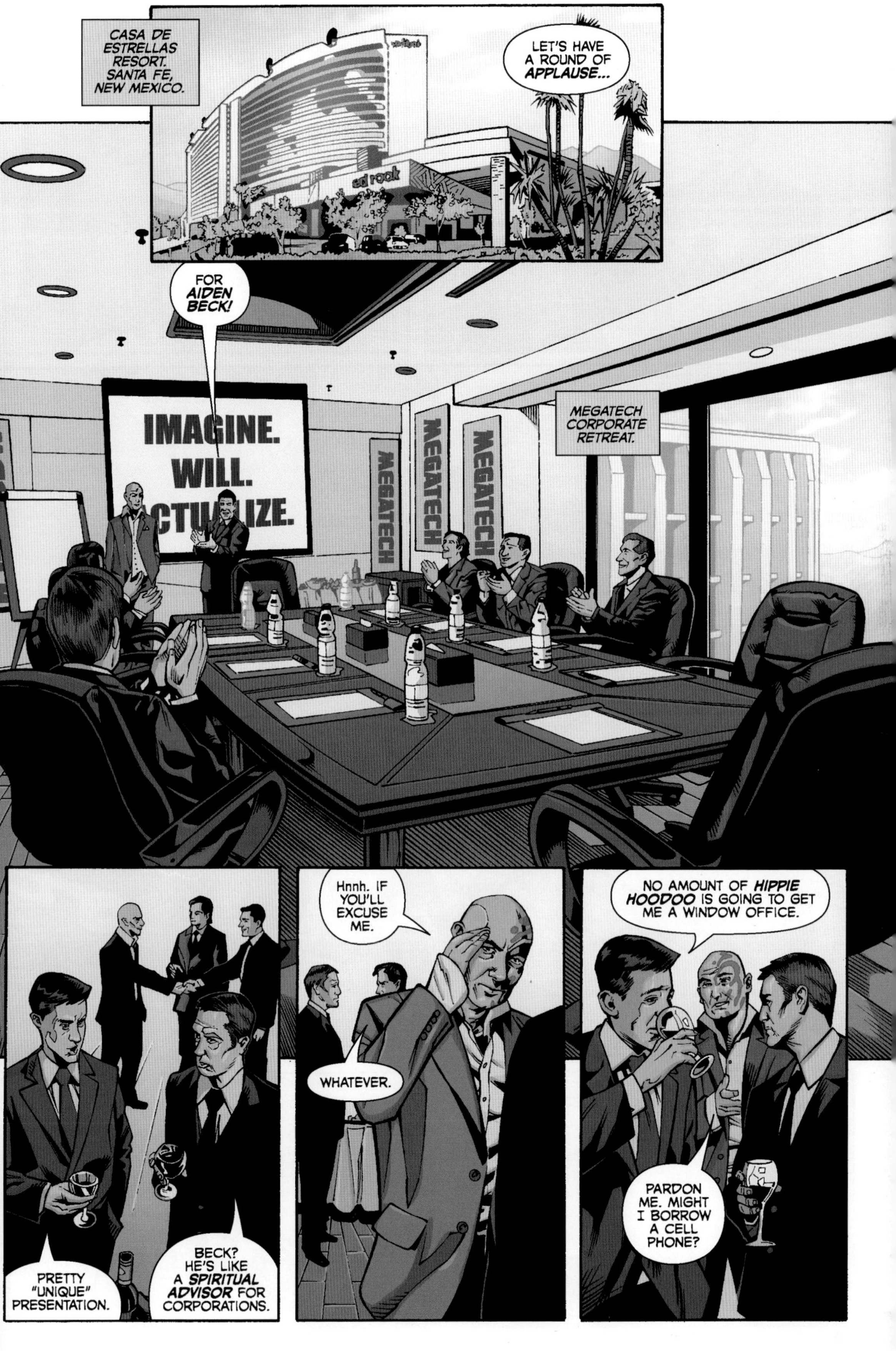
CASA DE ESTRELLAS RESORT. SANTA FE, NEW MEXICO.
LET'S HAVE A ROUND OF *APPLAUSE...*
FOR *AIDEN BECK!*
IMAGINE. WILL. CTUALIZE.
MEGATECH
MEGATECH
MEGATECH
MEGATECH CORPORATE RETREAT.
PRETTY "UNIQUE" PRESENTATION.
BECK? HE'S LIKE A *SPIRITUAL ADVISOR* FOR CORPORATIONS.
Hnnh. IF YOU'LL EXCUSE ME.
WHATEVER.
NO AMOUNT OF *HIPPIE HOODOO* IS GOING TO GET ME A WINDOW OFFICE.
PARDON ME. MIGHT I BORROW A CELL PHONE?

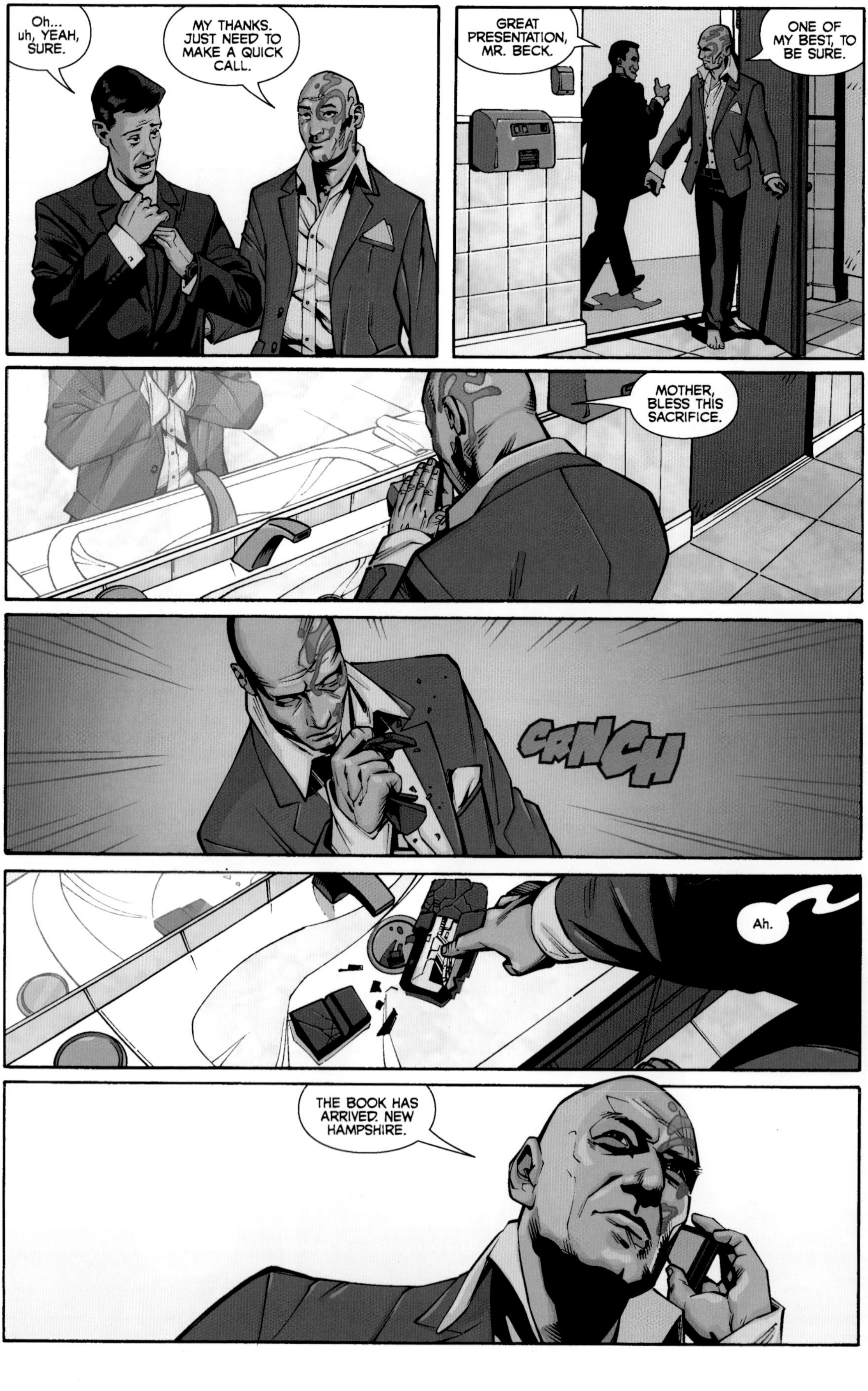
Oh... uh, YEAH, SURE.
MY THANKS. JUST NEED TO MAKE A QUICK CALL.
GREAT PRESENTATION, MR. BECK.
ONE OF MY BEST, TO BE SURE.
MOTHER, BLESS THIS SACRIFICE.
CRNCH
Ah.
THE BOOK HAS ARRIVED. NEW HAMPSHIRE.

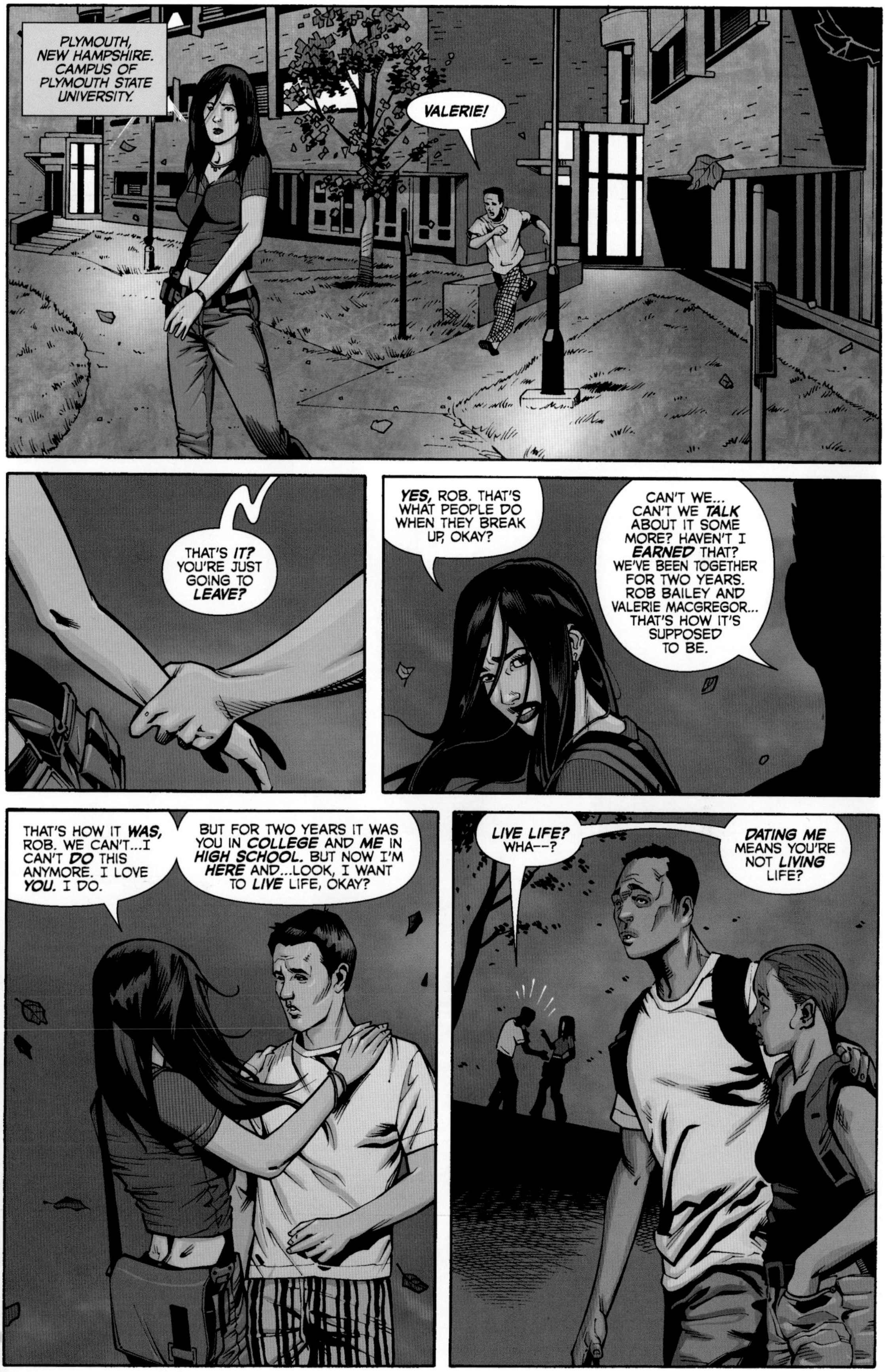
PLYMOUTH, NEW HAMPSHIRE. CAMPUS OF PLYMOUTH STATE UNIVERSITY.
VALERIE!
THAT'S IT? YOU'RE JUST GOING TO LEAVE?
YES, ROB. THAT'S WHAT PEOPLE DO WHEN THEY BREAK UP, OKAY?
CAN'T WE... CAN'T WE TALK ABOUT IT SOME MORE? HAVEN'T I EARNED THAT? WE'VE BEEN TOGETHER FOR TWO YEARS. ROB BAILEY AND VALERIE MACGREGOR... THAT'S HOW IT'S SUPPOSED TO BE.
THAT'S HOW IT WAS, ROB. WE CAN'T...I CAN'T DO THIS ANYMORE. I LOVE YOU. I DO.
BUT FOR TWO YEARS IT WAS YOU IN COLLEGE AND ME IN HIGH SCHOOL. BUT NOW I'M HERE AND...LOOK, I WANT TO LIVE LIFE, OKAY?
LIVE LIFE? WHA--?
DATING ME MEANS YOU'RE NOT LIVING LIFE?

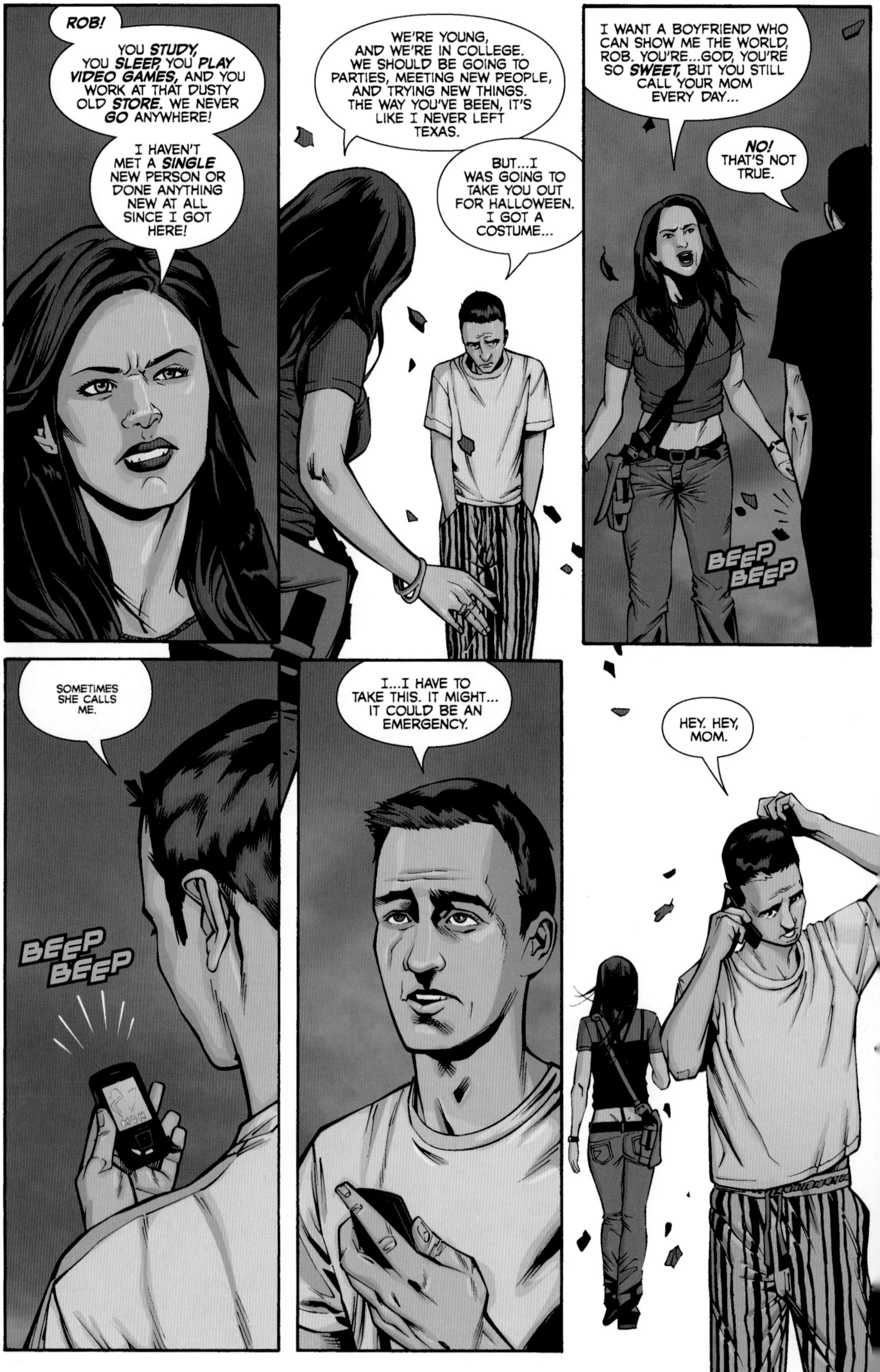
ROB!
YOU STUDY, YOU SLEEP, YOU PLAY VIDEO GAMES, AND YOU WORK AT THAT DUSTY OLD STORE. WE NEVER GO ANYWHERE!
I HAVEN'T MET A SINGLE NEW PERSON OR DONE ANYTHING NEW AT ALL SINCE I GOT HERE!
WE'RE YOUNG, AND WE'RE IN COLLEGE. WE SHOULD BE GOING TO PARTIES, MEETING NEW PEOPLE, AND TRYING NEW THINGS. THE WAY YOU'VE BEEN, IT'S LIKE I NEVER LEFT TEXAS.
BUT...I WAS GOING TO TAKE YOU OUT FOR HALLOWEEN. I GOT A COSTUME...
I WANT A BOYFRIEND WHO CAN SHOW ME THE WORLD, ROB. YOU'RE...GOD, YOU'RE SO SWEET, BUT YOU STILL CALL YOUR MOM EVERY DAY...
NO! THAT'S NOT TRUE.
BEEP BEEP
SOMETIMES SHE CALLS ME.
BEEP BEEP
I...I HAVE TO TAKE THIS. IT MIGHT... IT COULD BE AN EMERGENCY.
HEY. HEY, MOM.

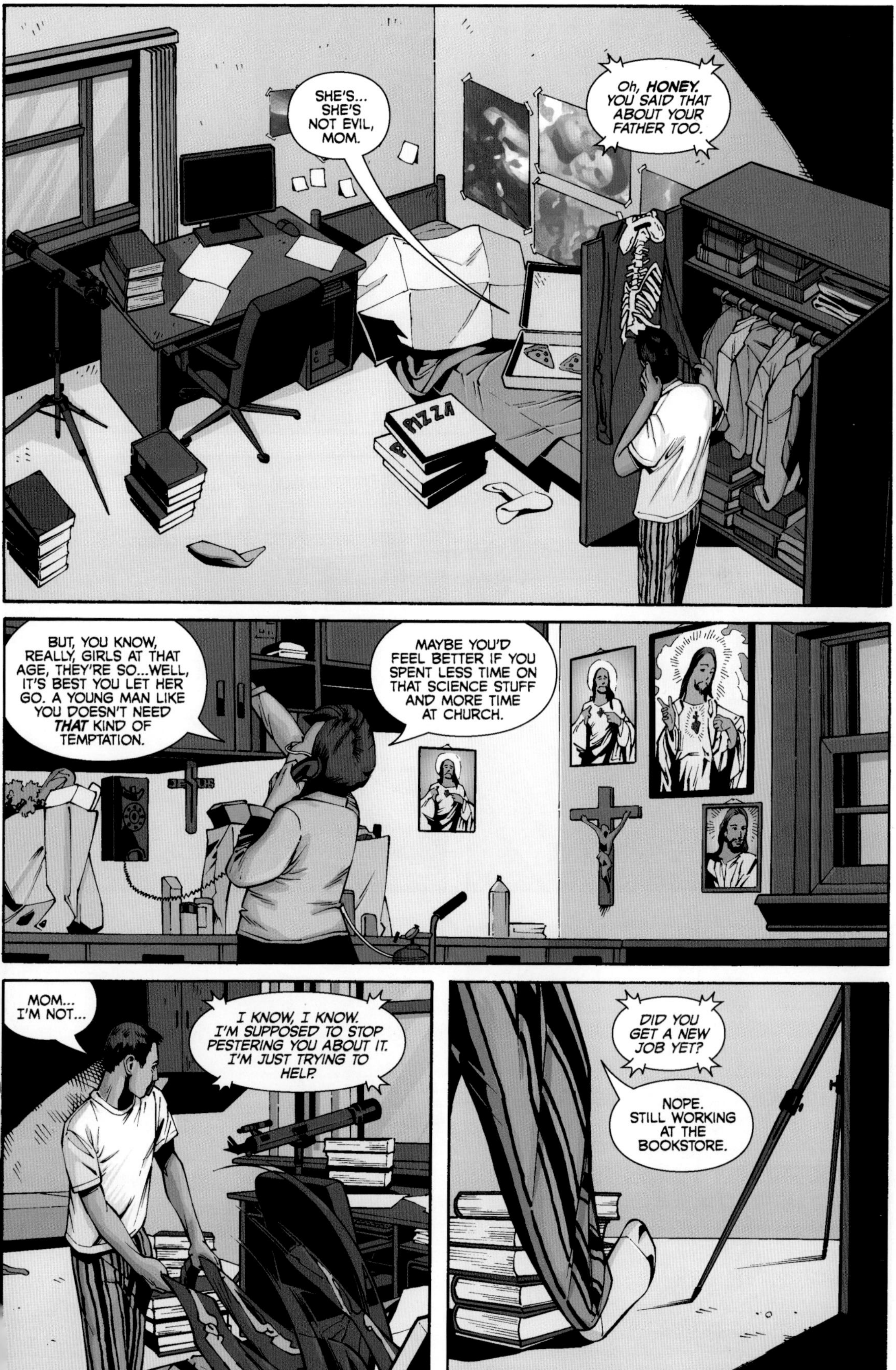

SHE'S... SHE'S NOT EVIL, MOM.
Oh, HONEY. YOU SAID THAT ABOUT YOUR FATHER TOO.
PIZZA
BUT, YOU KNOW, REALLY, GIRLS AT THAT AGE, THEY'RE SO...WELL, IT'S BEST YOU LET HER GO. A YOUNG MAN LIKE YOU DOESN'T NEED THAT KIND OF TEMPTATION.
MAYBE YOU'D FEEL BETTER IF YOU SPENT LESS TIME ON THAT SCIENCE STUFF AND MORE TIME AT CHURCH.
MOM... I'M NOT...
I KNOW, I KNOW. I'M SUPPOSED TO STOP PESTERING YOU ABOUT IT. I'M JUST TRYING TO HELP.
DID YOU GET A NEW JOB YET?
NOPE. STILL WORKING AT THE BOOKSTORE.

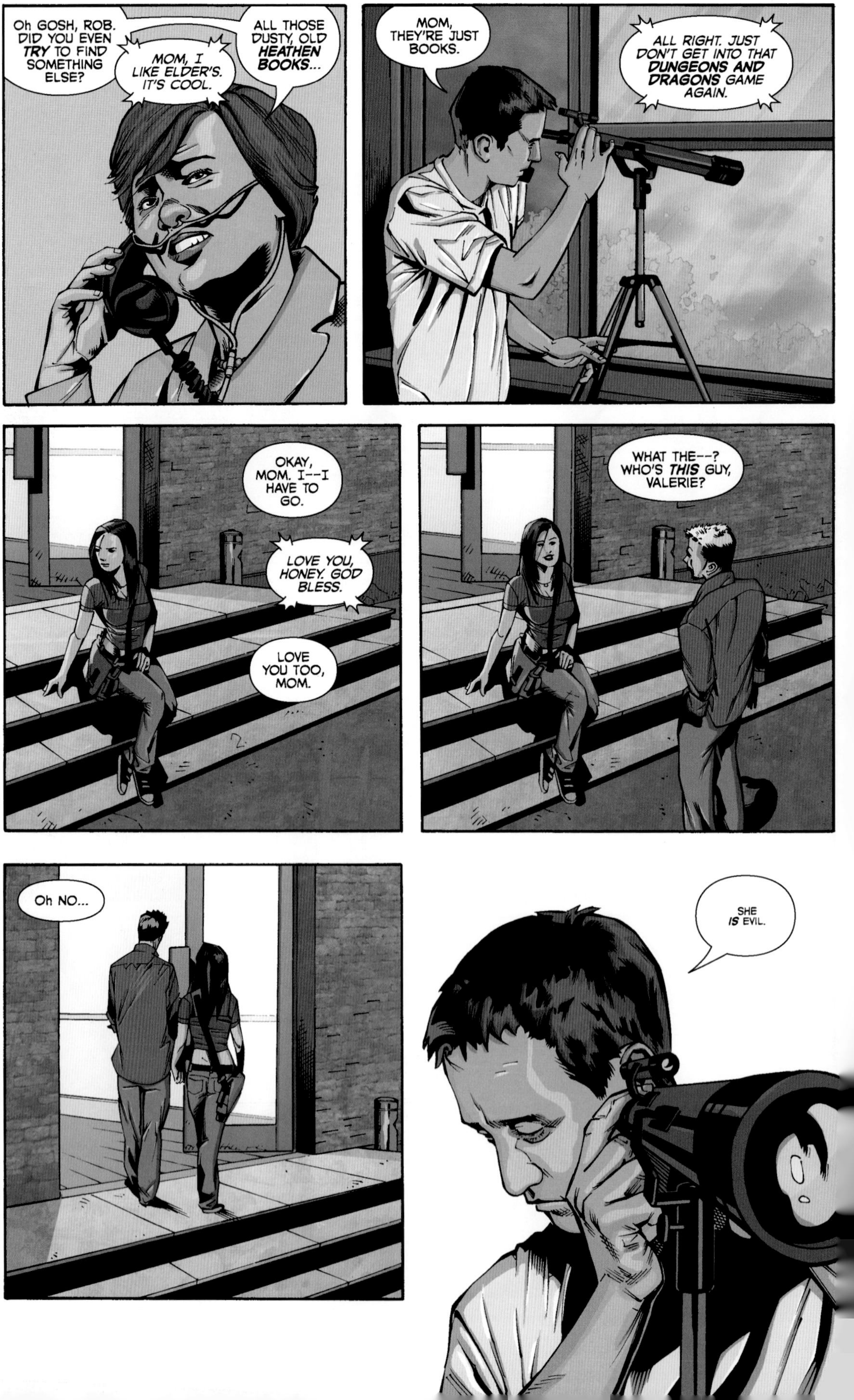
Oh GOSH, ROB. DID YOU EVEN TRY TO FIND SOMETHING ELSE?
MOM, I LIKE ELDER'S. IT'S COOL.
ALL THOSE DUSTY, OLD HEATHEN BOOKS...
MOM, THEY'RE JUST BOOKS.
ALL RIGHT. JUST DON'T GET INTO THAT DUNGEONS AND DRAGONS GAME AGAIN.
OKAY, MOM. I--I HAVE TO GO.
LOVE YOU, HONEY. GOD BLESS.
LOVE YOU TOO, MOM.
WHAT THE--? WHO'S THIS GUY, VALERIE?
Oh NO...
SHE IS EVIL.

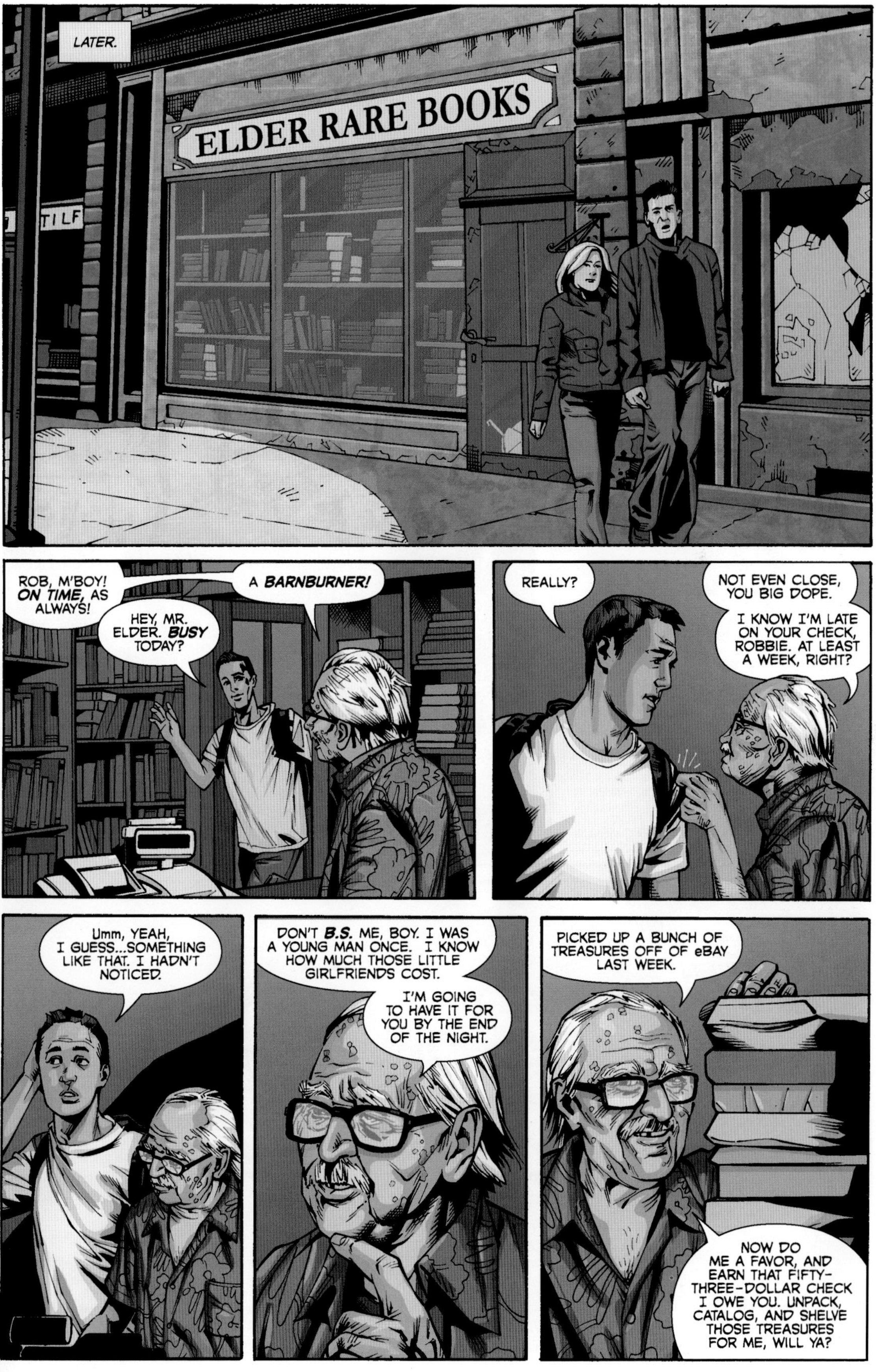
LATER.
ELDER RARE BOOKS
TILF
ROB, M'BOY! ON TIME, AS ALWAYS!
A BARNBURNER!
HEY, MR. ELDER. BUSY TODAY?
REALLY?
NOT EVEN CLOSE, YOU BIG DOPE.
I KNOW I'M LATE ON YOUR CHECK, ROBBIE. AT LEAST A WEEK, RIGHT?
Umm, YEAH, I GUESS...SOMETHING LIKE THAT. I HADN'T NOTICED.
DON'T B.S. ME, BOY. I WAS A YOUNG MAN ONCE. I KNOW HOW MUCH THOSE LITTLE GIRLFRIENDS COST.
I'M GOING TO HAVE IT FOR YOU BY THE END OF THE NIGHT.
PICKED UP A BUNCH OF TREASURES OFF OF eBAY LAST WEEK.
NOW DO ME A FAVOR, AND EARN THAT FIFTY-THREE-DOLLAR CHECK I OWE YOU. UNPACK, CATALOG, AND SHELVE THOSE TREASURES FOR ME, WILL YA?

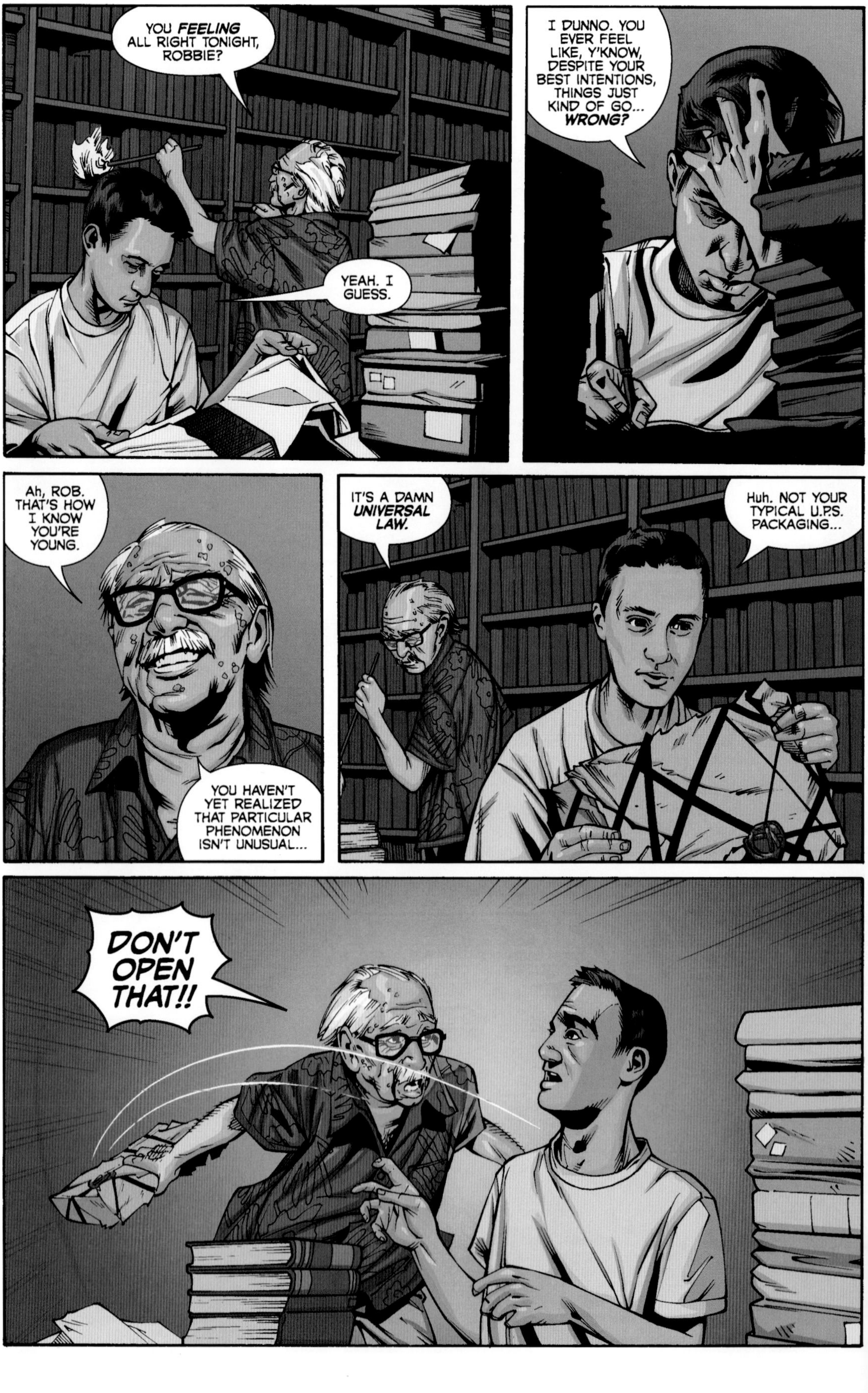
YOU *FEELING* ALL RIGHT TONIGHT, ROBBIE?
YEAH. I GUESS.
I DUNNO. YOU EVER FEEL LIKE, Y'KNOW, DESPITE YOUR BEST INTENTIONS, THINGS JUST KIND OF GO... *WRONG?*
Ah, ROB. THAT'S HOW I KNOW YOU'RE YOUNG.
YOU HAVEN'T YET REALIZED THAT PARTICULAR PHENOMENON ISN'T UNUSUAL...
IT'S A DAMN *UNIVERSAL LAW.*
Huh. NOT YOUR TYPICAL U.P.S. PACKAGING...
DON'T OPEN THAT!!

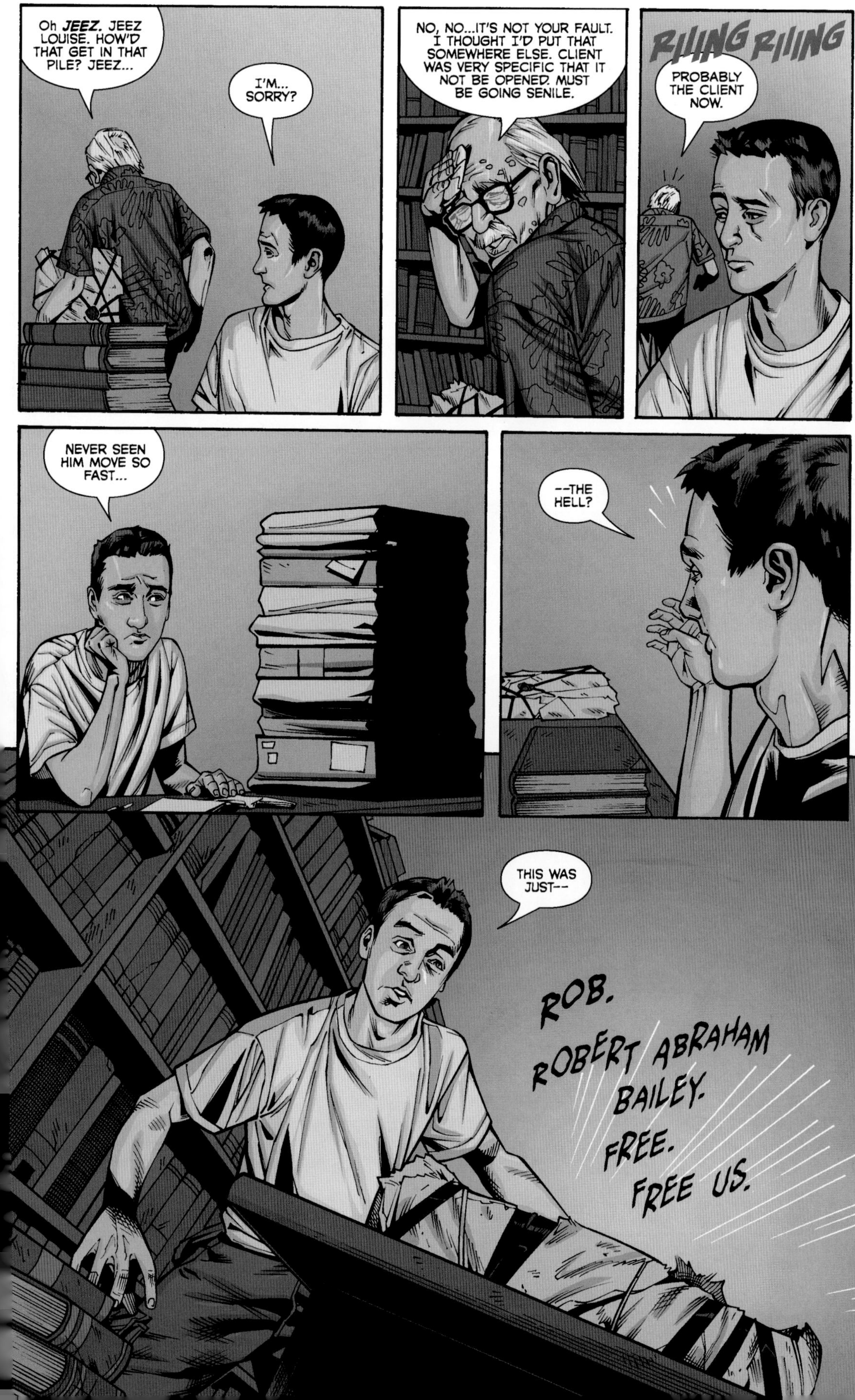
Oh JEEZ. JEEZ LOUISE. HOW'D THAT GET IN THAT PILE? JEEZ...
I'M... SORRY?
NO, NO...IT'S NOT YOUR FAULT. I THOUGHT I'D PUT THAT SOMEWHERE ELSE. CLIENT WAS VERY SPECIFIC THAT IT NOT BE OPENED. MUST BE GOING SENILE.
RIIING RIIING
PROBABLY THE CLIENT NOW.
NEVER SEEN HIM MOVE SO FAST...
--THE HELL?
THIS WAS JUST--
ROB.
ROBERT ABRAHAM BAILEY.
FREE.
FREE US.

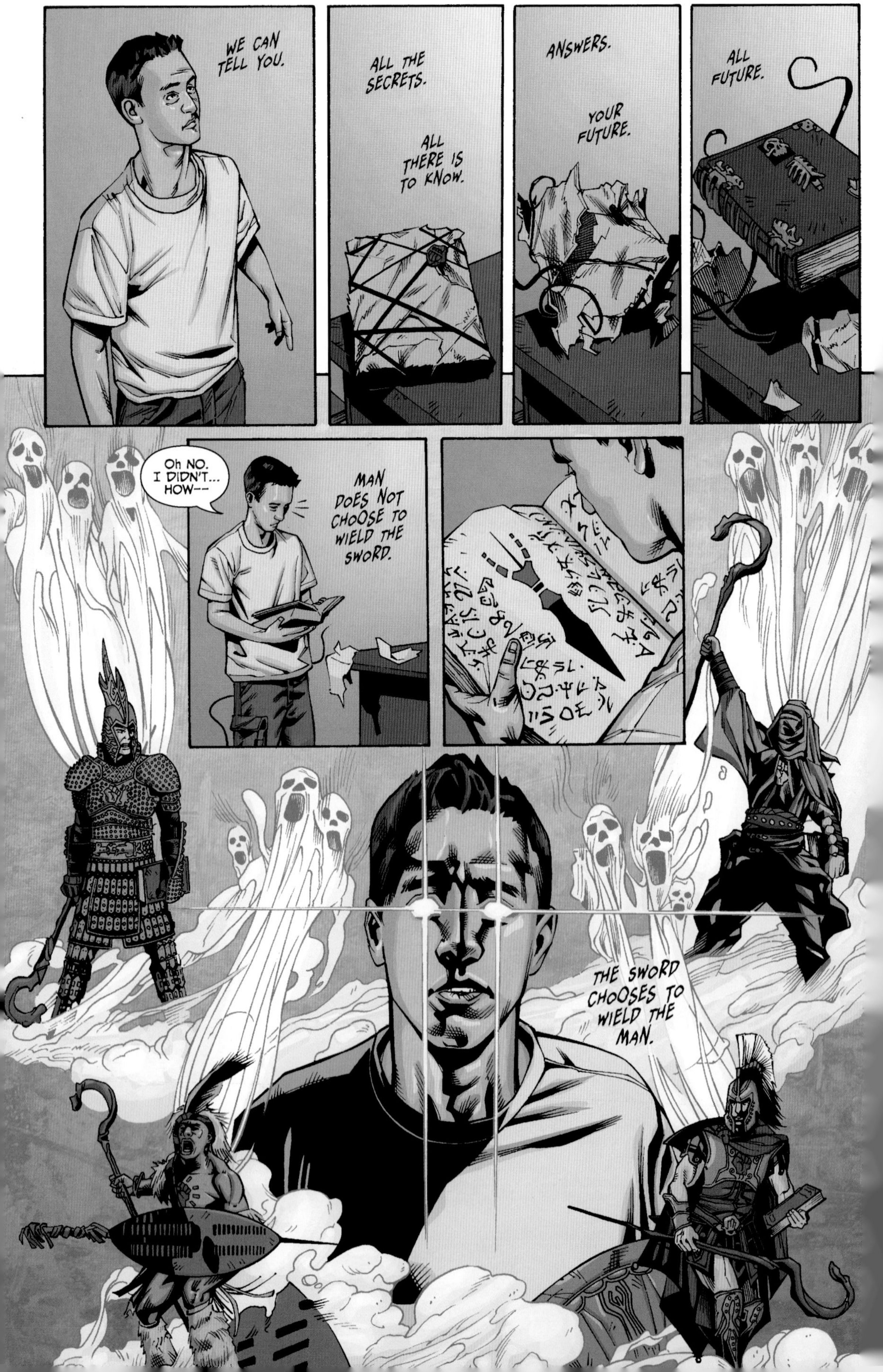
WE CAN TELL YOU.
ALL THE SECRETS.
ALL THERE IS TO KNOW.
ANSWERS.
YOUR FUTURE.
ALL FUTURE.
Oh NO. I DIDN'T... HOW--
MAN DOES NOT CHOOSE TO WIELD THE SWORD.
THE SWORD CHOOSES TO WIELD THE MAN.

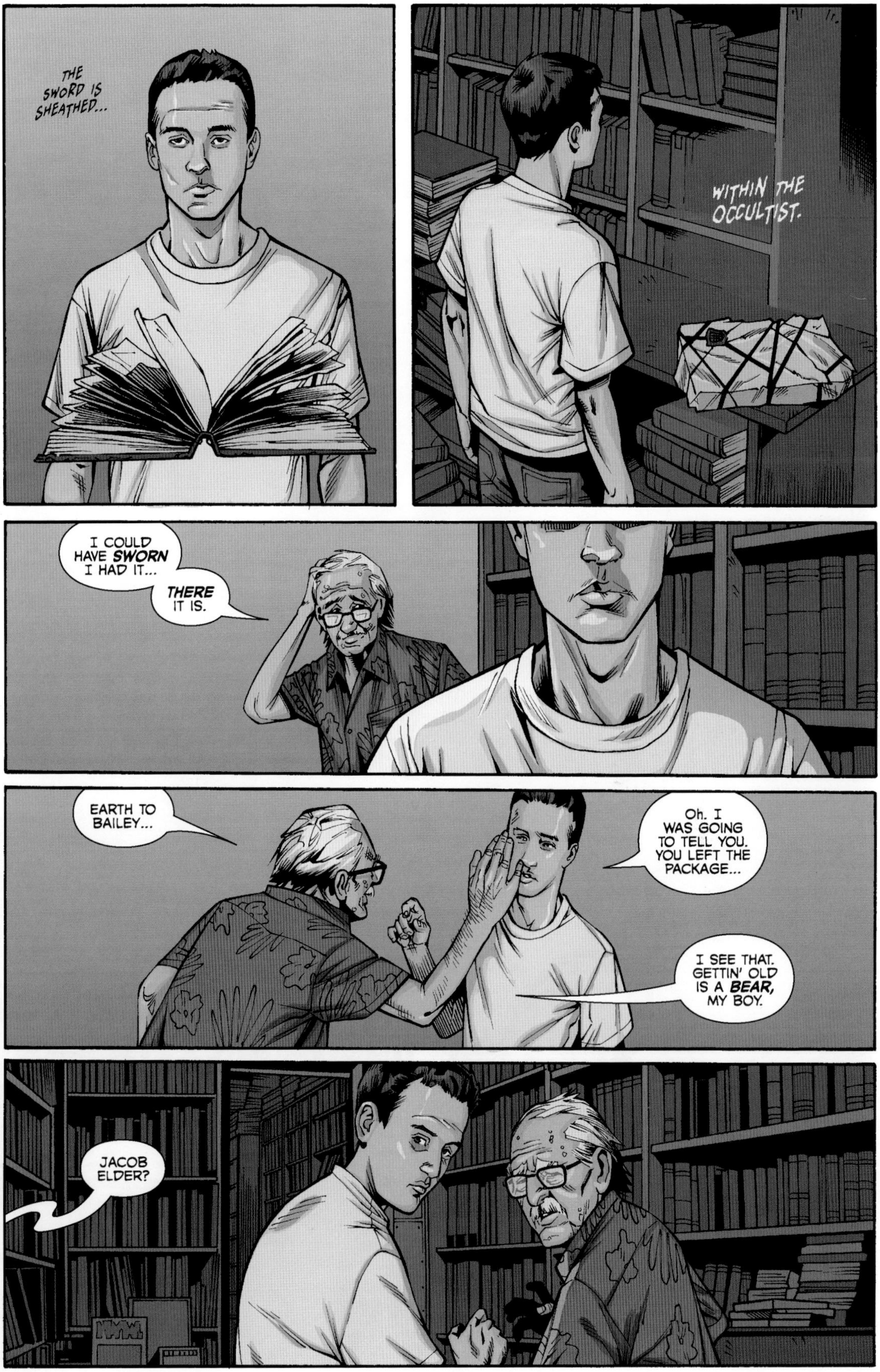
THE SWORD IS SHEATHED...
WITHIN THE OCCULTIST.
I COULD HAVE SWORN I HAD IT...
THERE IT IS.
EARTH TO BAILEY...
Oh. I WAS GOING TO TELL YOU. YOU LEFT THE PACKAGE...
I SEE THAT. GETTIN' OLD IS A BEAR, MY BOY.
JACOB ELDER?

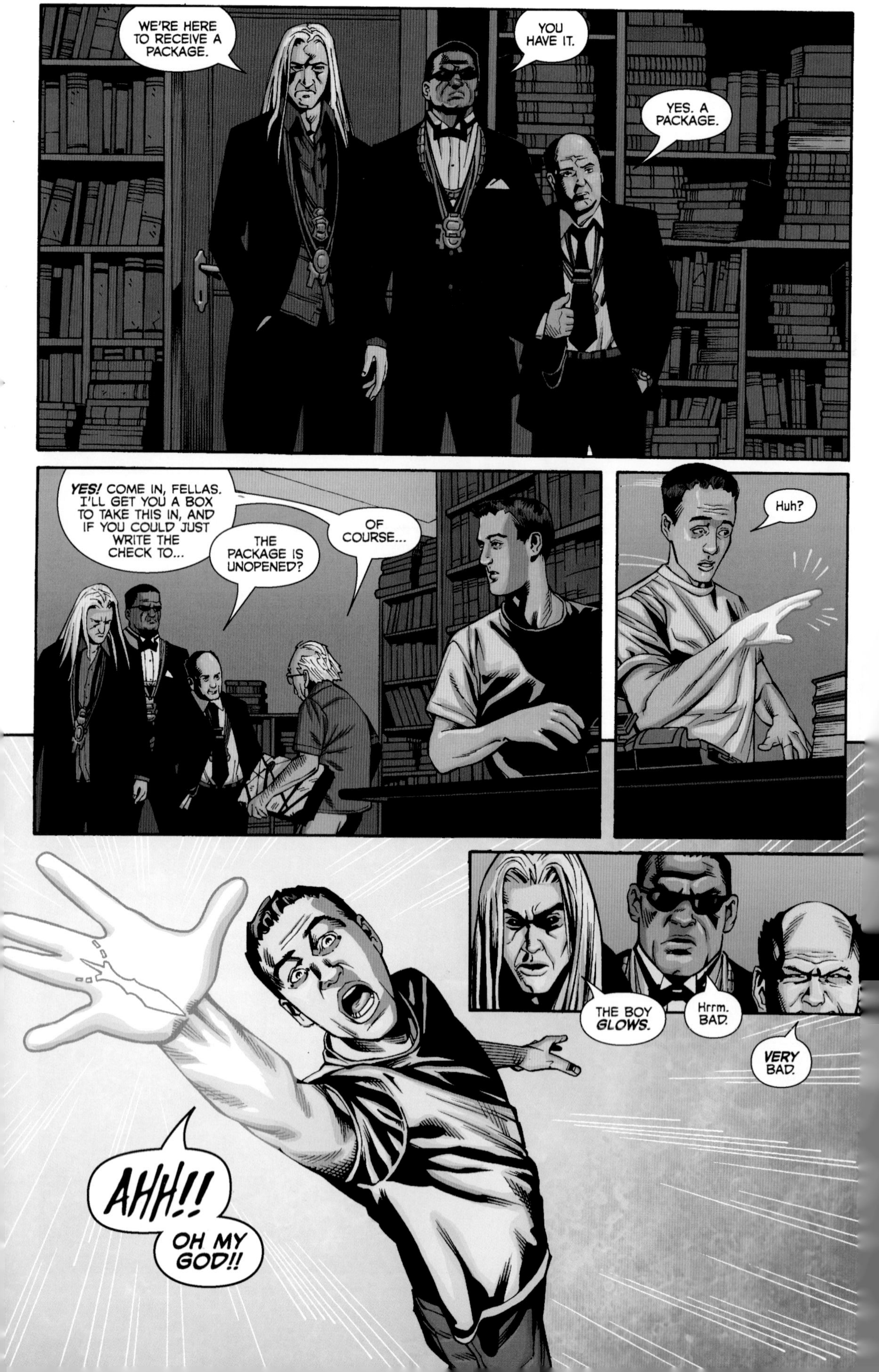
WE'RE HERE TO RECEIVE A PACKAGE.
YOU HAVE IT.
YES. A PACKAGE.
YES! COME IN, FELLAS. I'LL GET YOU A BOX TO TAKE THIS IN, AND IF YOU COULD JUST WRITE THE CHECK TO...
THE PACKAGE IS UNOPENED?
OF COURSE...
Huh?
AHH!!
OH MY GOD!!
THE BOY GLOWS.
Hrrm. BAD.
VERY BAD.

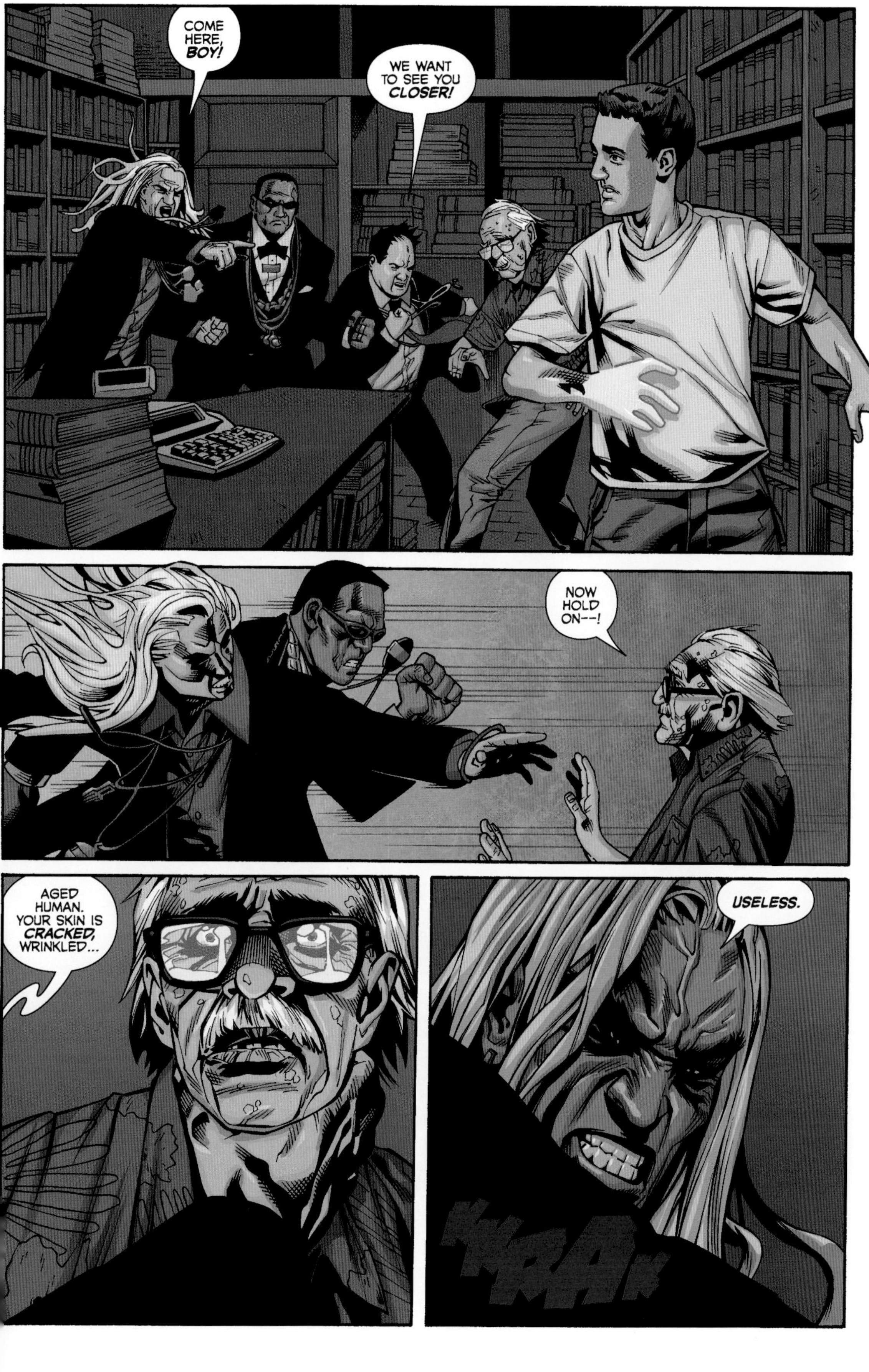
COME HERE, BOY!
WE WANT TO SEE YOU CLOSER!
NOW HOLD ON--!
AGED HUMAN. YOUR SKIN IS CRACKED, WRINKLED...
USELESS.
KRAK

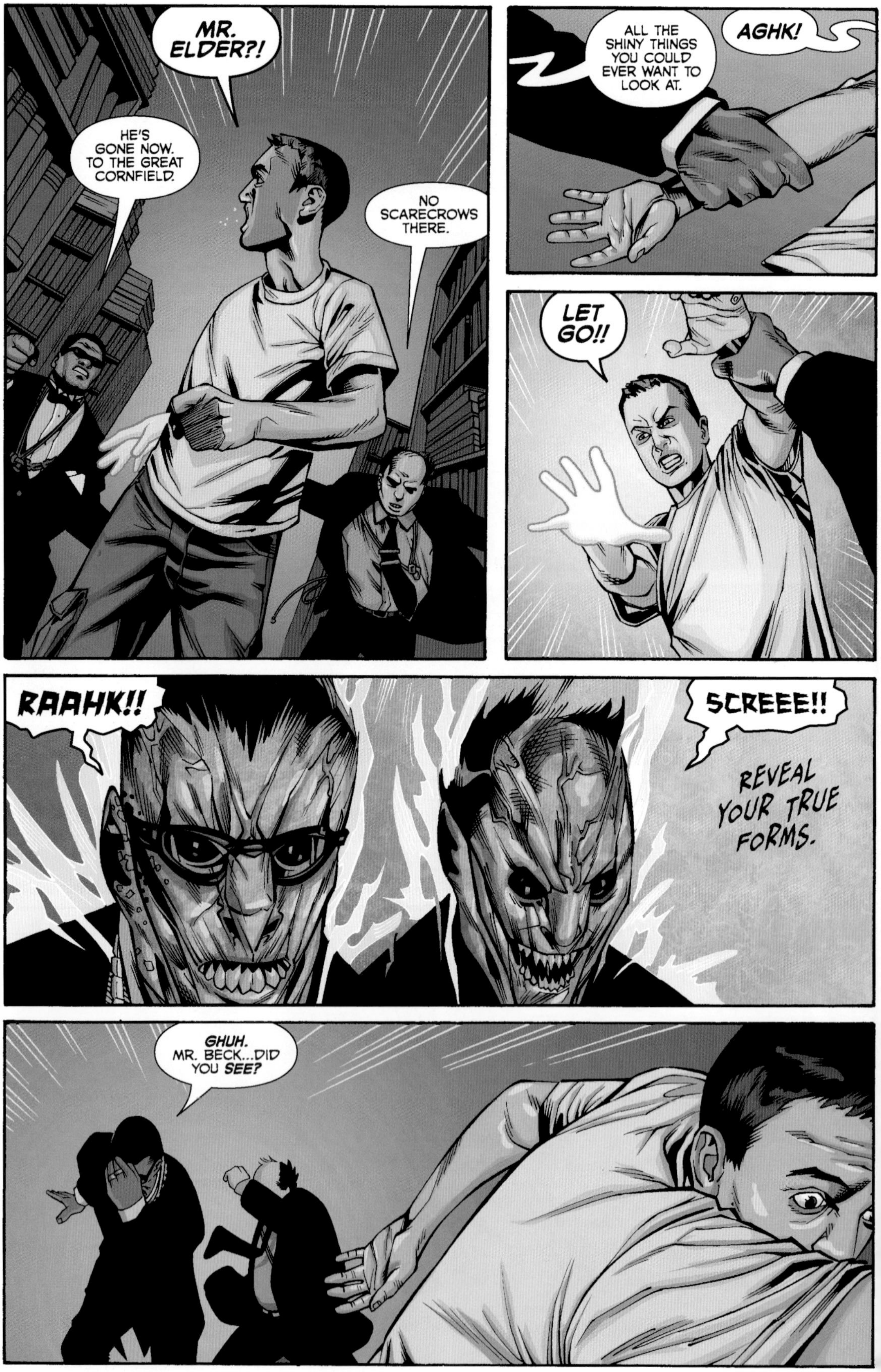
MR. ELDER?!
HE'S GONE NOW. TO THE GREAT CORNFIELD.
NO SCARECROWS THERE.
ALL THE SHINY THINGS YOU COULD EVER WANT TO LOOK AT.
AGHK!
LET GO!!
RAAHK!!
SCREEE!!
REVEAL YOUR TRUE FORMS.
GHUH. MR. BECK...DID YOU SEE?

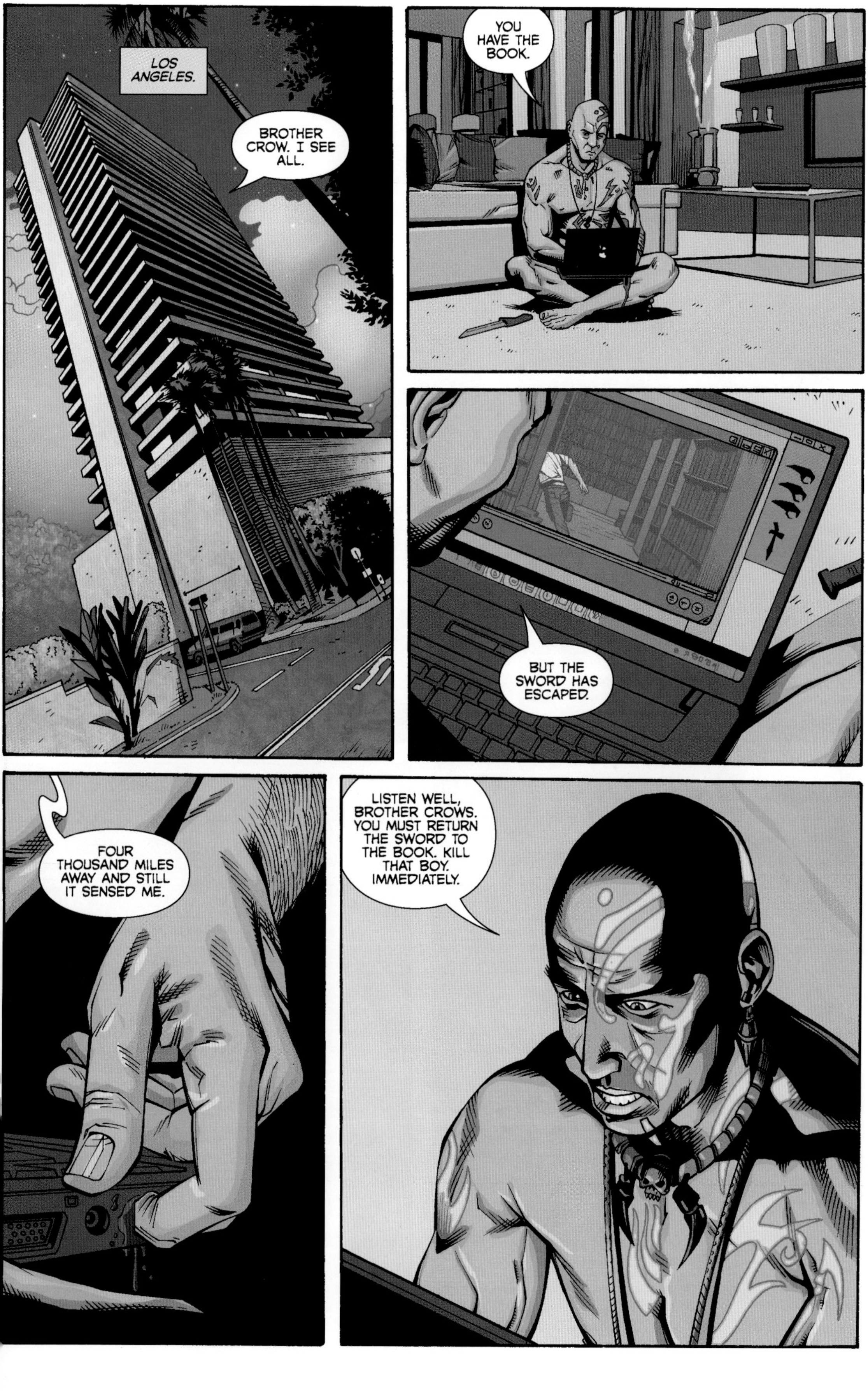
LOS ANGELES.
BROTHER CROW. I SEE ALL.
YOU HAVE THE BOOK.
BUT THE SWORD HAS ESCAPED.
FOUR THOUSAND MILES AWAY AND STILL IT SENSED ME.
LISTEN WELL, BROTHER CROWS. YOU MUST RETURN THE SWORD TO THE BOOK. KILL THAT BOY. IMMEDIATELY.

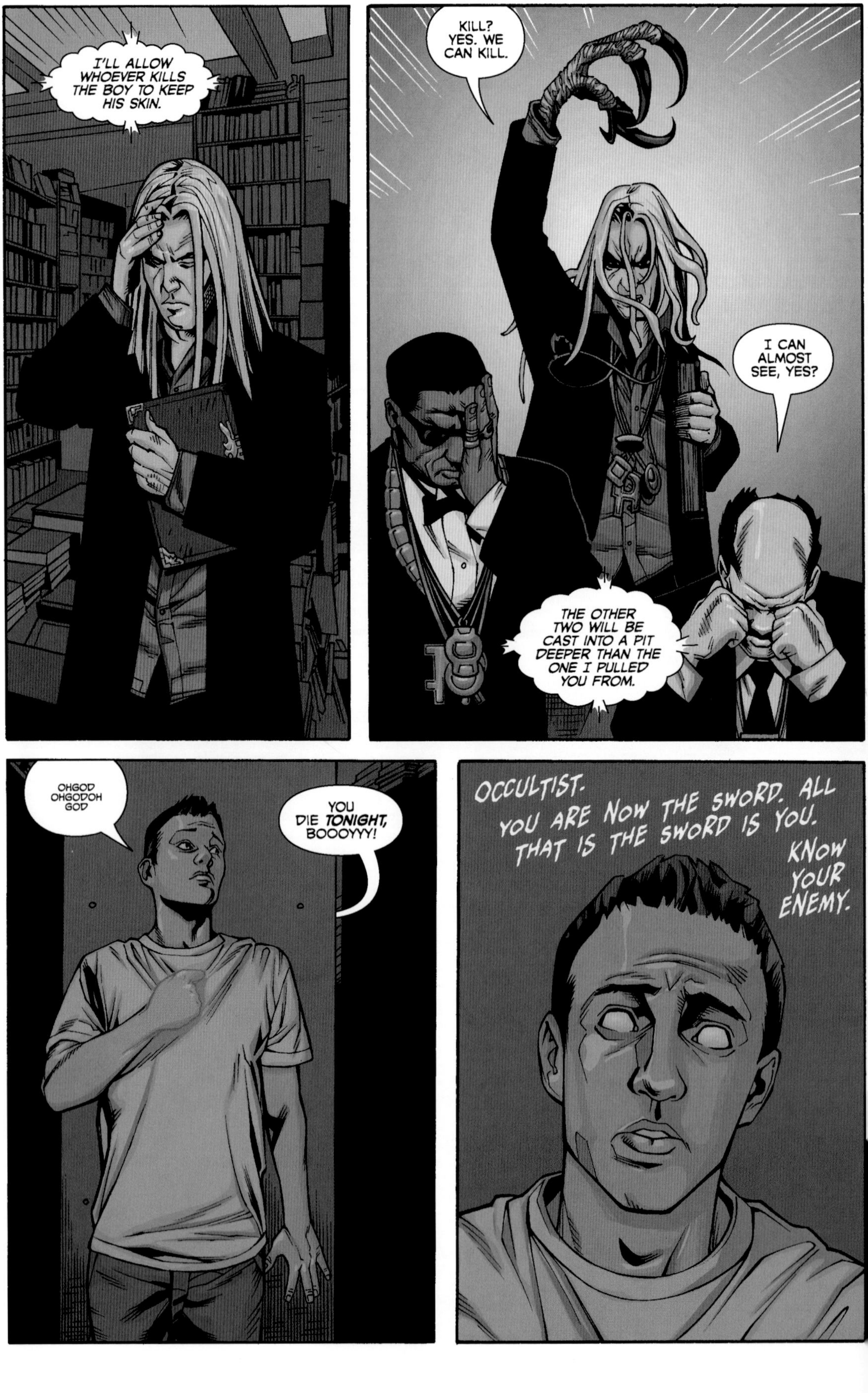
I'LL ALLOW WHOEVER KILLS THE BOY TO KEEP HIS SKIN.
KILL? YES. WE CAN KILL.
I CAN ALMOST SEE, YES?
THE OTHER TWO WILL BE CAST INTO A PIT DEEPER THAN THE ONE I PULLED YOU FROM.
OHGOD OHGODOH GOD
YOU DIE TONIGHT, BOOOYYY!
OCCULTIST.
YOU ARE NOW THE SWORD. ALL THAT IS THE SWORD IS YOU.
KNOW YOUR ENEMY.

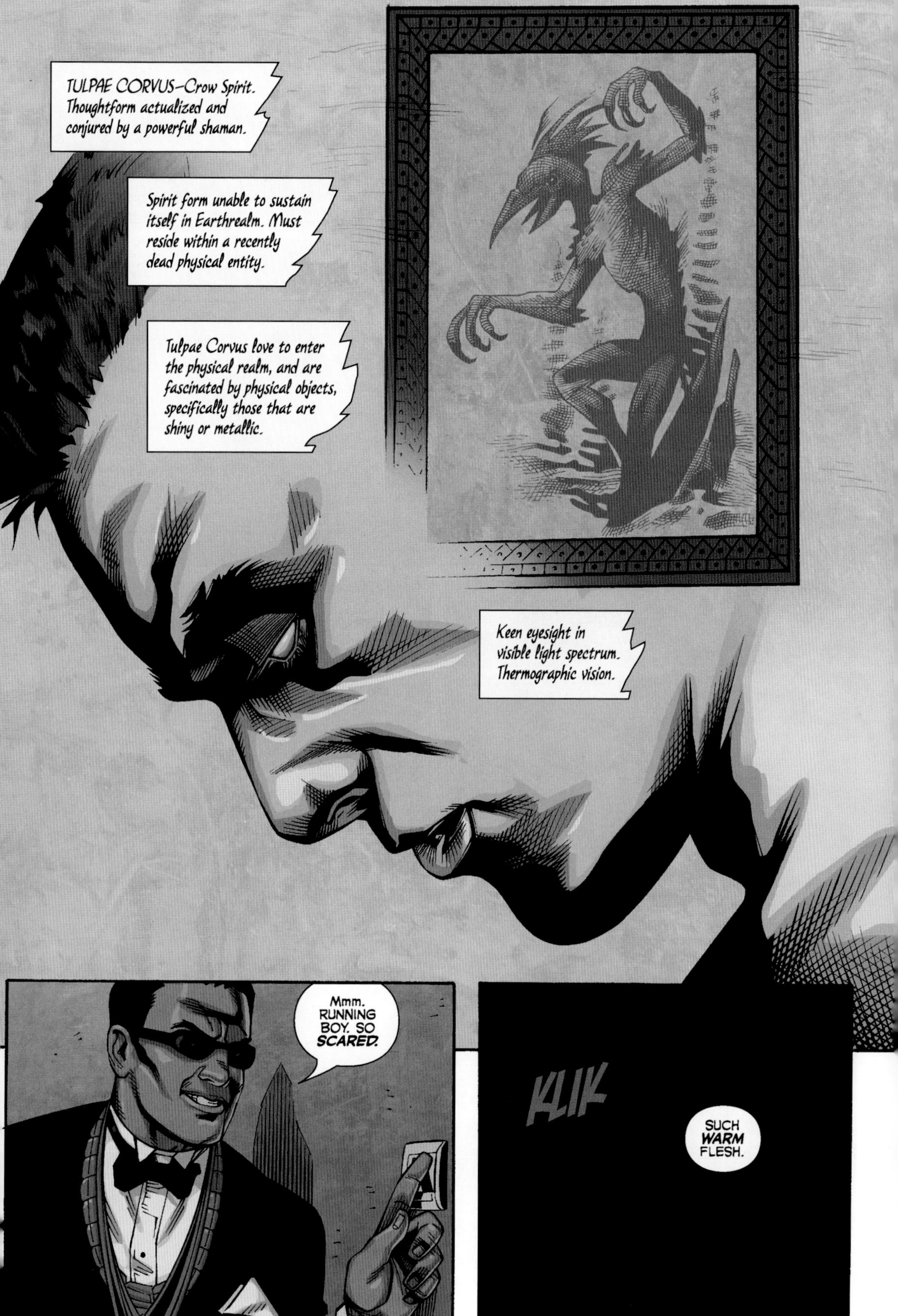

TULPAE CORVUS—Crow Spirit. Thoughtform actualized and conjured by a powerful shaman.
Spirit form unable to sustain itself in Earthrealm. Must reside within a recently dead physical entity.
Tulpae Corvus love to enter the physical realm, and are fascinated by physical objects, specifically those that are shiny or metallic.
Keen eyesight in visible light spectrum. Thermographic vision.
Mmm. RUNNING BOY. SO *SCARED.*
KLIK
SUCH *WARM* FLESH.

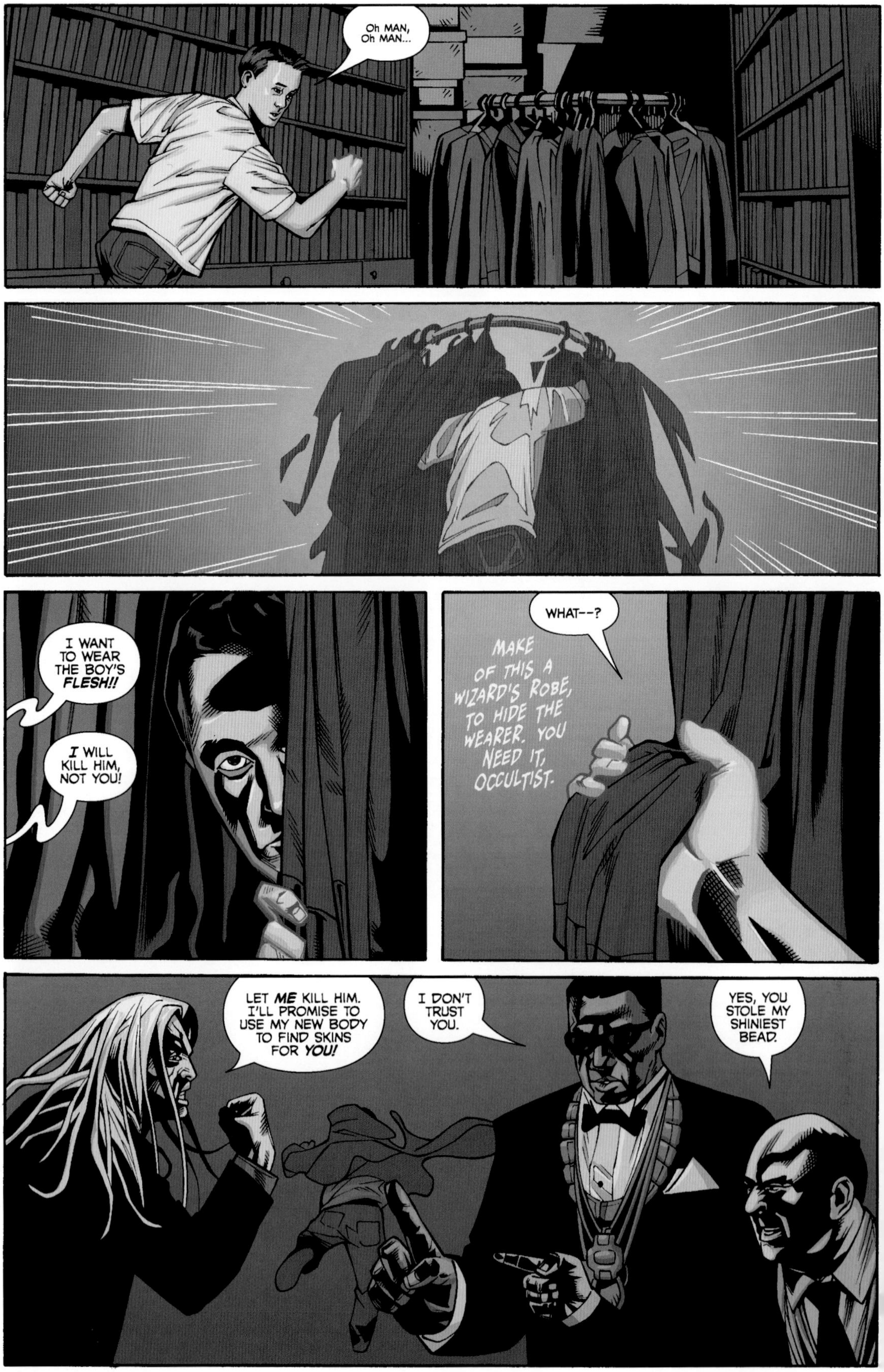
Oh MAN, Oh MAN...
I WANT TO WEAR THE BOY'S FLESH!!
I WILL KILL HIM, NOT YOU!
WHAT--?
MAKE OF THIS A WIZARD'S ROBE, TO HIDE THE WEARER. YOU NEED IT, OCCULTIST.
LET ME KILL HIM. I'LL PROMISE TO USE MY NEW BODY TO FIND SKINS FOR YOU!
I DON'T TRUST YOU.
YES, YOU STOLE MY SHINIEST BEAD.

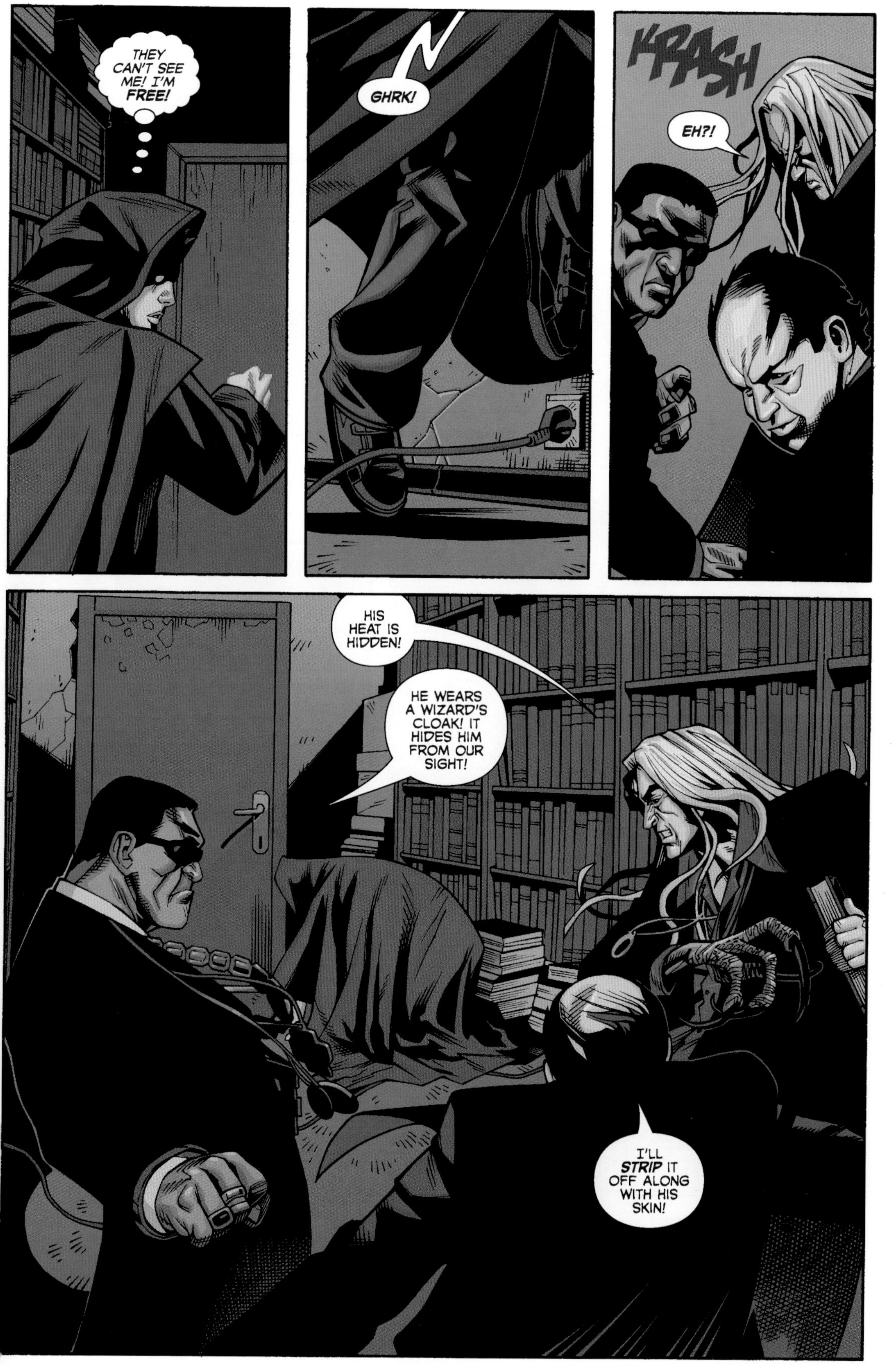
THEY CAN'T SEE ME! I'M FREE!
GHRK!
KRASH
EH?!
HIS HEAT IS HIDDEN!
HE WEARS A WIZARD'S CLOAK! IT HIDES HIM FROM OUR SIGHT!
I'LL STRIP IT OFF ALONG WITH HIS SKIN!

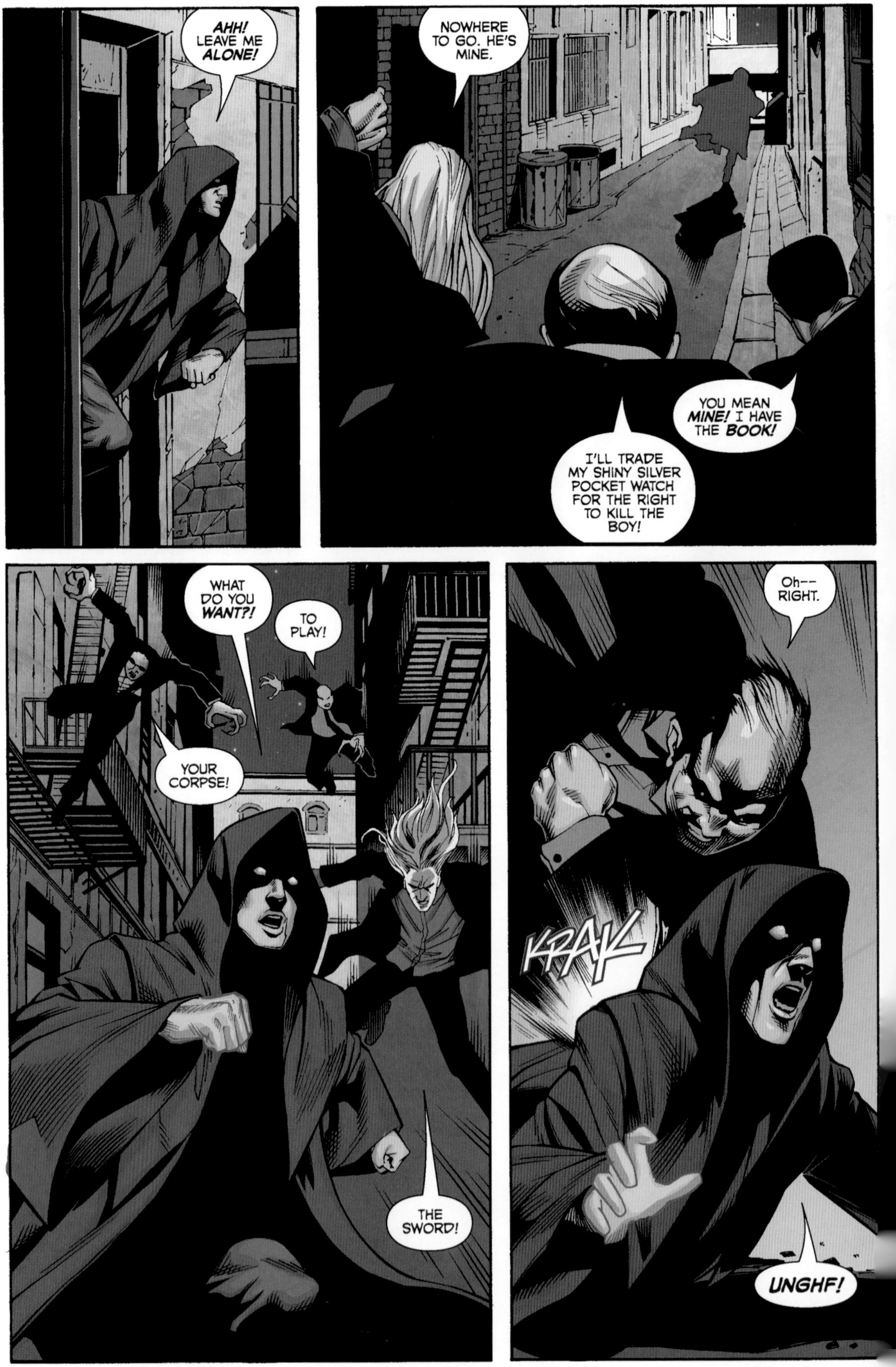
AHH! LEAVE ME ALONE!
NOWHERE TO GO. HE'S MINE.
YOU MEAN MINE! I HAVE THE BOOK!
I'LL TRADE MY SHINY SILVER POCKET WATCH FOR THE RIGHT TO KILL THE BOY!
WHAT DO YOU WANT?!
TO PLAY!
YOUR CORPSE!
THE SWORD!
Oh-- RIGHT.
KRAK
UNGHF!

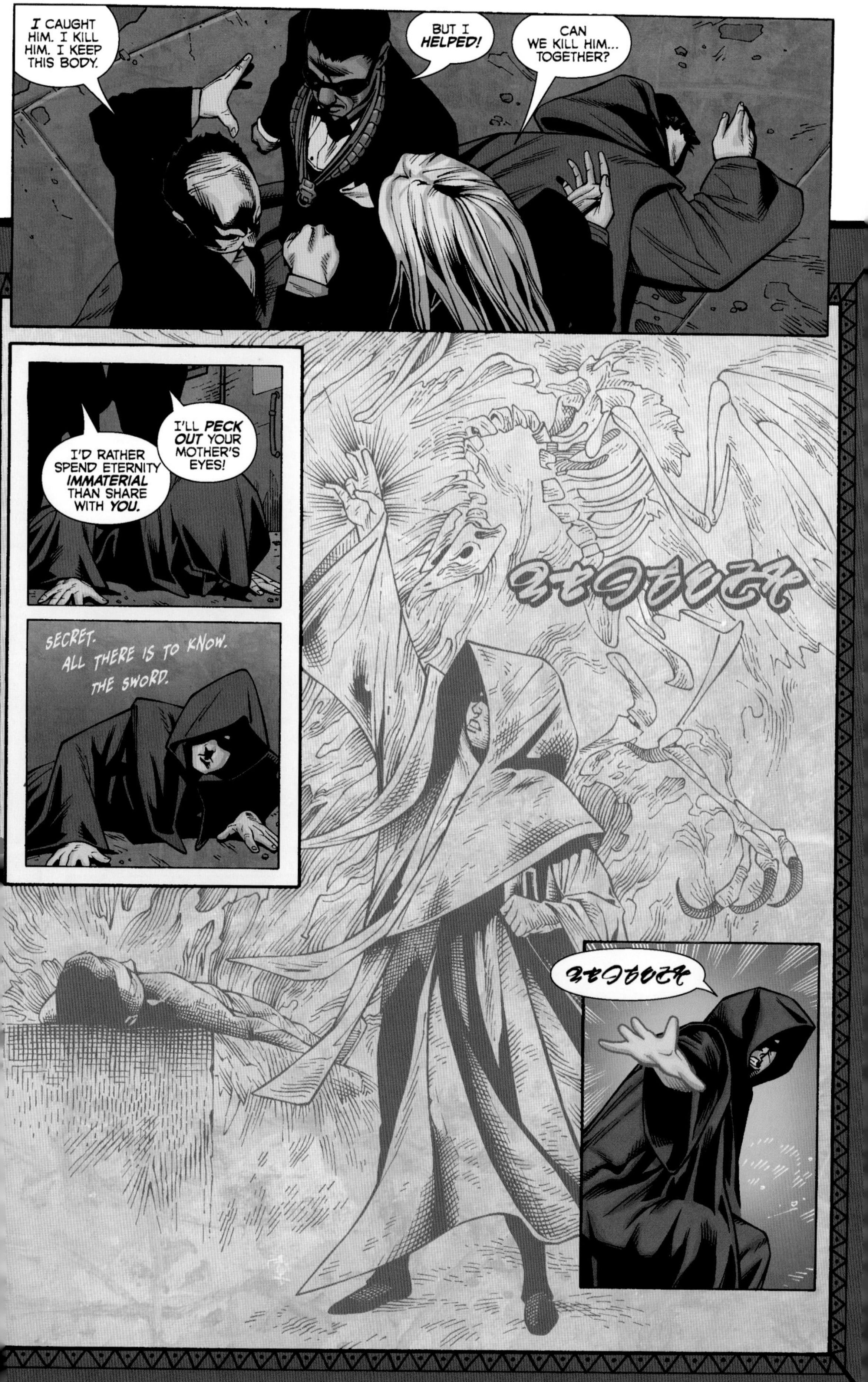
I CAUGHT HIM. I KILL HIM. I KEEP THIS BODY.
BUT I HELPED!
CAN WE KILL HIM... TOGETHER?
I'D RATHER SPEND ETERNITY IMMATERIAL THAN SHARE WITH YOU.
I'LL PECK OUT YOUR MOTHER'S EYES!
SECRET.
ALL THERE IS TO KNOW.
THE SWORD.

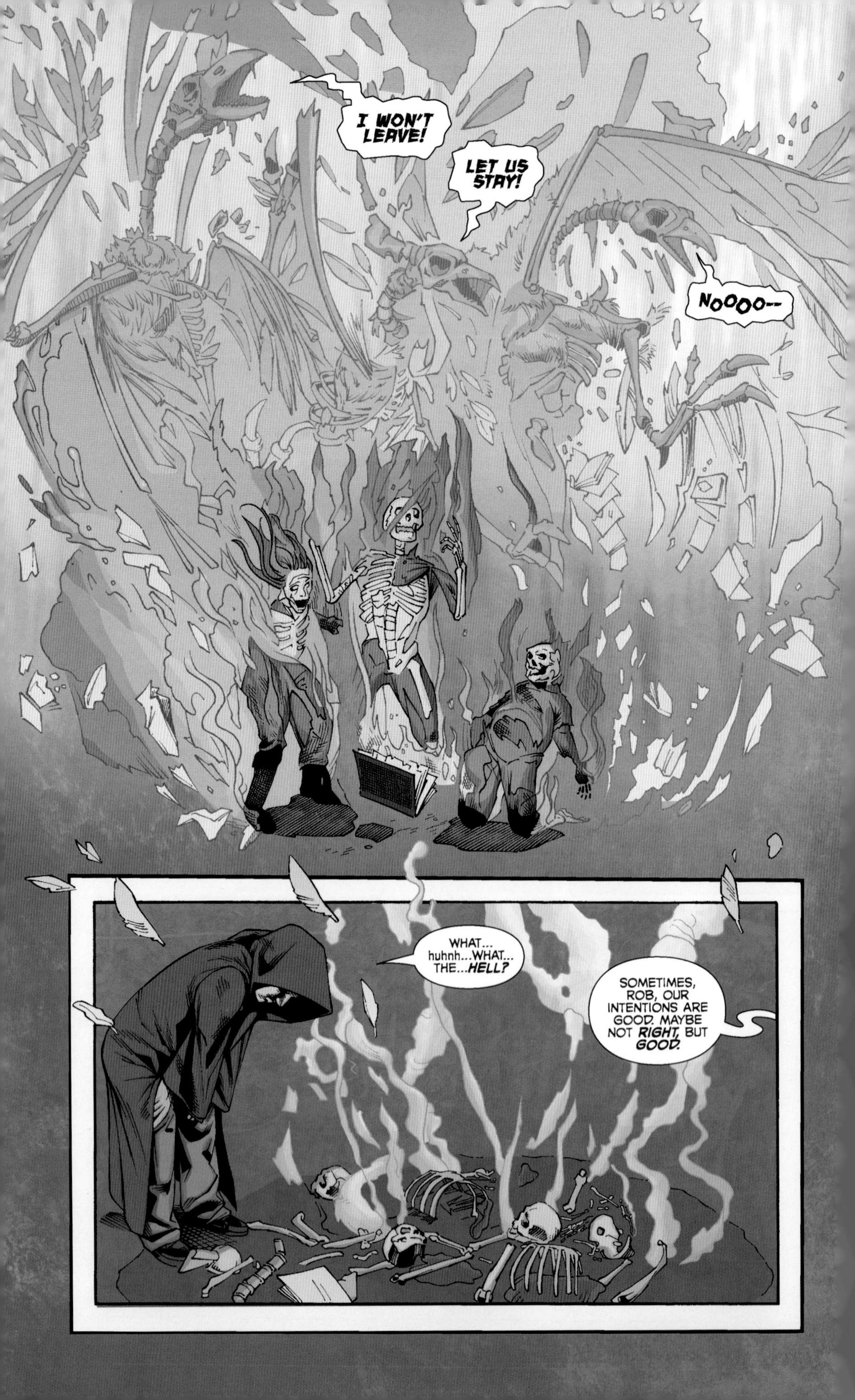
I WON'T LEAVE!
LET US STAY!
NOOOO--
WHAT... huhnh...WHAT... THE...HELL?
SOMETIMES, ROB, OUR INTENTIONS ARE GOOD. MAYBE NOT RIGHT, BUT GOOD.

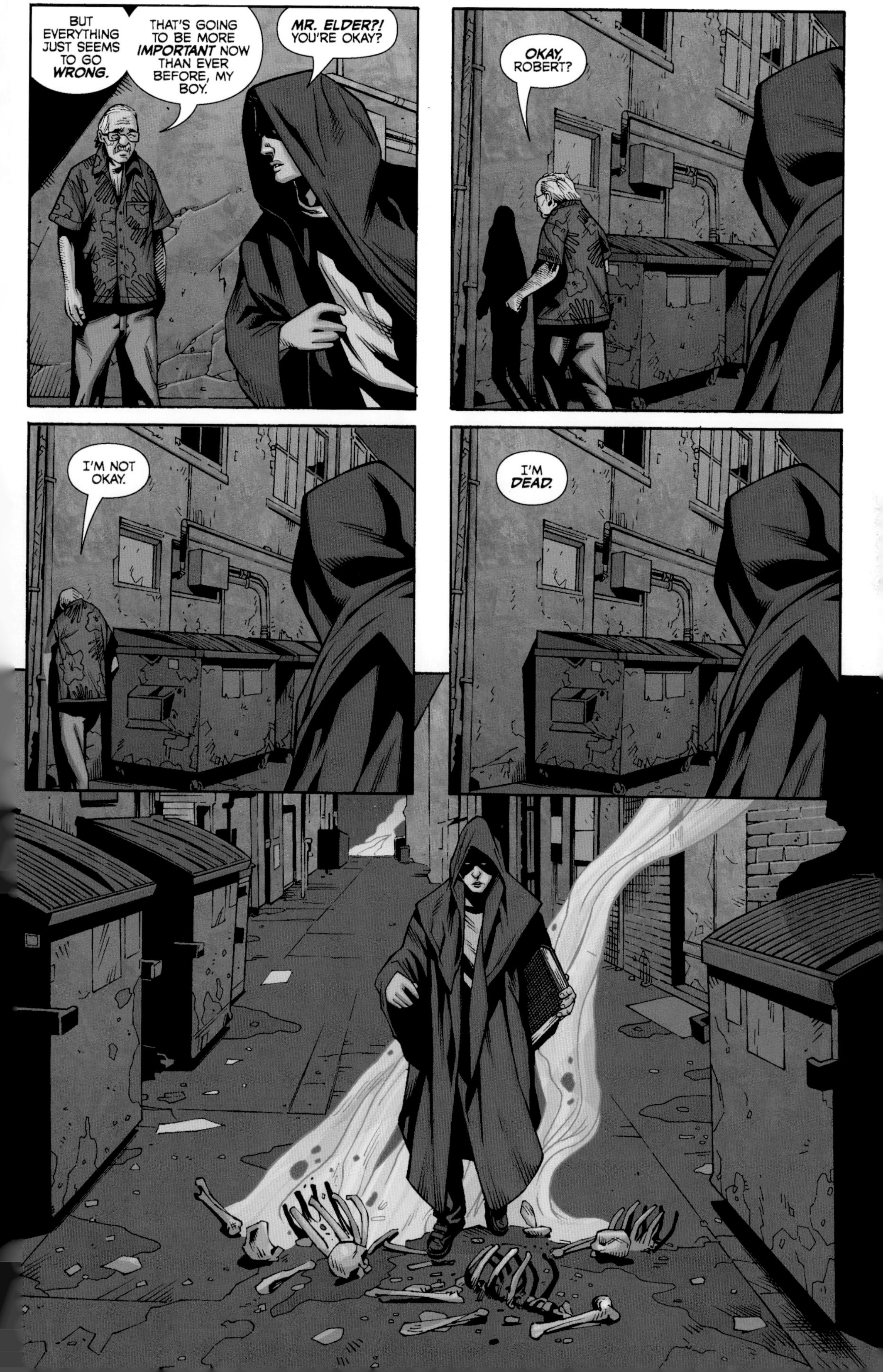
BUT EVERYTHING JUST SEEMS TO GO WRONG.
THAT'S GOING TO BE MORE IMPORTANT NOW THAN EVER BEFORE, MY BOY.
MR. ELDER?! YOU'RE OKAY?
OKAY, ROBERT?
I'M NOT OKAY.
I'M DEAD.

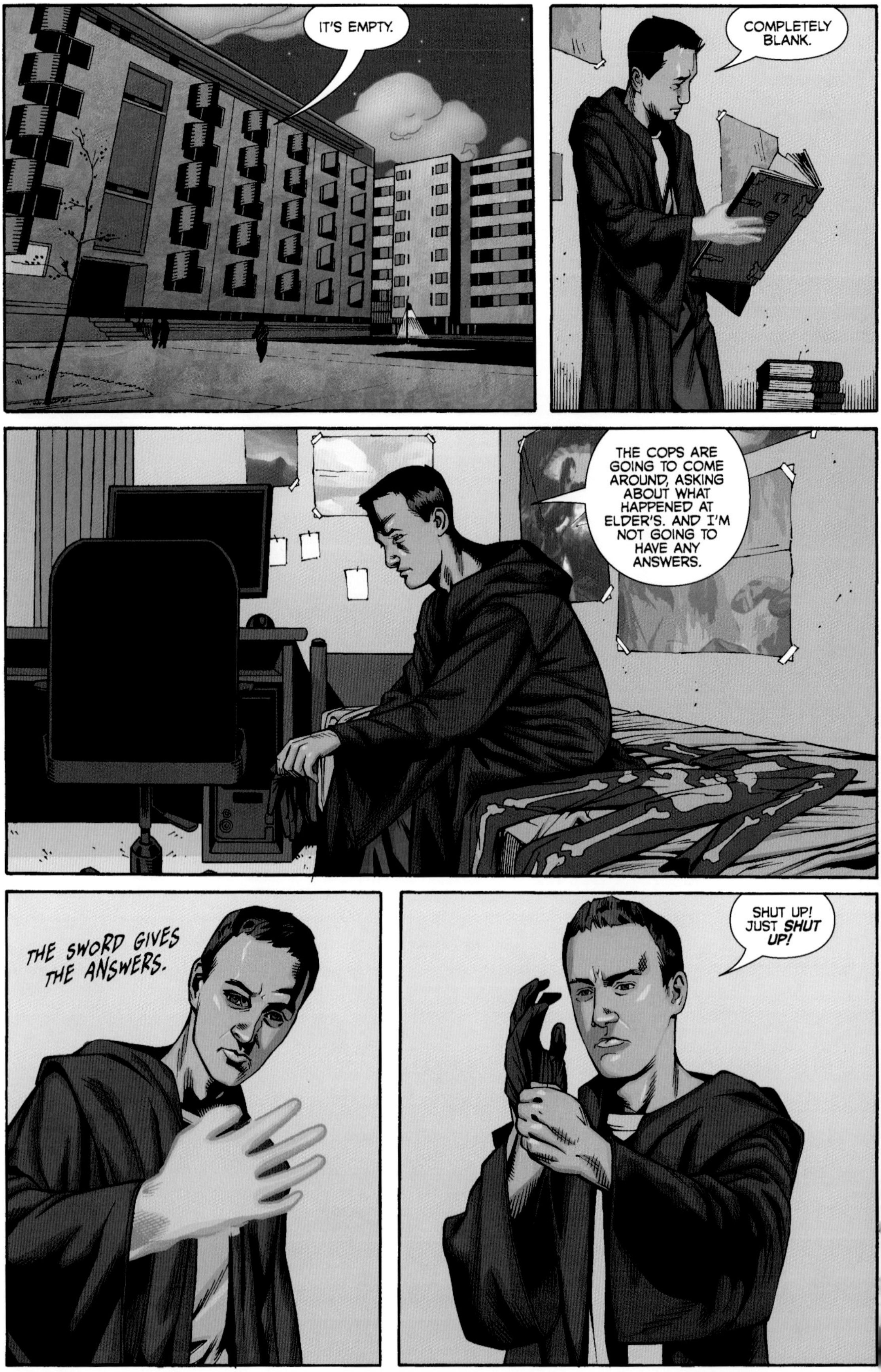
IT'S EMPTY.
COMPLETELY BLANK.
THE COPS ARE GOING TO COME AROUND, ASKING ABOUT WHAT HAPPENED AT ELDER'S. AND I'M NOT GOING TO HAVE ANY ANSWERS.
THE SWORD GIVES THE ANSWERS.
SHUT UP! JUST SHUT UP!

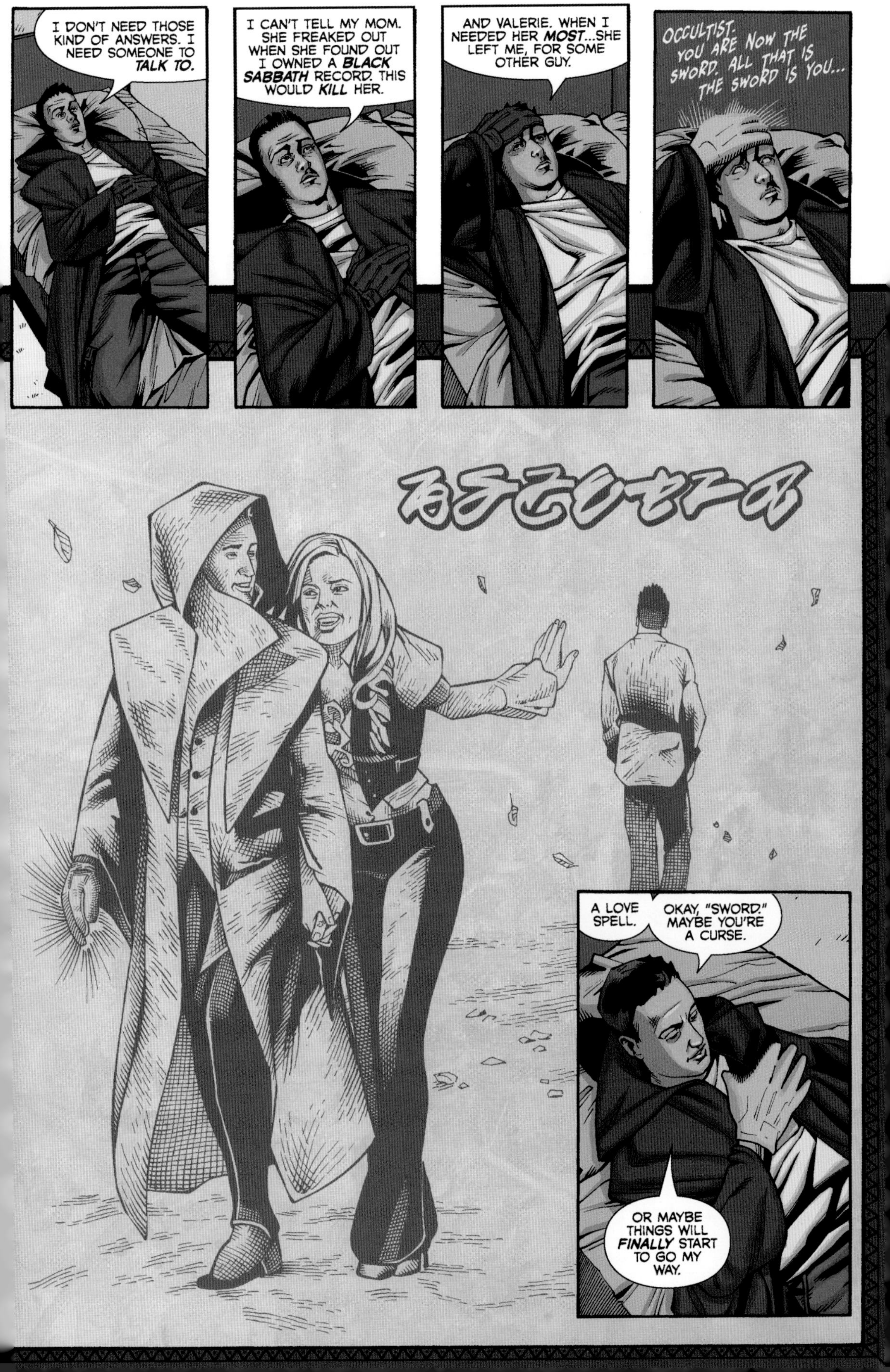
I DON'T NEED THOSE KIND OF ANSWERS. I NEED SOMEONE TO *TALK TO.*
I CAN'T TELL MY MOM. SHE FREAKED OUT WHEN SHE FOUND OUT I OWNED A *BLACK SABBATH* RECORD. THIS WOULD *KILL* HER.
AND VALERIE. WHEN I NEEDED HER *MOST*...SHE LEFT ME, FOR SOME OTHER GUY.
OCCULTIST. YOU ARE NOW THE SWORD. ALL THAT IS THE SWORD IS YOU...
A LOVE SPELL.
OKAY, "SWORD." MAYBE YOU'RE A CURSE.
OR MAYBE THINGS WILL *FINALLY* START TO GO MY WAY.

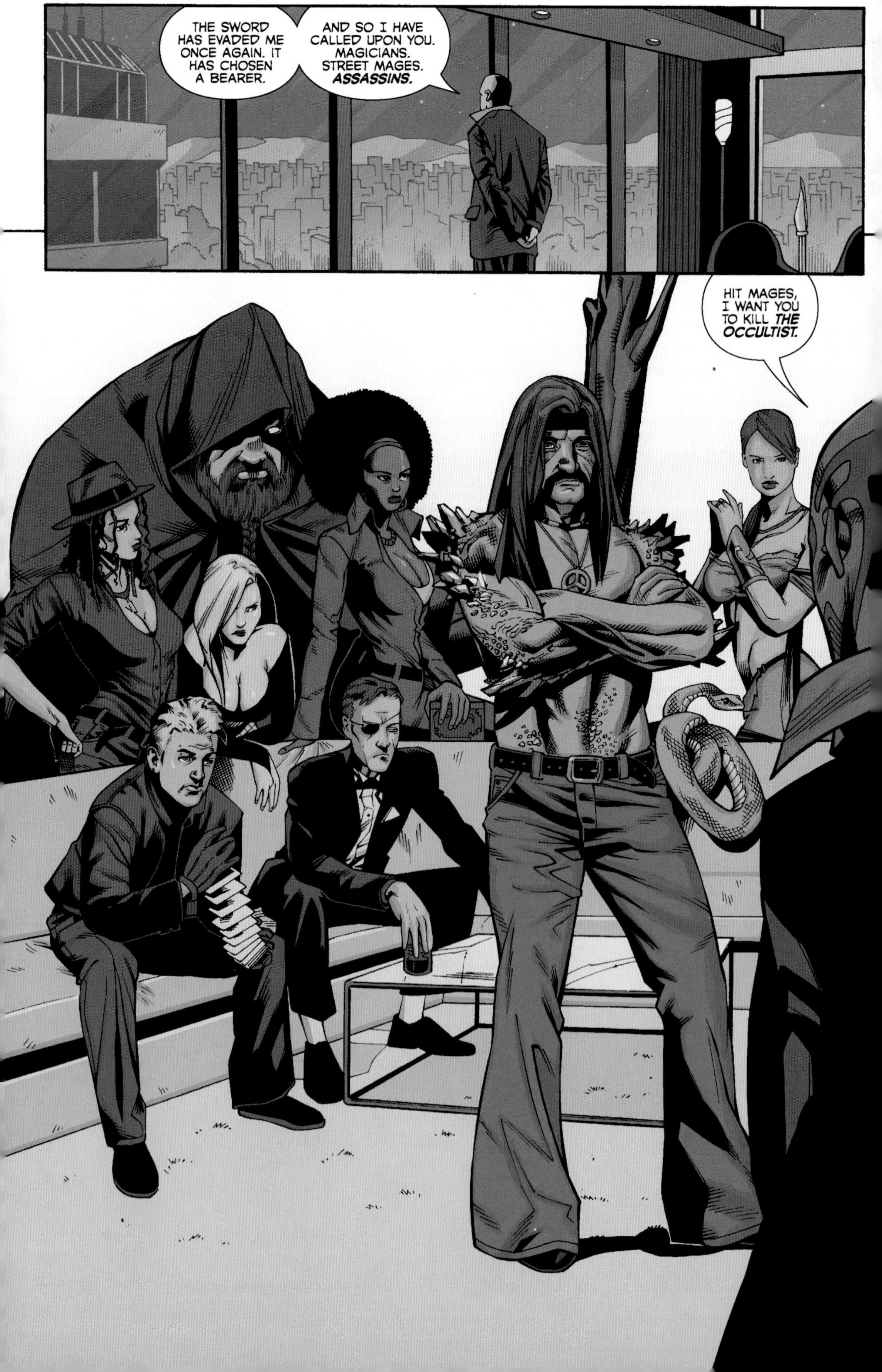
THE SWORD HAS EVADED ME ONCE AGAIN. IT HAS CHOSEN A BEARER.
AND SO I HAVE CALLED UPON YOU. MAGICIANS. STREET MAGES. ASSASSINS.
HIT MAGES, I WANT YOU TO KILL THE OCCULTIST.

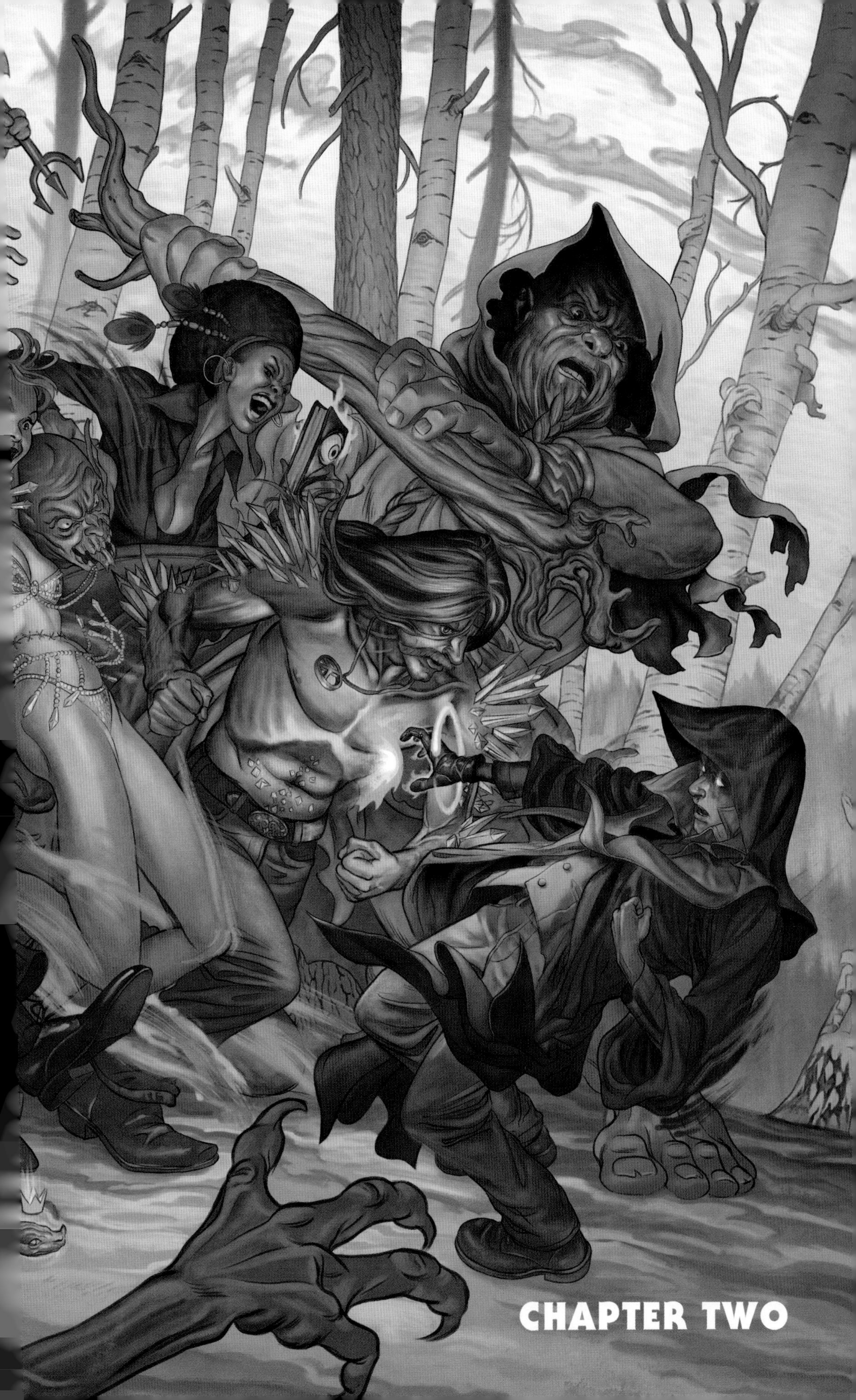

CHAPTER TWO

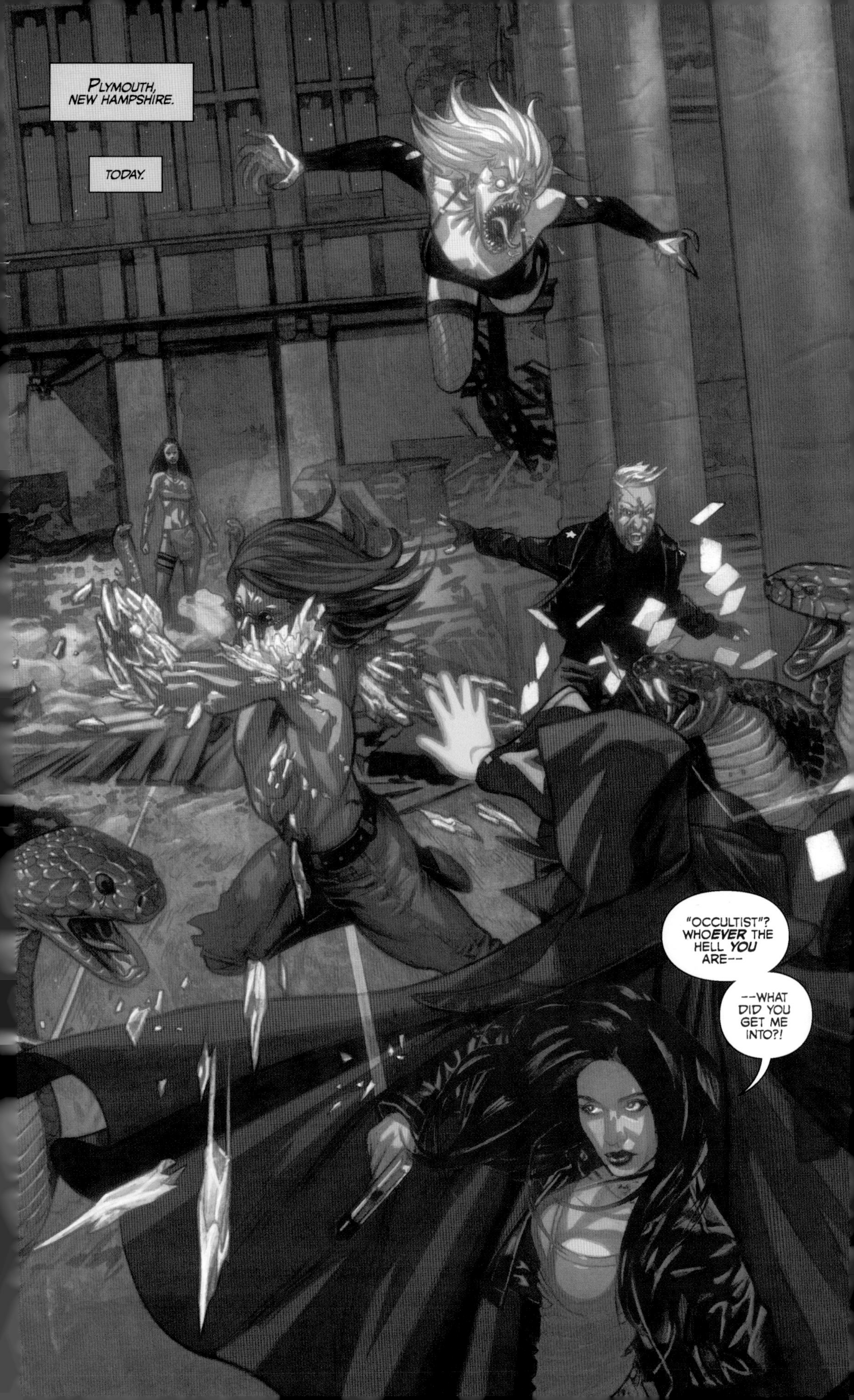
PLYMOUTH, NEW HAMPSHIRE.
TODAY.
"OCCULTIST"? WHOEVER THE HELL YOU ARE--
--WHAT DID YOU GET ME INTO?!

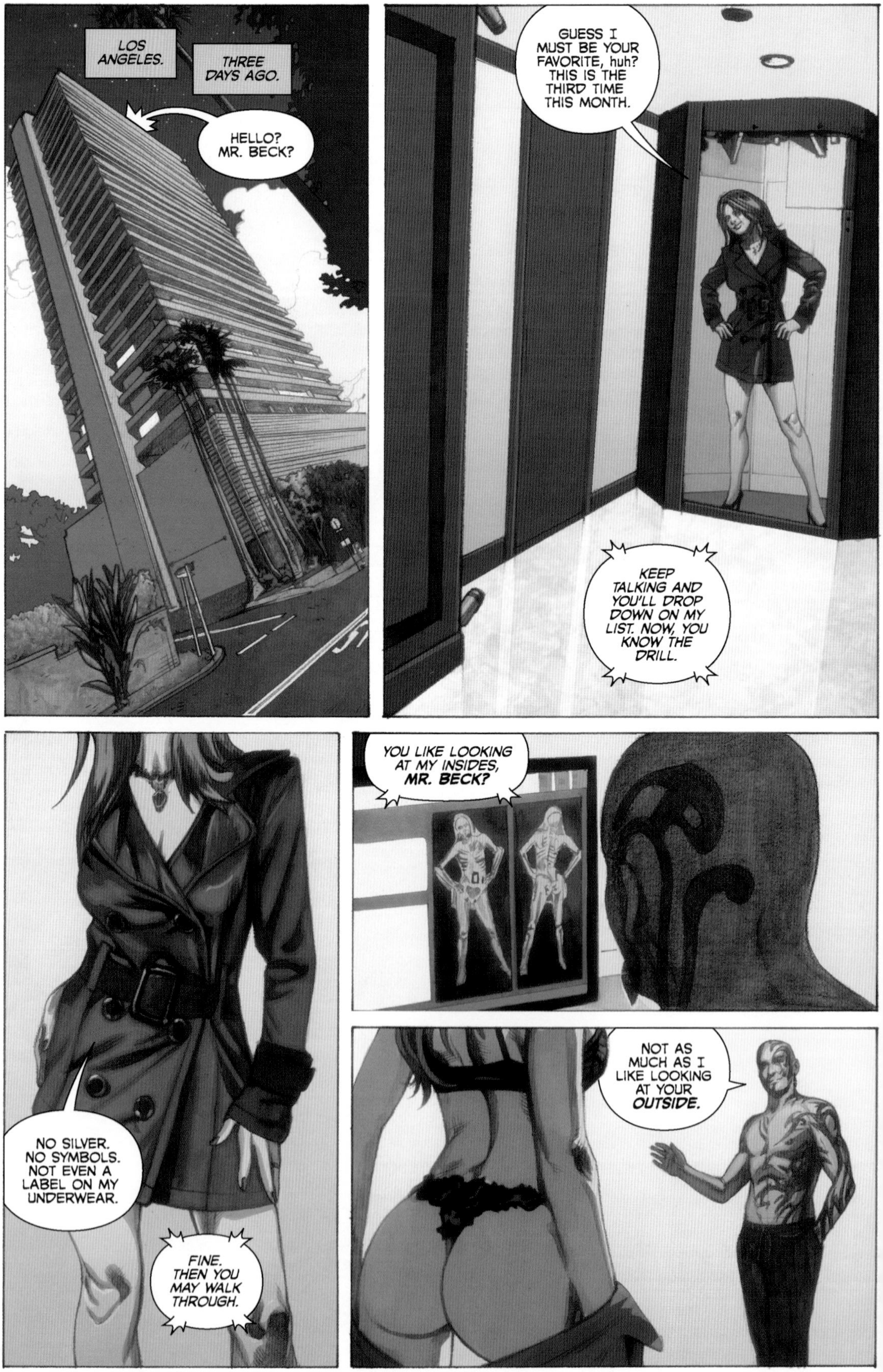
LOS ANGELES.
THREE DAYS AGO.
HELLO? MR. BECK?
GUESS I MUST BE YOUR FAVORITE, huh? THIS IS THE THIRD TIME THIS MONTH.
KEEP TALKING AND YOU'LL DROP DOWN ON MY LIST. NOW, YOU KNOW THE DRILL.
NO SILVER. NO SYMBOLS. NOT EVEN A LABEL ON MY UNDERWEAR.
FINE. THEN YOU MAY WALK THROUGH.
YOU LIKE LOOKING AT MY INSIDES, MR. BECK?
NOT AS MUCH AS I LIKE LOOKING AT YOUR OUTSIDE.

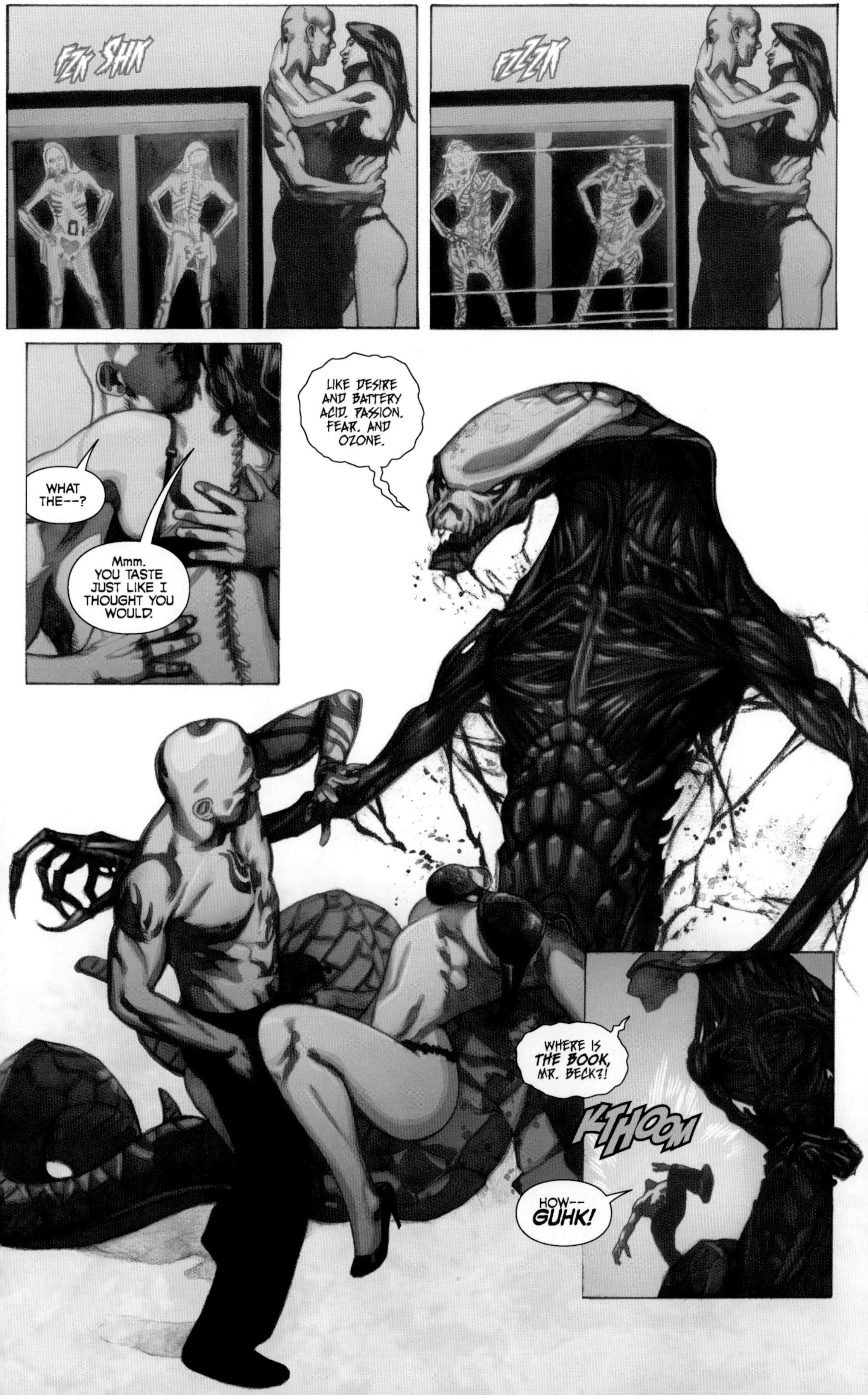
FZK SHK
FZZZK
WHAT THE--?
Mmm. YOU TASTE JUST LIKE I THOUGHT YOU WOULD.
LIKE DESIRE AND BATTERY ACID. PASSION. FEAR. AND OZONE.
WHERE IS THE BOOK, MR. BECK?!
K-THOOM
HOW-- GUHK!

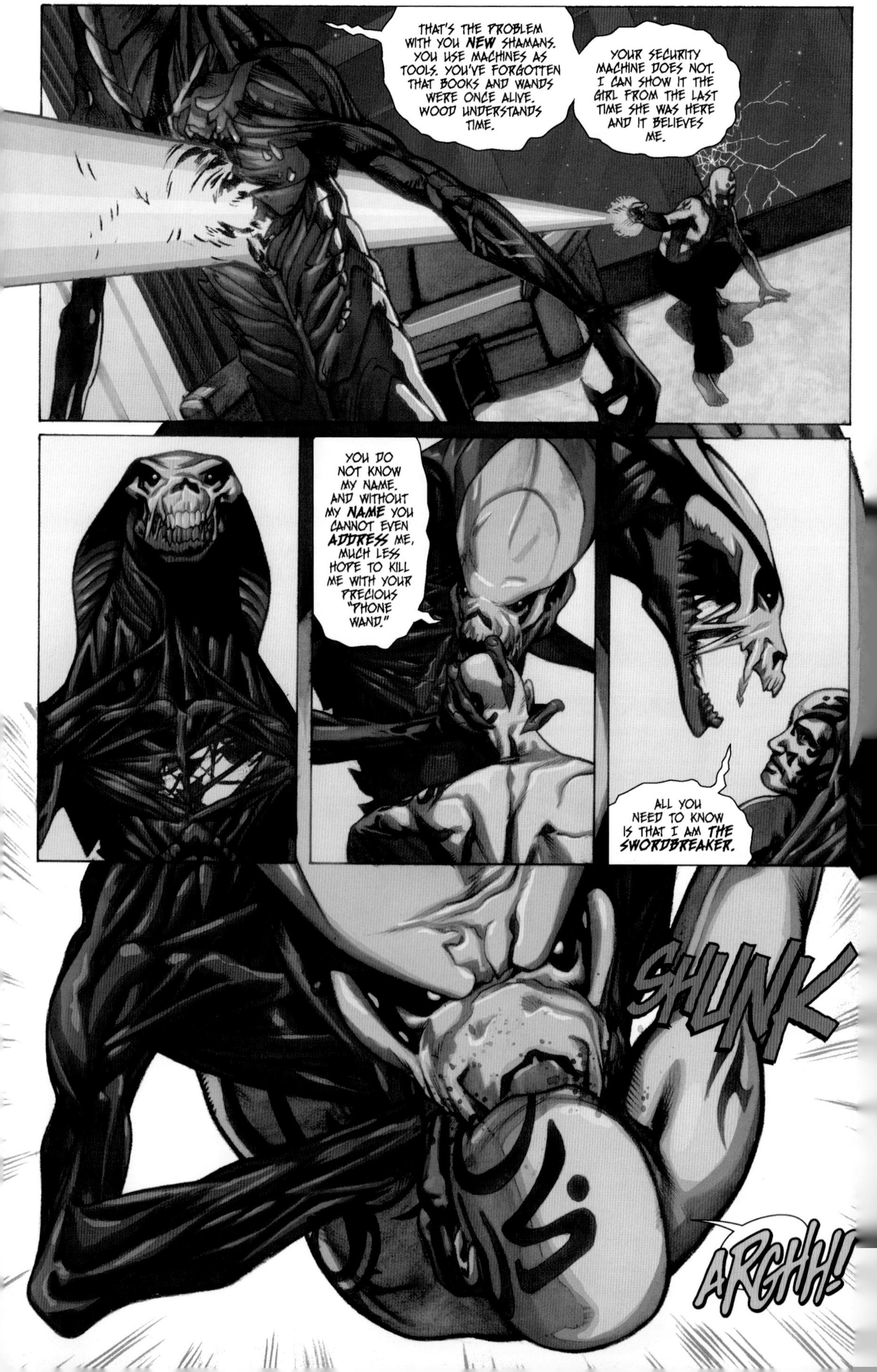
THAT'S THE PROBLEM WITH YOU NEW SHAMANS. YOU USE MACHINES AS TOOLS. YOU'VE FORGOTTEN THAT BOOKS AND WANDS WERE ONCE ALIVE. WOOD UNDERSTANDS TIME.
YOUR SECURITY MACHINE DOES NOT. I CAN SHOW IT THE GIRL FROM THE LAST TIME SHE WAS HERE AND IT BELIEVES ME.
YOU DO NOT KNOW MY NAME. AND WITHOUT MY NAME YOU CANNOT EVEN ADDRESS ME, MUCH LESS HOPE TO KILL ME WITH YOUR PRECIOUS "PHONE WAND."
ALL YOU NEED TO KNOW IS THAT I AM THE SWORDBREAKER.
SHUNK!
ARGHH!

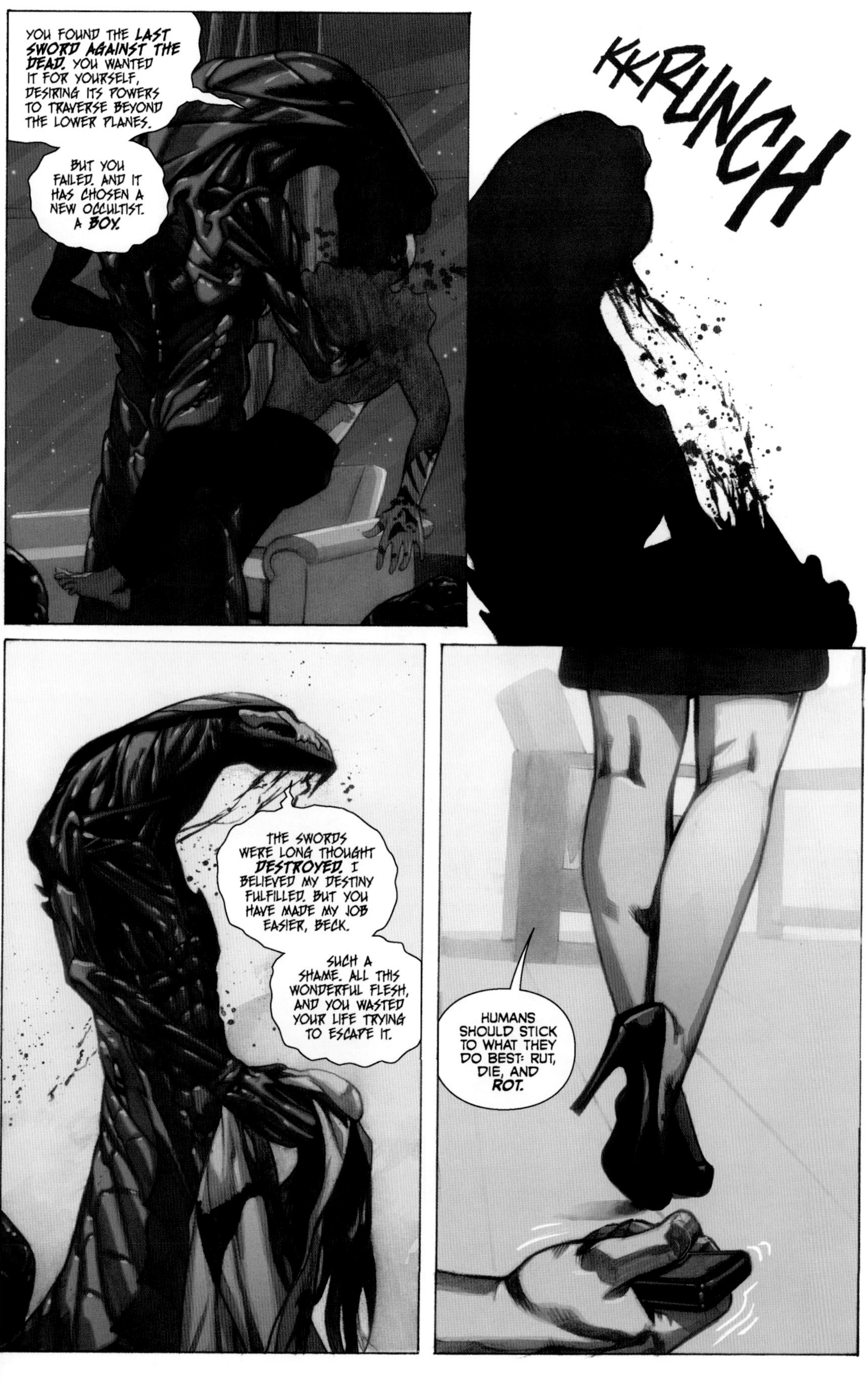
YOU FOUND THE LAST SWORD AGAINST THE DEAD. YOU WANTED IT FOR YOURSELF, DESIRING ITS POWERS TO TRAVERSE BEYOND THE LOWER PLANES.
BUT YOU FAILED. AND IT HAS CHOSEN A NEW OCCULTIST. A BOY.
KKRUNCH
THE SWORDS WERE LONG THOUGHT DESTROYED. I BELIEVED MY DESTINY FULFILLED. BUT YOU HAVE MADE MY JOB EASIER, BECK.
SUCH A SHAME. ALL THIS WONDERFUL FLESH, AND YOU WASTED YOUR LIFE TRYING TO ESCAPE IT.
HUMANS SHOULD STICK TO WHAT THEY DO BEST: RUT, DIE, AND ROT.

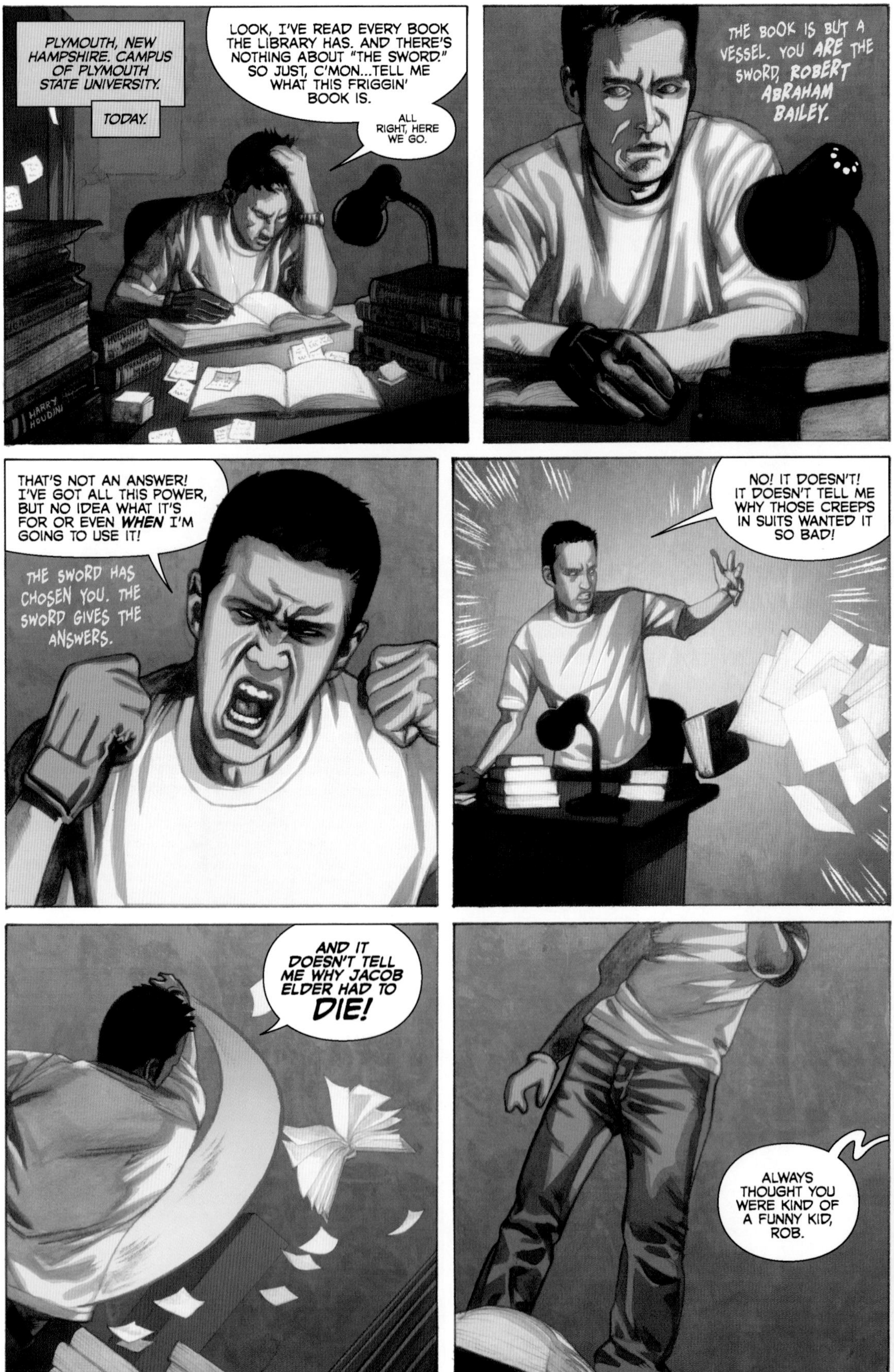
PLYMOUTH, NEW HAMPSHIRE. CAMPUS OF PLYMOUTH STATE UNIVERSITY.
TODAY.
LOOK, I'VE READ EVERY BOOK THE LIBRARY HAS. AND THERE'S NOTHING ABOUT "THE SWORD." SO JUST, C'MON...TELL ME WHAT THIS FRIGGIN' BOOK IS.
ALL RIGHT, HERE WE GO.
THE BOOK IS BUT A VESSEL. YOU ARE THE SWORD, ROBERT ABRAHAM BAILEY.
THAT'S NOT AN ANSWER! I'VE GOT ALL THIS POWER, BUT NO IDEA WHAT IT'S FOR OR EVEN WHEN I'M GOING TO USE IT!
THE SWORD HAS CHOSEN YOU. THE SWORD GIVES THE ANSWERS.
NO! IT DOESN'T! IT DOESN'T TELL ME WHY THOSE CREEPS IN SUITS WANTED IT SO BAD!
AND IT DOESN'T TELL ME WHY JACOB ELDER HAD TO DIE!
ALWAYS THOUGHT YOU WERE KIND OF A FUNNY KID, ROB.

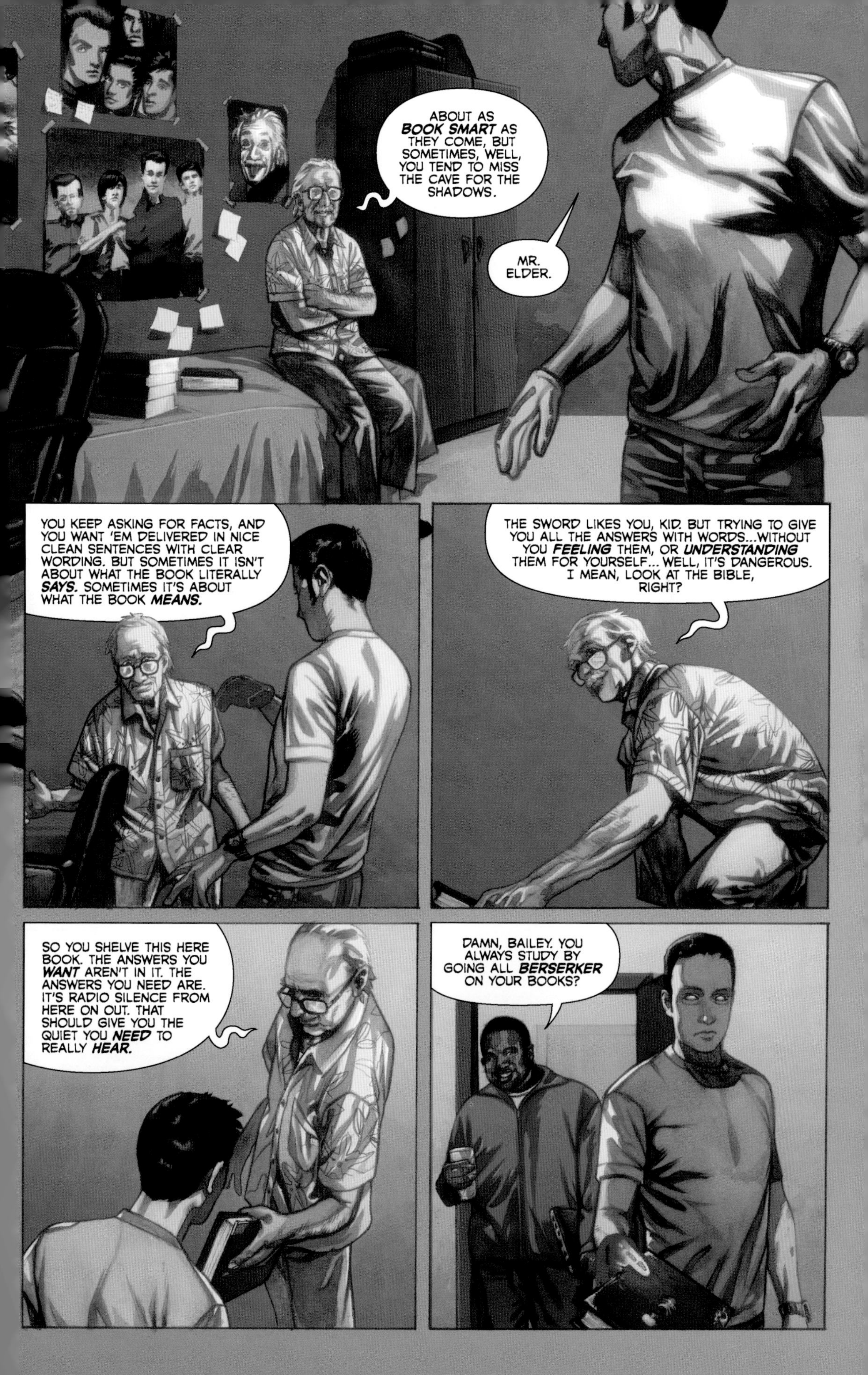
ABOUT AS BOOK SMART AS THEY COME, BUT SOMETIMES, WELL, YOU TEND TO MISS THE CAVE FOR THE SHADOWS.
MR. ELDER.
YOU KEEP ASKING FOR FACTS, AND YOU WANT 'EM DELIVERED IN NICE CLEAN SENTENCES WITH CLEAR WORDING. BUT SOMETIMES IT ISN'T ABOUT WHAT THE BOOK LITERALLY SAYS. SOMETIMES IT'S ABOUT WHAT THE BOOK MEANS.
THE SWORD LIKES YOU, KID. BUT TRYING TO GIVE YOU ALL THE ANSWERS WITH WORDS...WITHOUT YOU FEELING THEM, OR UNDERSTANDING THEM FOR YOURSELF... WELL, IT'S DANGEROUS. I MEAN, LOOK AT THE BIBLE, RIGHT?
SO YOU SHELVE THIS HERE BOOK. THE ANSWERS YOU WANT AREN'T IN IT. THE ANSWERS YOU NEED ARE. IT'S RADIO SILENCE FROM HERE ON OUT. THAT SHOULD GIVE YOU THE QUIET YOU NEED TO REALLY HEAR.
DAMN, BAILEY. YOU ALWAYS STUDY BY GOING ALL BERSERKER ON YOUR BOOKS?

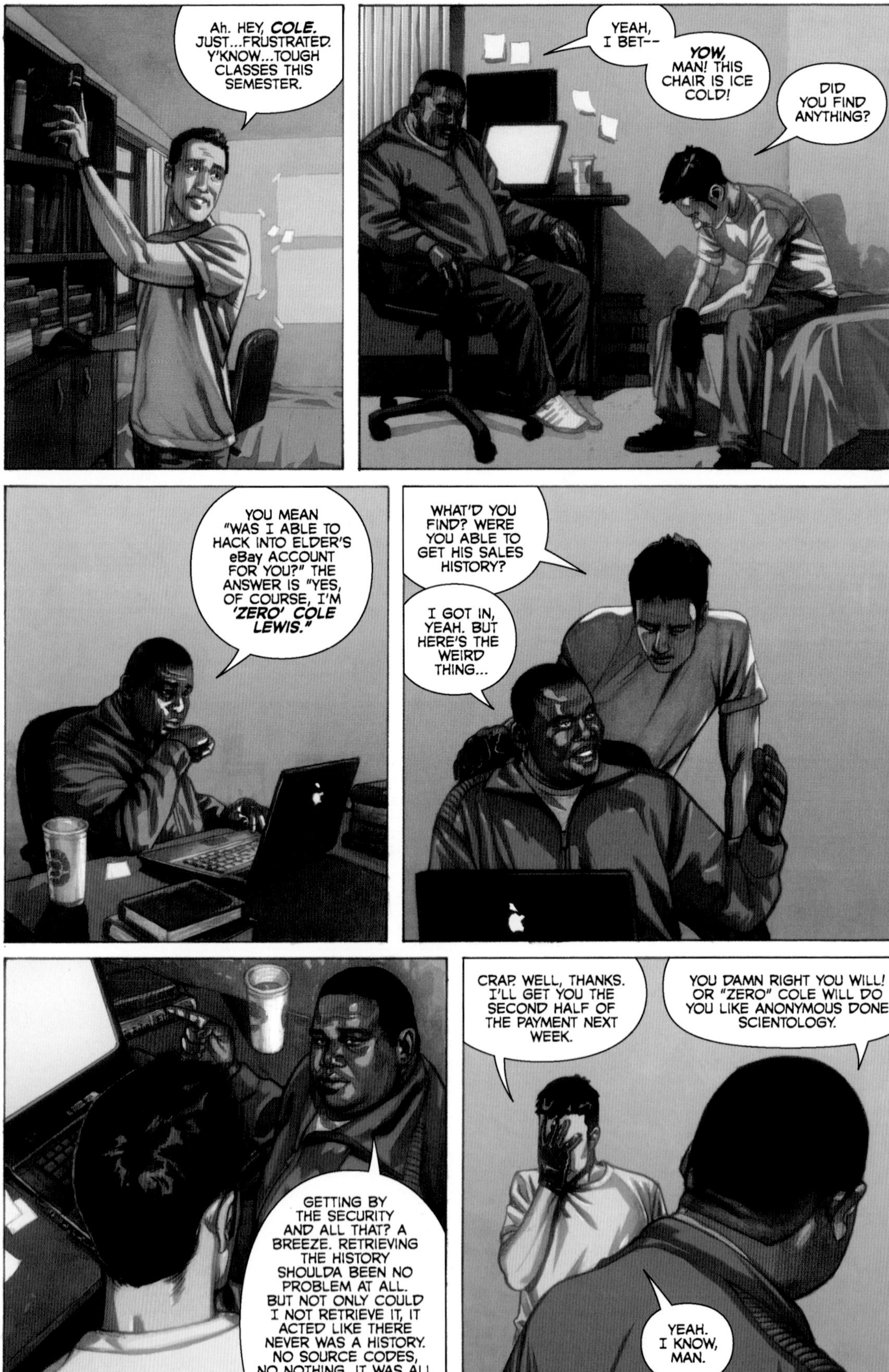

Ah. HEY, COLE. JUST...FRUSTRATED. Y'KNOW...TOUGH CLASSES THIS SEMESTER.
YEAH, I BET--
YOW, MAN! THIS CHAIR IS ICE COLD!
DID YOU FIND ANYTHING?
YOU MEAN "WAS I ABLE TO HACK INTO ELDER'S eBay ACCOUNT FOR YOU?" THE ANSWER IS "YES, OF COURSE, I'M 'ZERO' COLE LEWIS."
WHAT'D YOU FIND? WERE YOU ABLE TO GET HIS SALES HISTORY?
I GOT IN, YEAH. BUT HERE'S THE WEIRD THING...
GETTING BY THE SECURITY AND ALL THAT? A BREEZE. RETRIEVING THE HISTORY SHOULDA BEEN NO PROBLEM AT ALL. BUT NOT ONLY COULD I NOT RETRIEVE IT, IT ACTED LIKE THERE NEVER WAS A HISTORY. NO SOURCE CODES, NO NOTHING. IT WAS ALL GONE...POOF. MAGIC.
CRAP. WELL, THANKS. I'LL GET YOU THE SECOND HALF OF THE PAYMENT NEXT WEEK.
YOU DAMN RIGHT YOU WILL! OR "ZERO" COLE WILL DO YOU LIKE ANONYMOUS DONE SCIENTOLOGY.
YEAH. I KNOW, MAN.

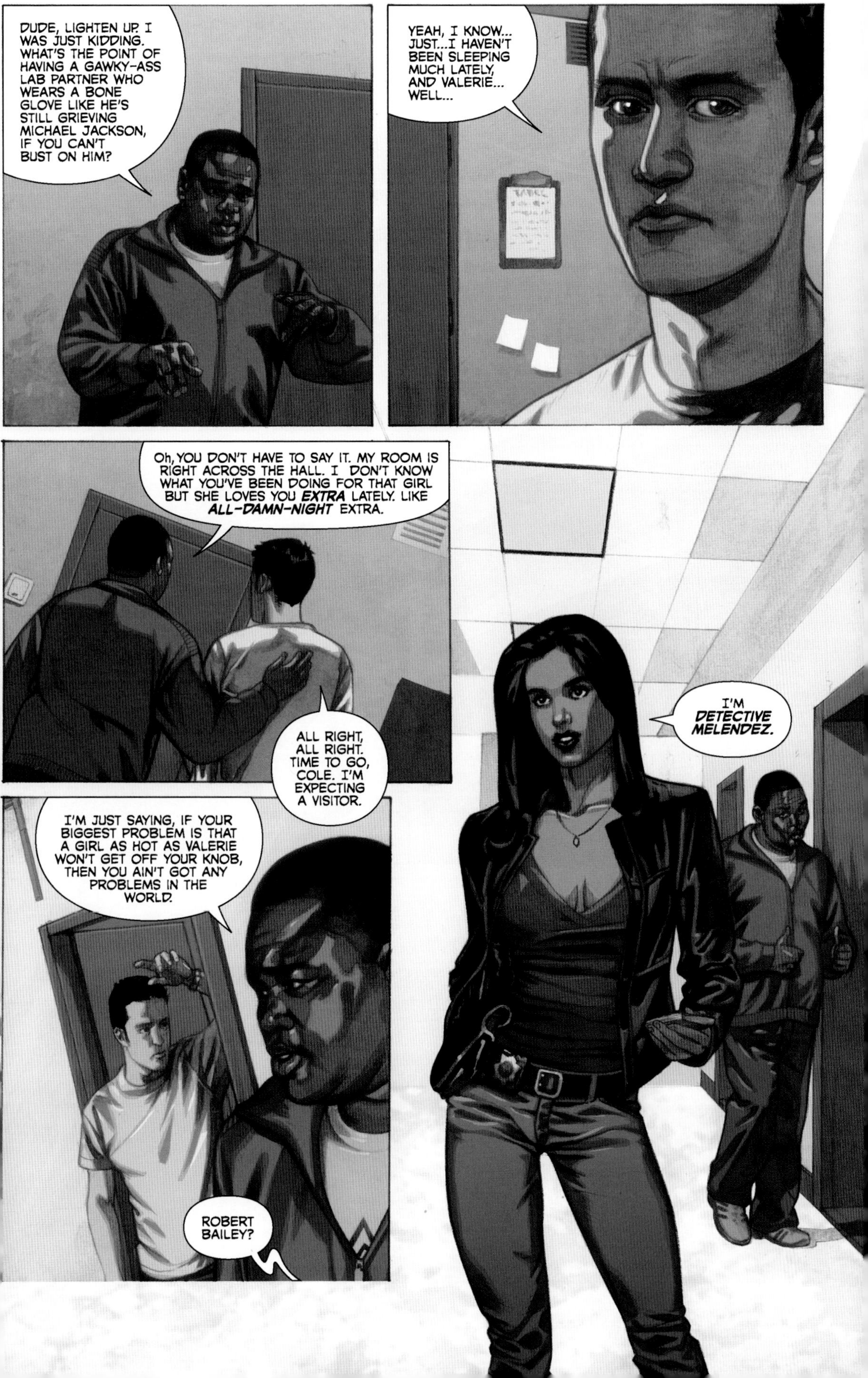
DUDE, LIGHTEN UP. I WAS JUST KIDDING. WHAT'S THE POINT OF HAVING A GAWKY-ASS LAB PARTNER WHO WEARS A BONE GLOVE LIKE HE'S STILL GRIEVING MICHAEL JACKSON, IF YOU CAN'T BUST ON HIM?
YEAH, I KNOW... JUST...I HAVEN'T BEEN SLEEPING MUCH LATELY, AND VALERIE... WELL...
OH, YOU DON'T HAVE TO SAY IT. MY ROOM IS RIGHT ACROSS THE HALL. I DON'T KNOW WHAT YOU'VE BEEN DOING FOR THAT GIRL BUT SHE LOVES YOU EXTRA LATELY. LIKE ALL-DAMN-NIGHT EXTRA.
ALL RIGHT, ALL RIGHT. TIME TO GO, COLE. I'M EXPECTING A VISITOR.
I'M JUST SAYING, IF YOUR BIGGEST PROBLEM IS THAT A GIRL AS HOT AS VALERIE WON'T GET OFF YOUR KNOB, THEN YOU AIN'T GOT ANY PROBLEMS IN THE WORLD.
ROBERT BAILEY?
I'M DETECTIVE MELENDEZ.

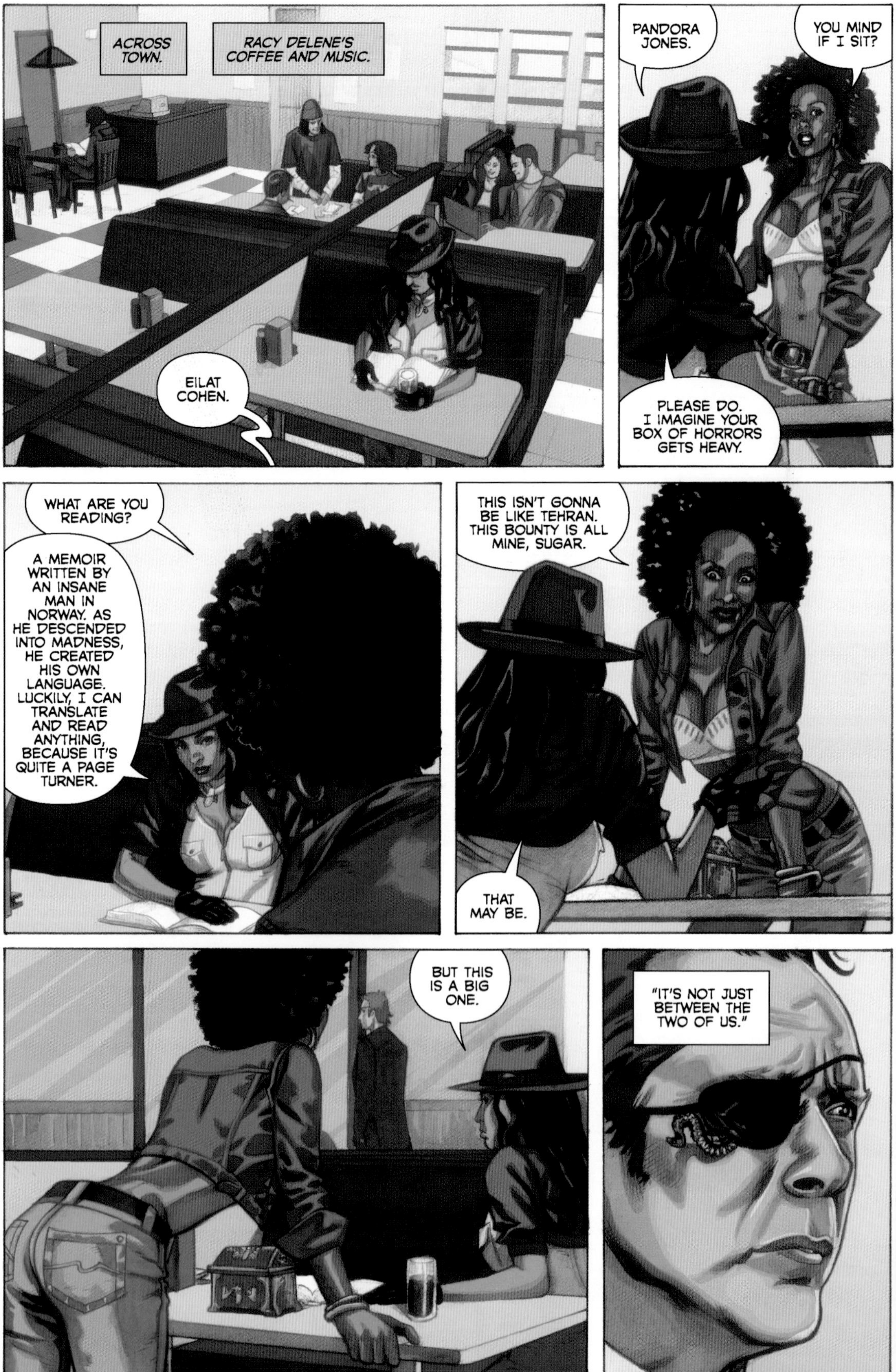
ACROSS TOWN.
RACY DELENE'S COFFEE AND MUSIC.
EILAT COHEN.
PANDORA JONES.
YOU MIND IF I SIT?
PLEASE DO. I IMAGINE YOUR BOX OF HORRORS GETS HEAVY.
WHAT ARE YOU READING?
A MEMOIR WRITTEN BY AN INSANE MAN IN NORWAY. AS HE DESCENDED INTO MADNESS, HE CREATED HIS OWN LANGUAGE. LUCKILY, I CAN TRANSLATE AND READ ANYTHING, BECAUSE IT'S QUITE A PAGE TURNER.
THIS ISN'T GONNA BE LIKE TEHRAN. THIS BOUNTY IS ALL MINE, SUGAR.
THAT MAY BE.
BUT THIS IS A BIG ONE.
"IT'S NOT JUST BETWEEN THE TWO OF US."

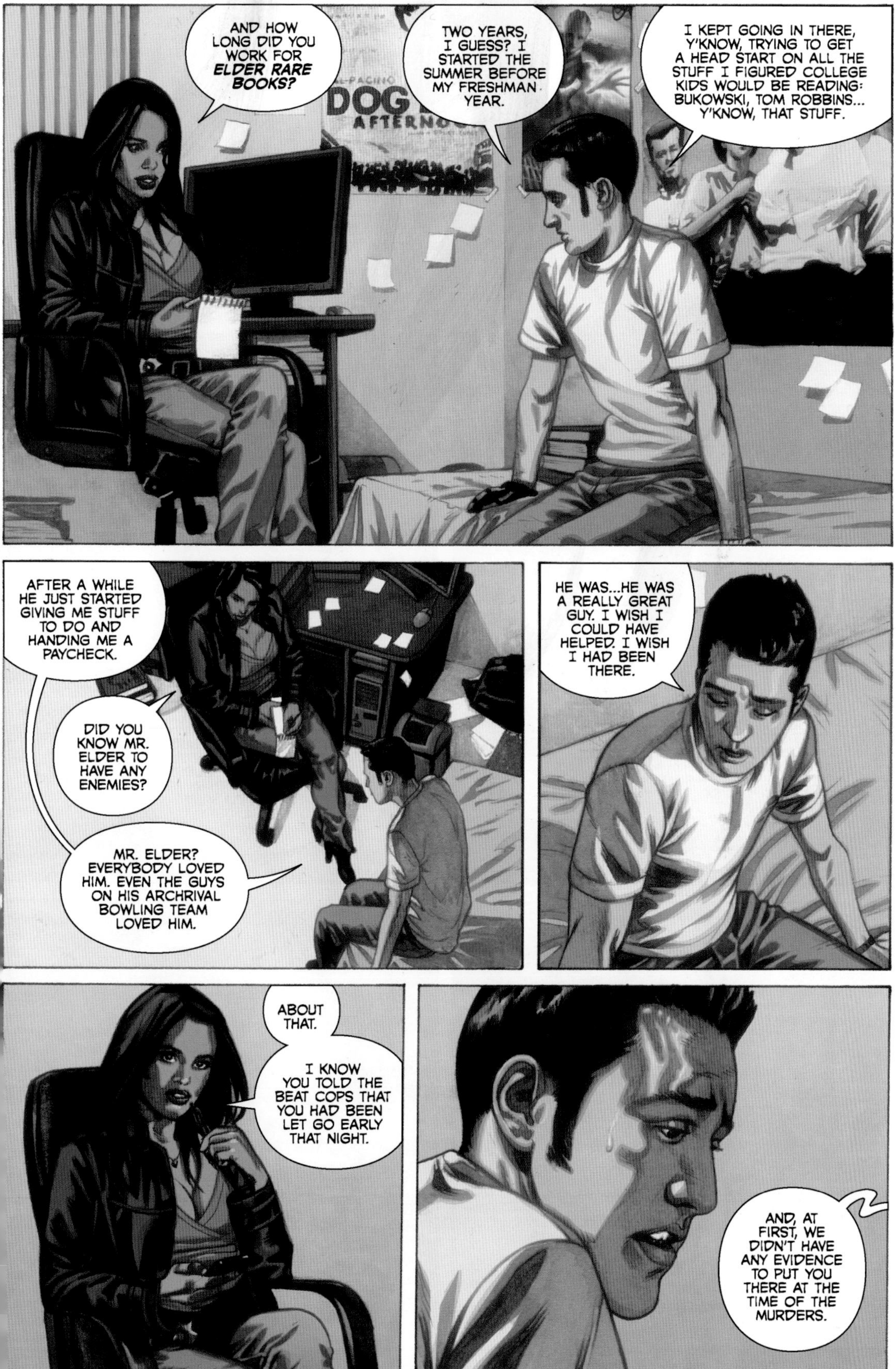
AND HOW LONG DID YOU WORK FOR ELDER RARE BOOKS?
TWO YEARS, I GUESS? I STARTED THE SUMMER BEFORE MY FRESHMAN YEAR.
I KEPT GOING IN THERE, Y'KNOW, TRYING TO GET A HEAD START ON ALL THE STUFF I FIGURED COLLEGE KIDS WOULD BE READING: BUKOWSKI, TOM ROBBINS... Y'KNOW, THAT STUFF.
AFTER A WHILE HE JUST STARTED GIVING ME STUFF TO DO AND HANDING ME A PAYCHECK.
DID YOU KNOW MR. ELDER TO HAVE ANY ENEMIES?
MR. ELDER? EVERYBODY LOVED HIM. EVEN THE GUYS ON HIS ARCHRIVAL BOWLING TEAM LOVED HIM.
HE WAS...HE WAS A REALLY GREAT GUY. I WISH I COULD HAVE HELPED. I WISH I HAD BEEN THERE.
ABOUT THAT.
I KNOW YOU TOLD THE BEAT COPS THAT YOU HAD BEEN LET GO EARLY THAT NIGHT.
AND, AT FIRST, WE DIDN'T HAVE ANY EVIDENCE TO PUT YOU THERE AT THE TIME OF THE MURDERS.

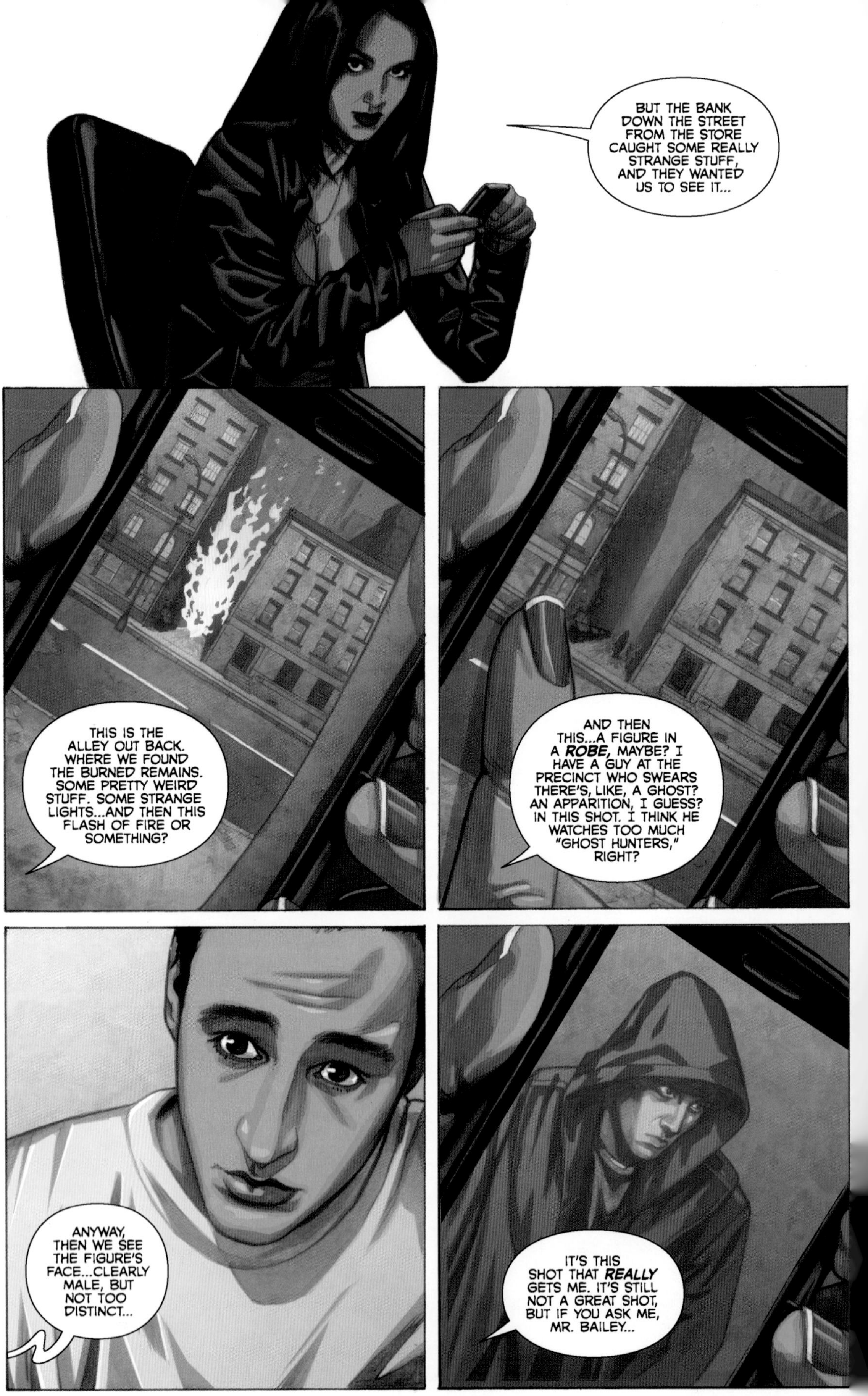
BUT THE BANK DOWN THE STREET FROM THE STORE CAUGHT SOME REALLY STRANGE STUFF, AND THEY WANTED US TO SEE IT...
THIS IS THE ALLEY OUT BACK. WHERE WE FOUND THE BURNED REMAINS. SOME PRETTY WEIRD STUFF. SOME STRANGE LIGHTS...AND THEN THIS FLASH OF FIRE OR SOMETHING?
AND THEN THIS...A FIGURE IN A *ROBE,* MAYBE? I HAVE A GUY AT THE PRECINCT WHO SWEARS THERE'S, LIKE, A GHOST? AN APPARITION, I GUESS? IN THIS SHOT. I THINK HE WATCHES TOO MUCH "GHOST HUNTERS," RIGHT?
ANYWAY, THEN WE SEE THE FIGURE'S FACE...CLEARLY MALE, BUT NOT TOO DISTINCT...
IT'S THIS SHOT THAT *REALLY* GETS ME. IT'S STILL NOT A GREAT SHOT, BUT IF YOU ASK ME, MR. BAILEY...

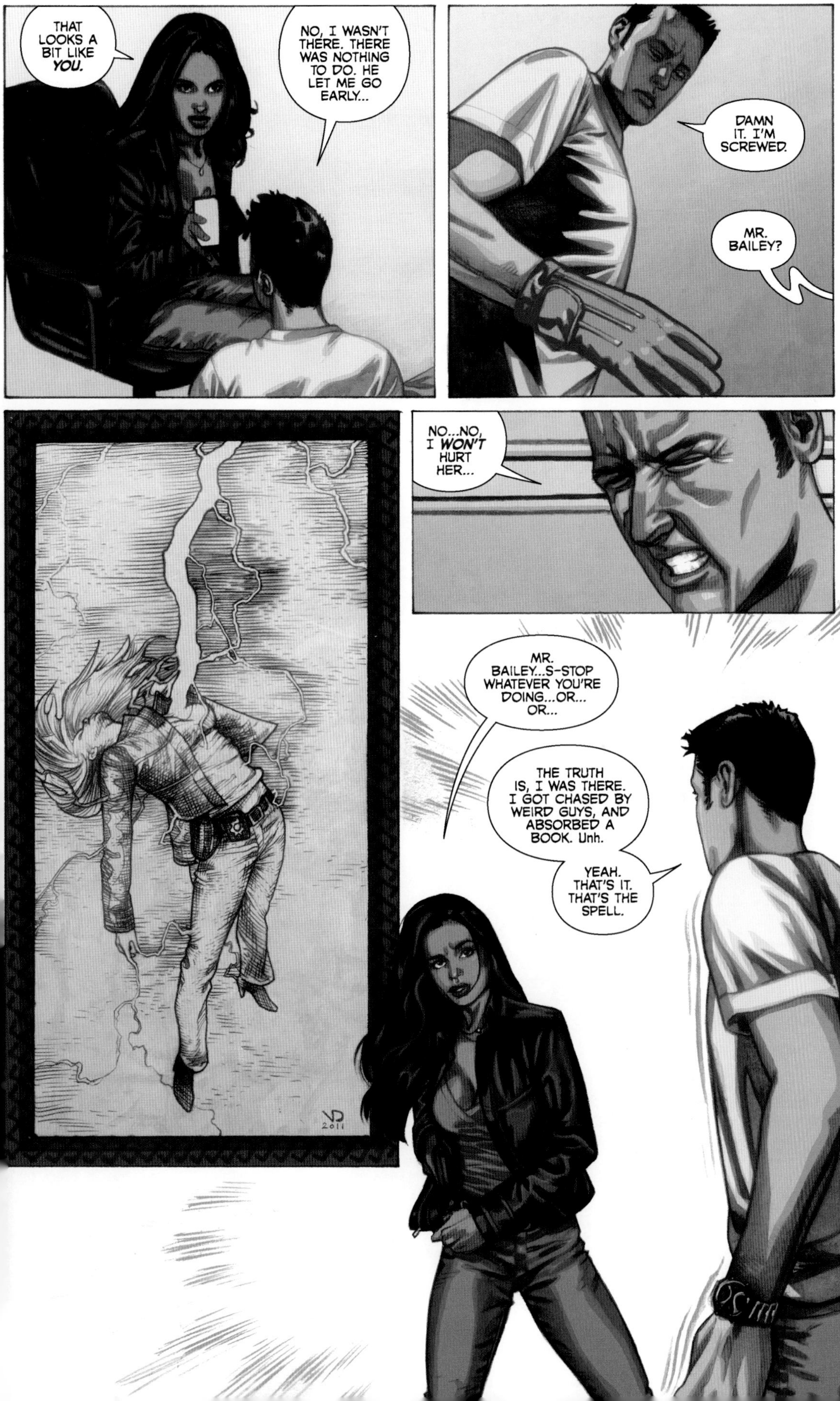
THAT LOOKS A BIT LIKE *YOU.*
NO, I WASN'T THERE. THERE WAS NOTHING TO DO. HE LET ME GO EARLY...
DAMN IT. I'M SCREWED.
MR. BAILEY?
NO...NO, I *WON'T* HURT HER...
MR. BAILEY...S-STOP WHATEVER YOU'RE DOING...OR... OR...
THE TRUTH IS, I WAS THERE. I GOT CHASED BY WEIRD GUYS, AND ABSORBED A BOOK. Unh.
YEAH. THAT'S IT. THAT'S THE SPELL.
VD 2011

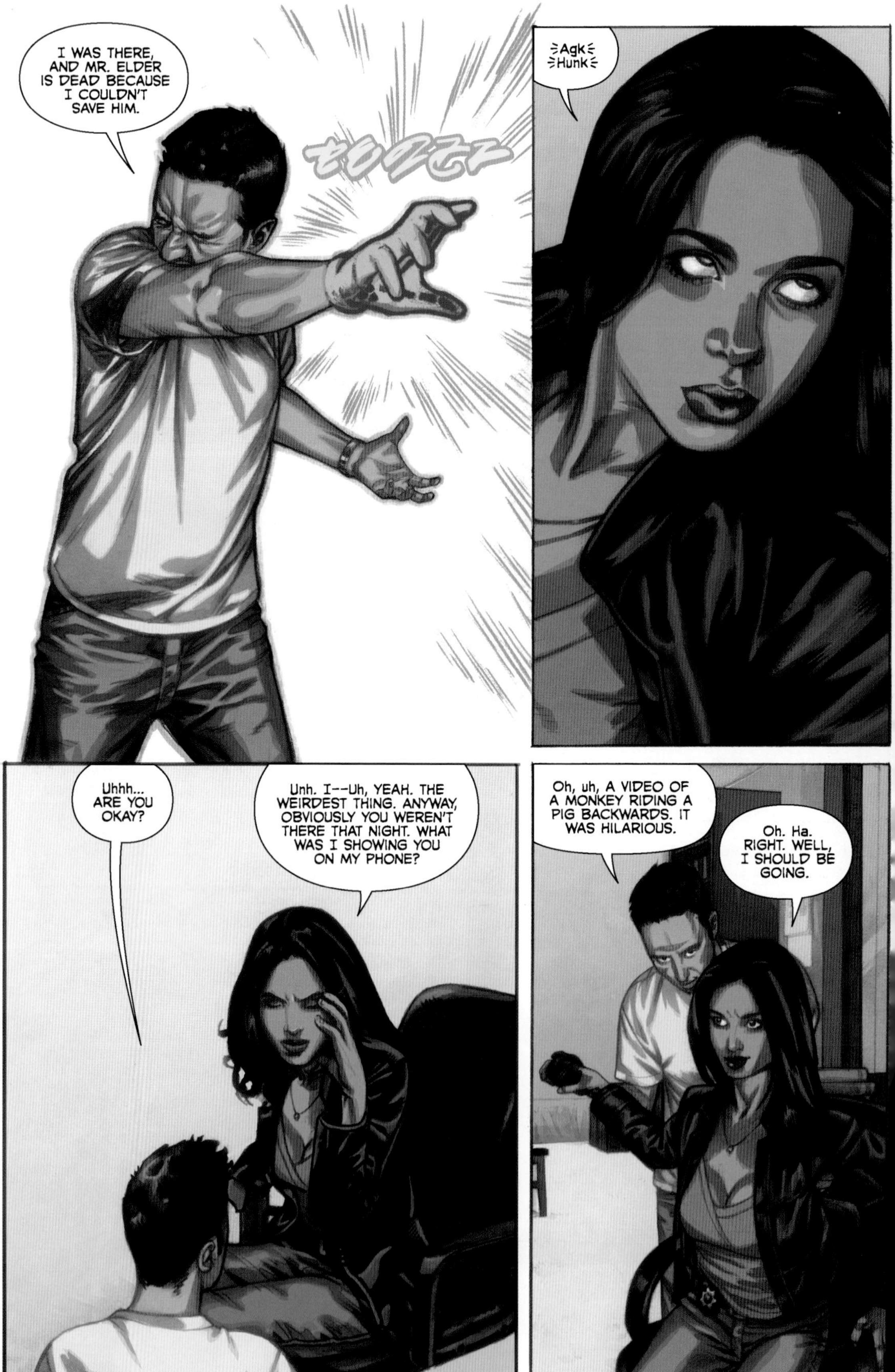
I WAS THERE, AND MR. ELDER IS DEAD BECAUSE I COULDN'T SAVE HIM.
Agk Hunk
Uhhh... ARE YOU OKAY?
Unh. I--Uh, YEAH. THE WEIRDEST THING. ANYWAY, OBVIOUSLY YOU WEREN'T THERE THAT NIGHT. WHAT WAS I SHOWING YOU ON MY PHONE?
Oh, uh, A VIDEO OF A MONKEY RIDING A PIG BACKWARDS. IT WAS HILARIOUS.
Oh. Ha. RIGHT. WELL, I SHOULD BE GOING.

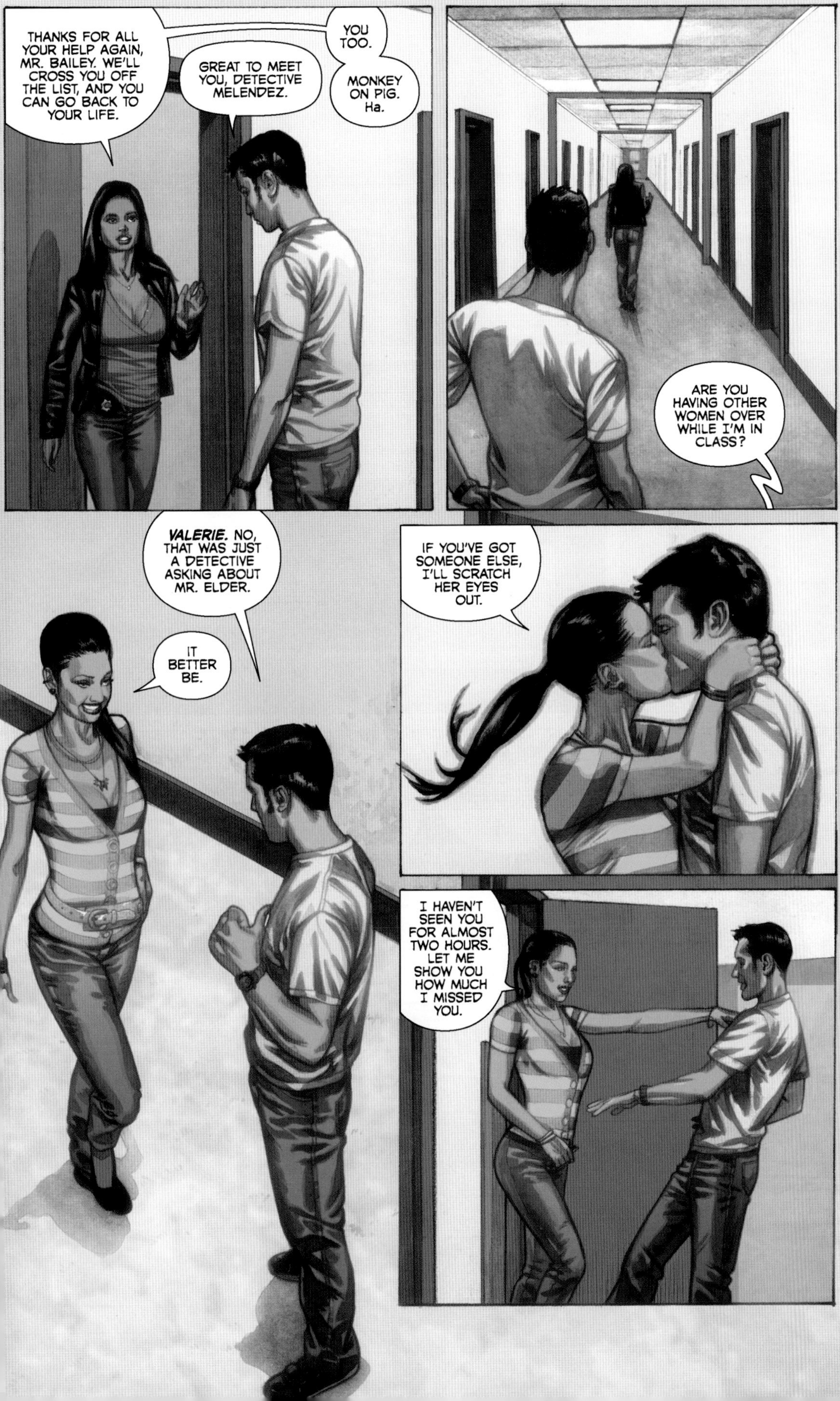
THANKS FOR ALL YOUR HELP AGAIN, MR. BAILEY. WE'LL CROSS YOU OFF THE LIST, AND YOU CAN GO BACK TO YOUR LIFE.
GREAT TO MEET YOU, DETECTIVE MELENDEZ.
YOU TOO.
MONKEY ON PIG. Ha.
ARE YOU HAVING OTHER WOMEN OVER WHILE I'M IN CLASS?
VALERIE. NO, THAT WAS JUST A DETECTIVE ASKING ABOUT MR. ELDER.
IT BETTER BE.
IF YOU'VE GOT SOMEONE ELSE, I'LL SCRATCH HER EYES OUT.
I HAVEN'T SEEN YOU FOR ALMOST TWO HOURS. LET ME SHOW YOU HOW MUCH I MISSED YOU.

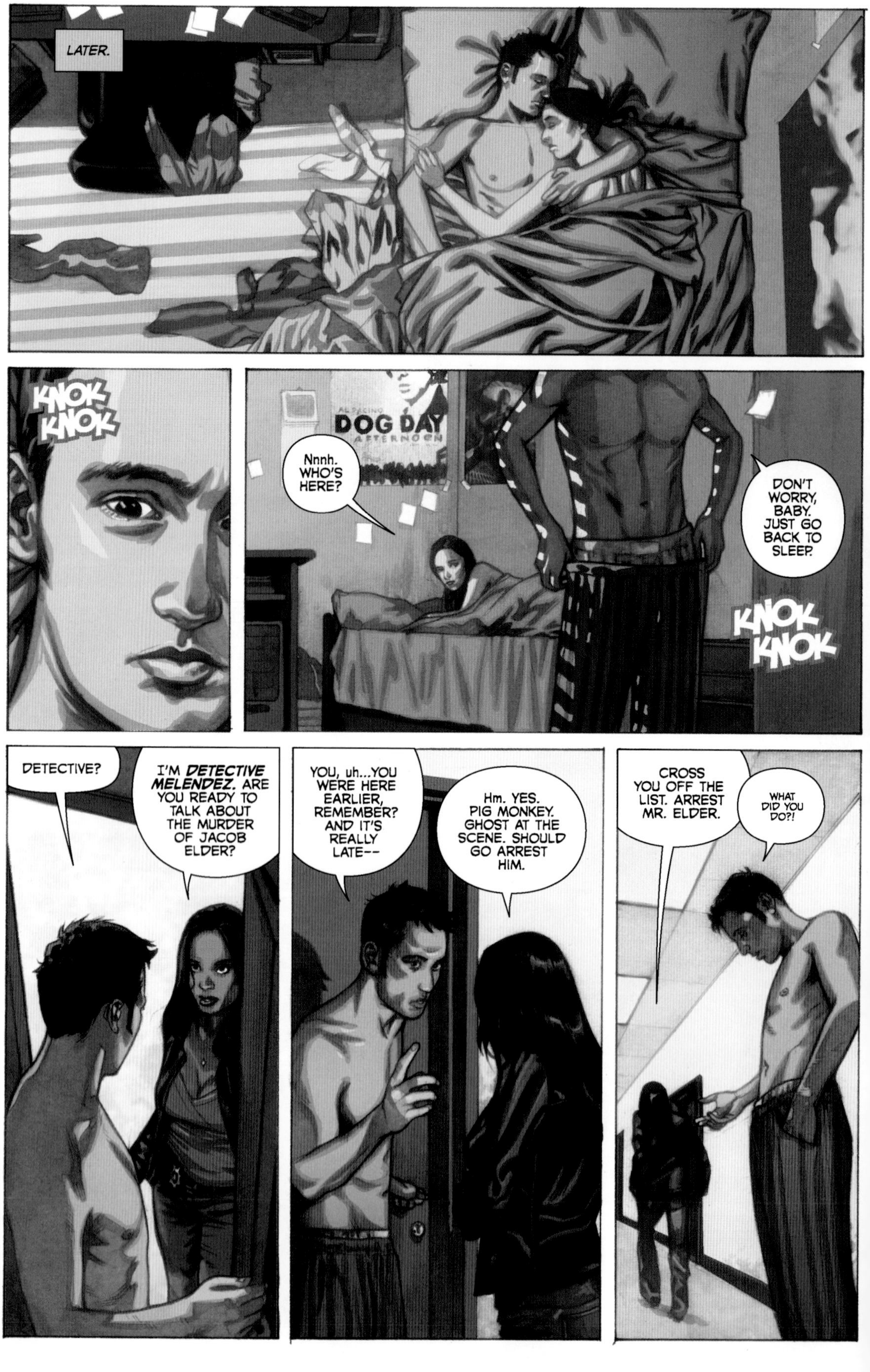
LATER.
KNOK KNOK
Nnnh. WHO'S HERE?
DOG DAY AFTERNOON
DON'T WORRY, BABY. JUST GO BACK TO SLEEP.
KNOK KNOK
DETECTIVE?
I'M DETECTIVE MELENDEZ. ARE YOU READY TO TALK ABOUT THE MURDER OF JACOB ELDER?
YOU, uh...YOU WERE HERE EARLIER, REMEMBER? AND IT'S REALLY LATE--
Hm. YES. PIG MONKEY. GHOST AT THE SCENE. SHOULD GO ARREST HIM.
CROSS YOU OFF THE LIST. ARREST MR. ELDER.
WHAT DID YOU DO?!

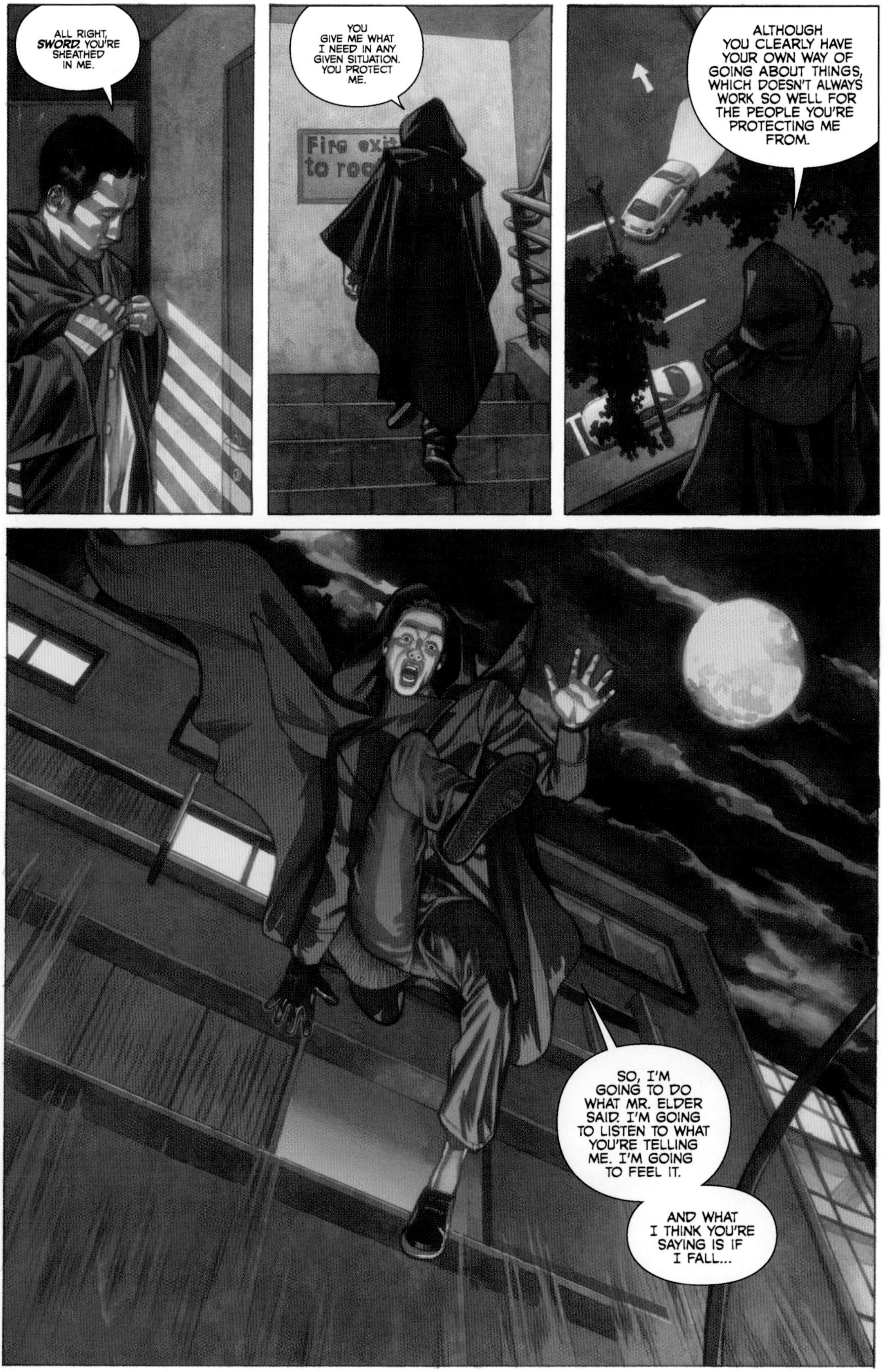
ALL RIGHT, SWORD. YOU'RE SHEATHED IN ME.
YOU GIVE ME WHAT I NEED IN ANY GIVEN SITUATION. YOU PROTECT ME.
Fire exit to roo
ALTHOUGH YOU CLEARLY HAVE YOUR OWN WAY OF GOING ABOUT THINGS, WHICH DOESN'T ALWAYS WORK SO WELL FOR THE PEOPLE YOU'RE PROTECTING ME FROM.
SO, I'M GOING TO DO WHAT MR. ELDER SAID. I'M GOING TO LISTEN TO WHAT YOU'RE TELLING ME. I'M GOING TO FEEL IT.
AND WHAT I THINK YOU'RE SAYING IS IF I FALL...

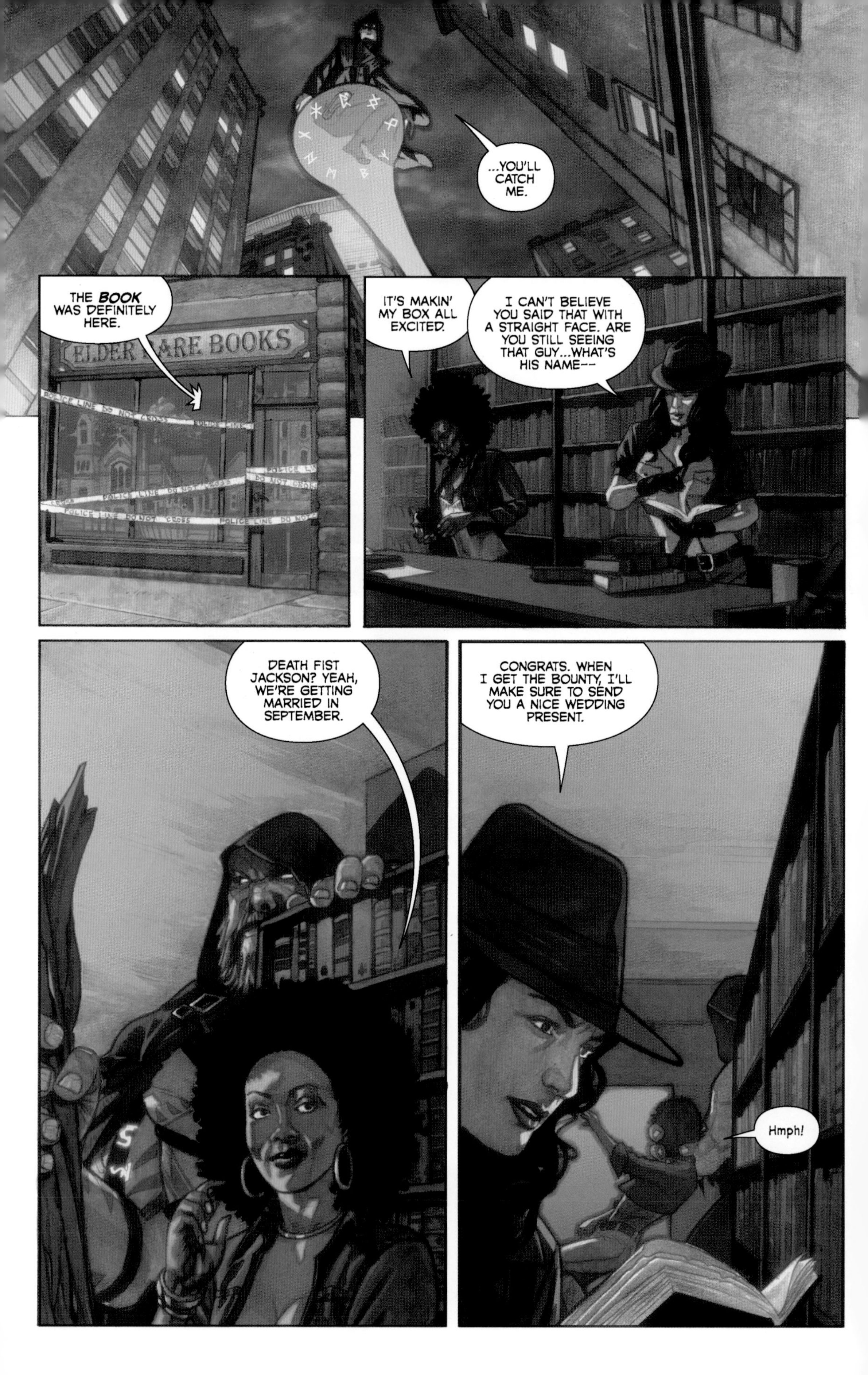
...YOU'LL CATCH ME.
THE BOOK WAS DEFINITELY HERE.
ELDER RARE BOOKS
POLICE LINE DO NOT CROSS
IT'S MAKIN' MY BOX ALL EXCITED.
I CAN'T BELIEVE YOU SAID THAT WITH A STRAIGHT FACE. ARE YOU STILL SEEING THAT GUY...WHAT'S HIS NAME--
DEATH FIST JACKSON? YEAH, WE'RE GETTING MARRIED IN SEPTEMBER.
CONGRATS. WHEN I GET THE BOUNTY, I'LL MAKE SURE TO SEND YOU A NICE WEDDING PRESENT.
Hmph!

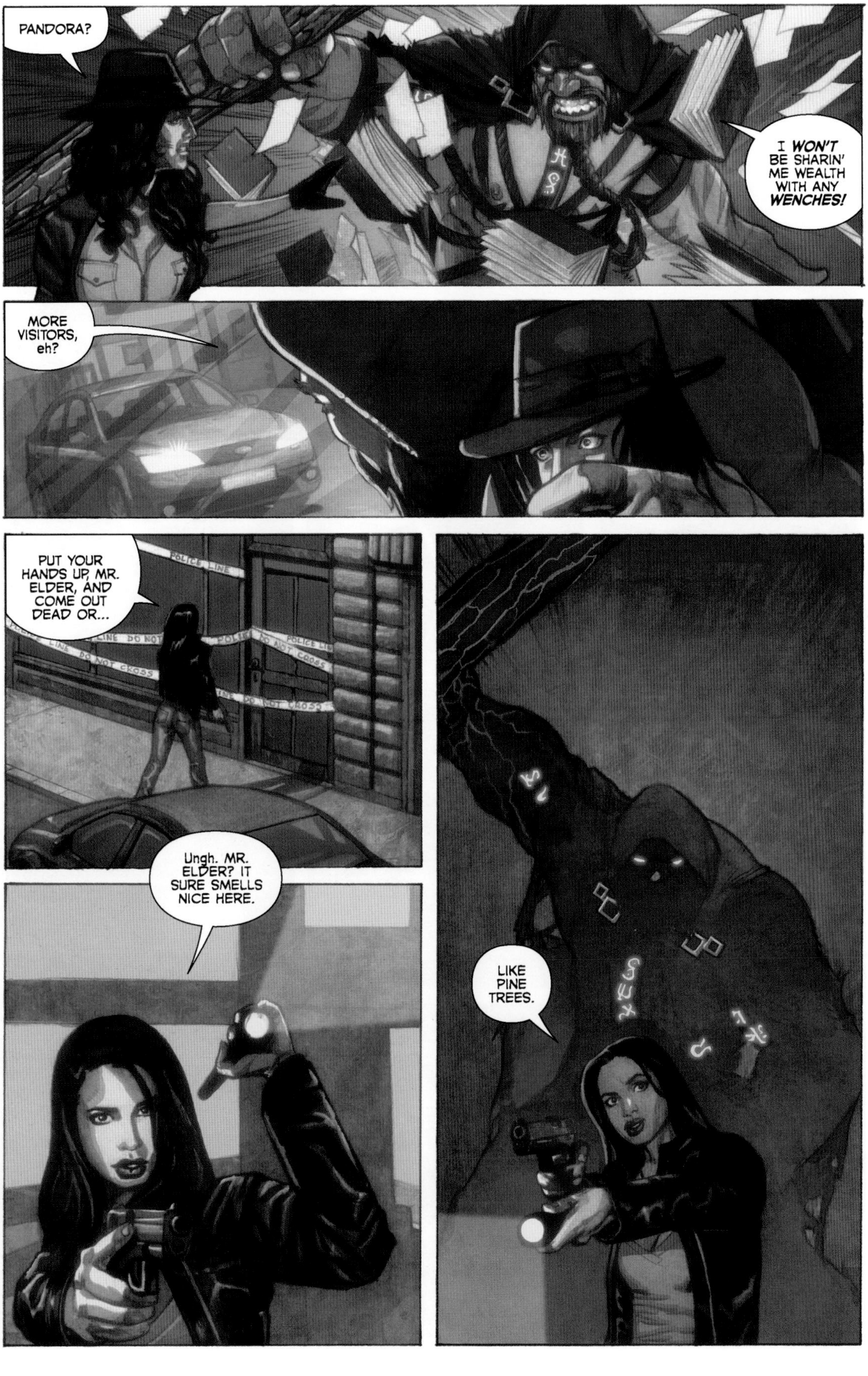
PANDORA?
I *WON'T* BE SHARIN' ME WEALTH WITH ANY *WENCHES!*
MORE VISITORS, eh?
PUT YOUR HANDS UP, MR. ELDER, AND COME OUT DEAD OR...
Ungh. MR. ELDER? IT SURE SMELLS NICE HERE.
LIKE PINE TREES.

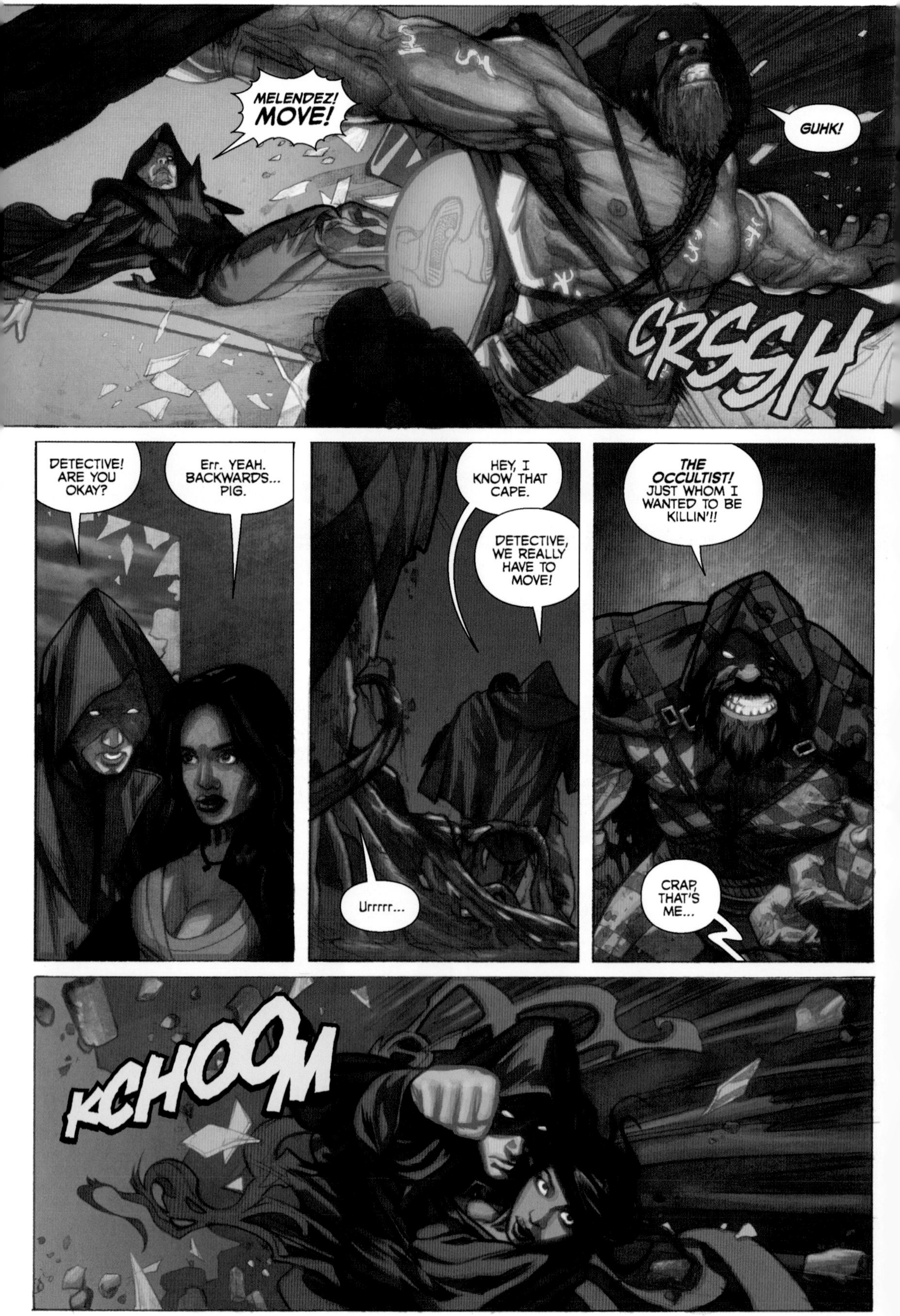
MELENDEZ! MOVE!
GUHK!
CRSSH
DETECTIVE! ARE YOU OKAY?
Err. YEAH. BACKWARDS... PIG.
HEY, I KNOW THAT CAPE.
DETECTIVE, WE REALLY HAVE TO MOVE!
Urrrrr...
THE OCCULTIST! JUST WHOM I WANTED TO BE KILLIN'!!
CRAP, THAT'S ME...
KCHOOM

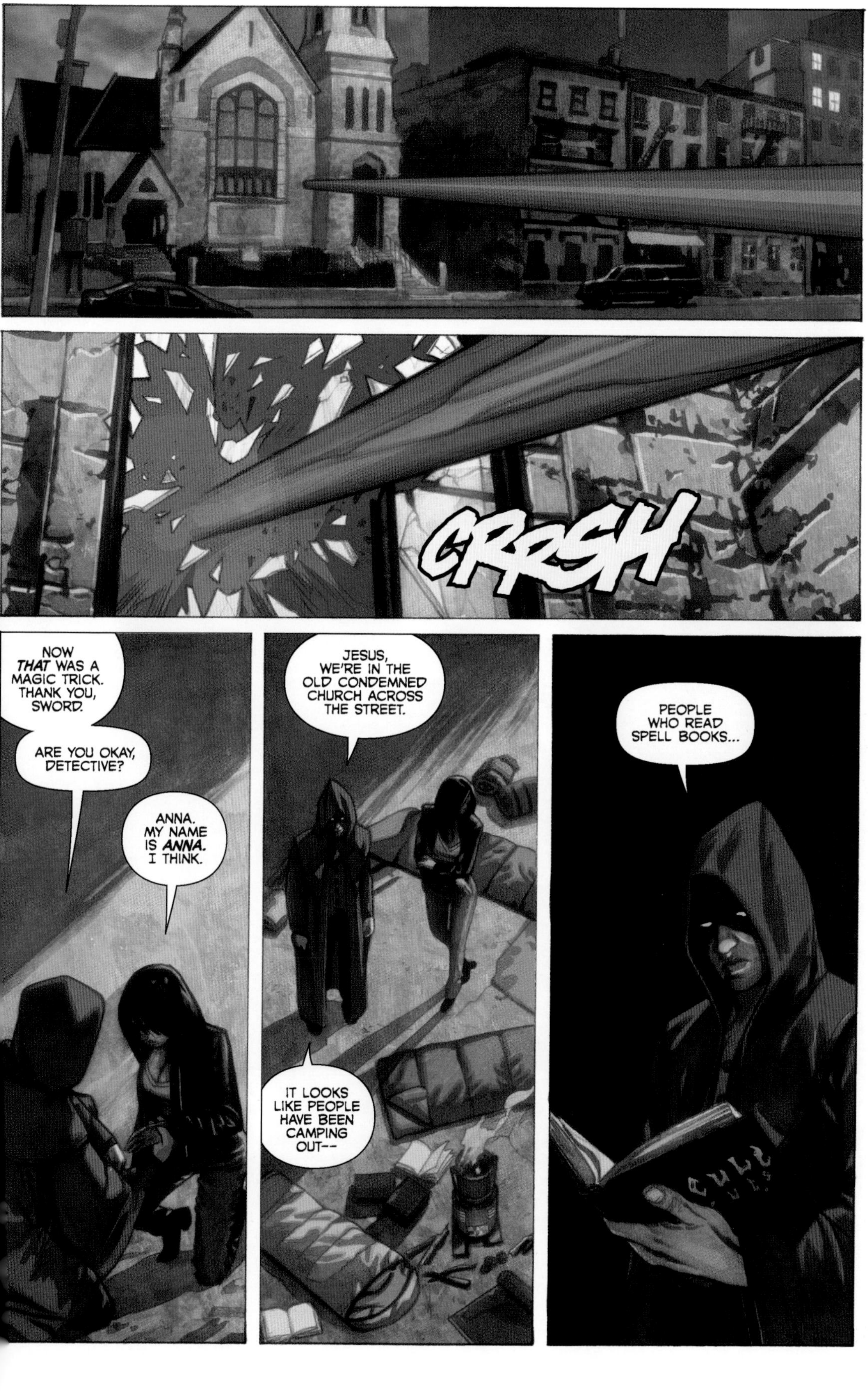

CRASH
NOW THAT WAS A MAGIC TRICK. THANK YOU, SWORD.
ARE YOU OKAY, DETECTIVE?
ANNA. MY NAME IS ANNA. I THINK.
JESUS, WE'RE IN THE OLD CONDEMNED CHURCH ACROSS THE STREET.
IT LOOKS LIKE PEOPLE HAVE BEEN CAMPING OUT--
PEOPLE WHO READ SPELL BOOKS...

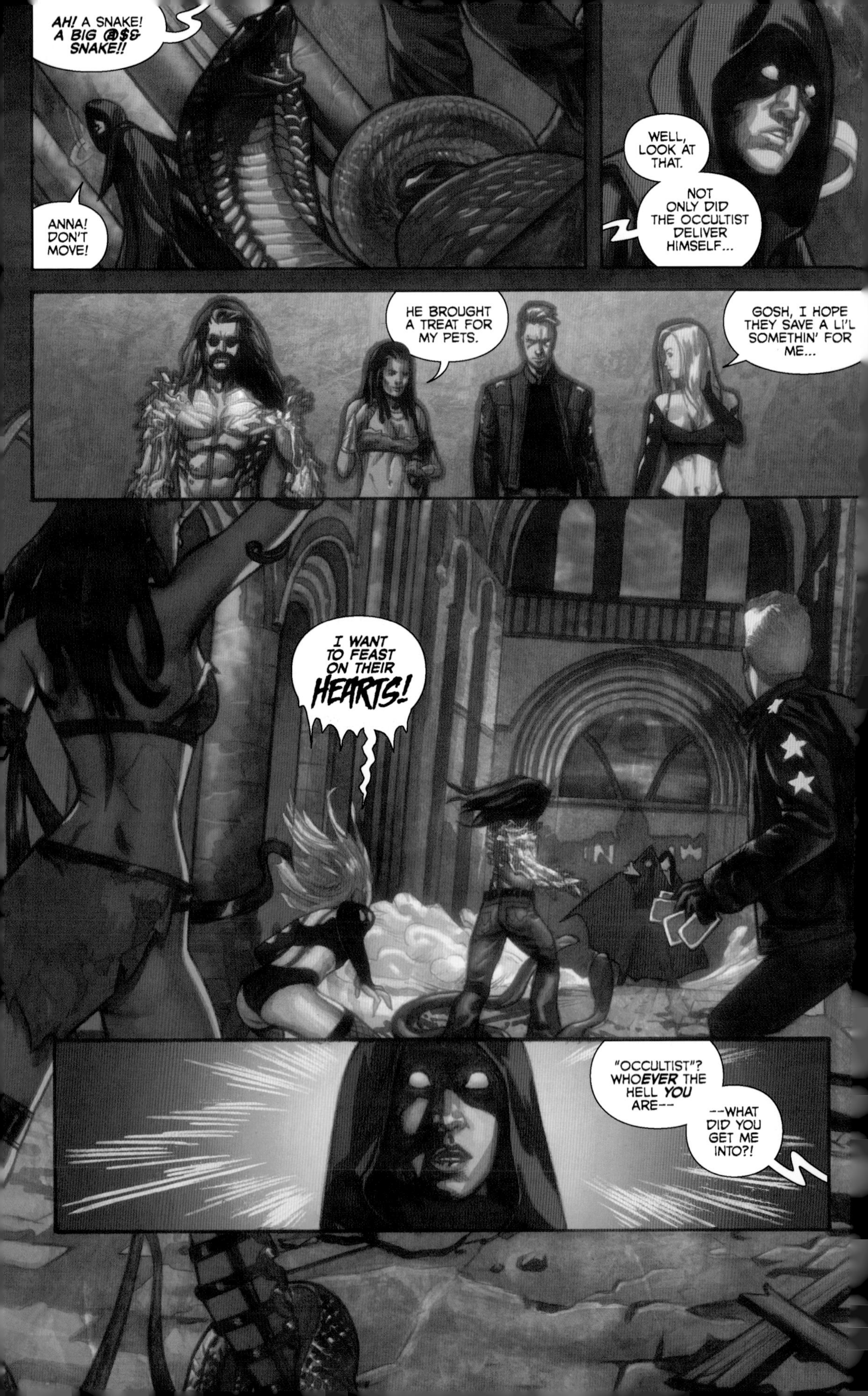
AH! A SNAKE! A BIG @$& SNAKE!!
ANNA! DON'T MOVE!
WELL, LOOK AT THAT.
NOT ONLY DID THE OCCULTIST DELIVER HIMSELF...
HE BROUGHT A TREAT FOR MY PETS.
GOSH, I HOPE THEY SAVE A LI'L SOMETHIN' FOR ME...
I WANT TO FEAST ON THEIR HEARTS!
"OCCULTIST"? WHOEVER THE HELL YOU ARE--
--WHAT DID YOU GET ME INTO?!

CHAPTER THREE

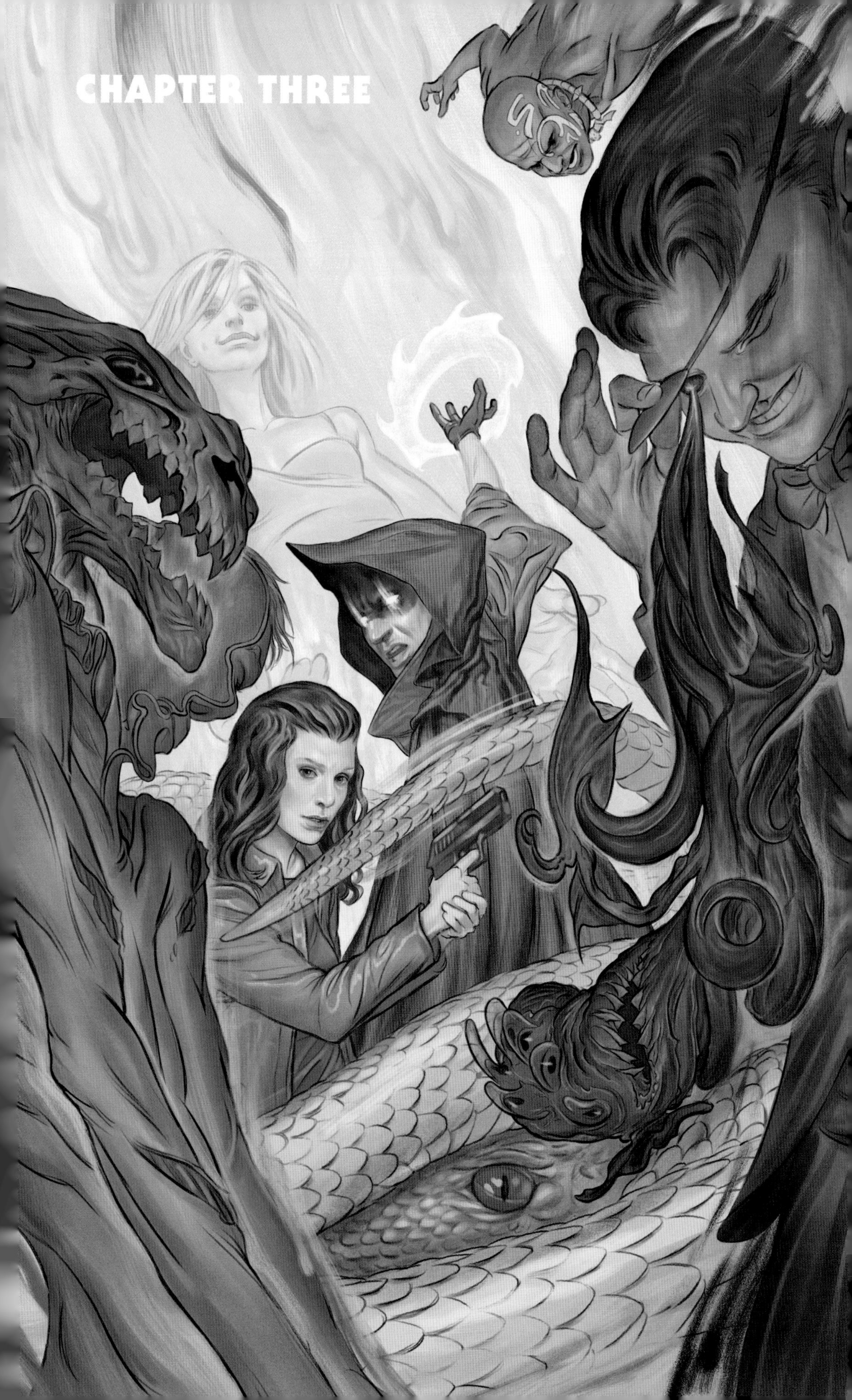

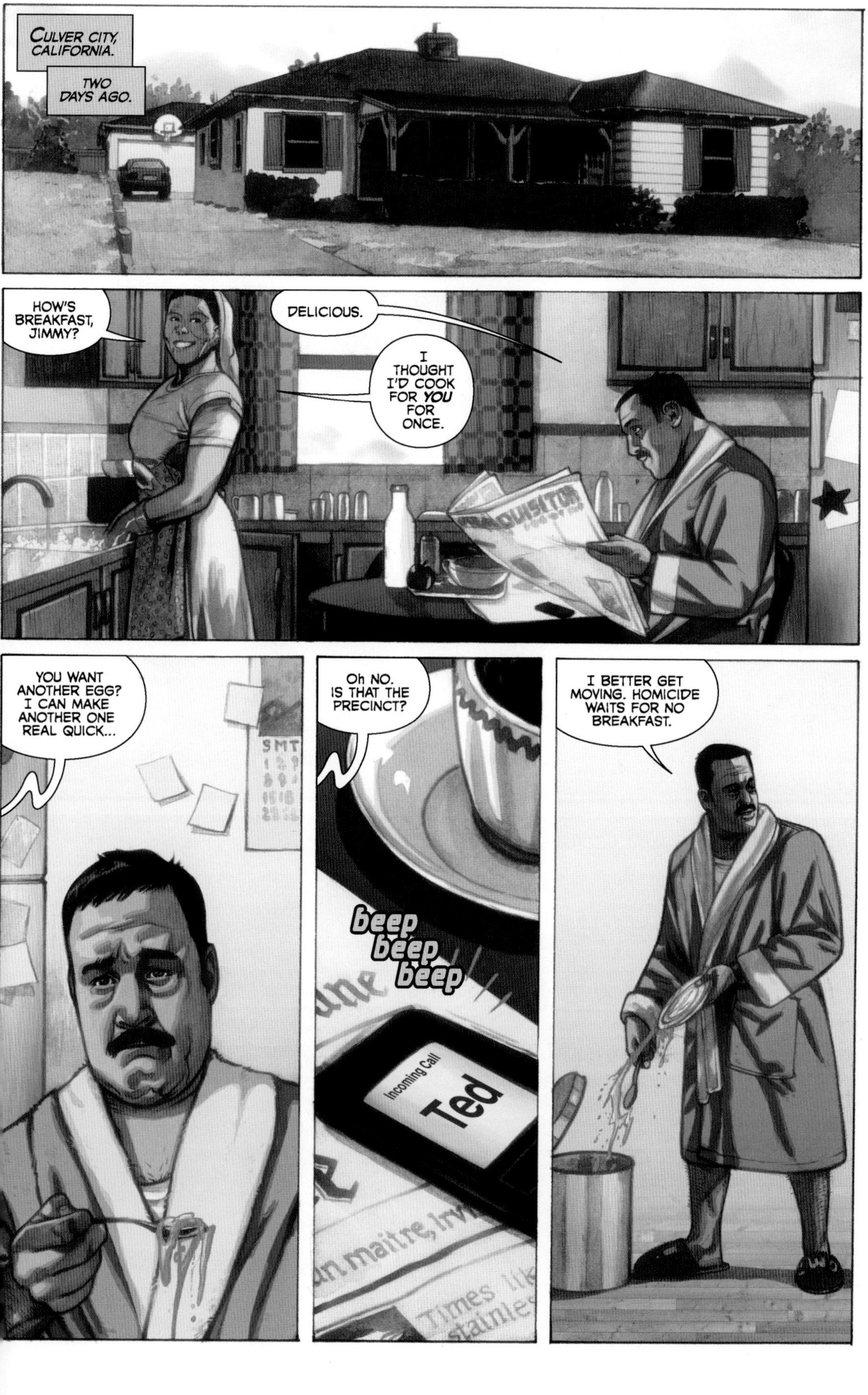
CULVER CITY, CALIFORNIA.
TWO DAYS AGO.
HOW'S BREAKFAST, JIMMY?
DELICIOUS.
I THOUGHT I'D COOK FOR *YOU* FOR ONCE.
YOU WANT ANOTHER EGG? I CAN MAKE ANOTHER ONE REAL QUICK...
Oh NO. IS THAT THE PRECINCT?
beep beep beep
Incoming Call
Ted
I BETTER GET MOVING. HOMICIDE WAITS FOR NO BREAKFAST.

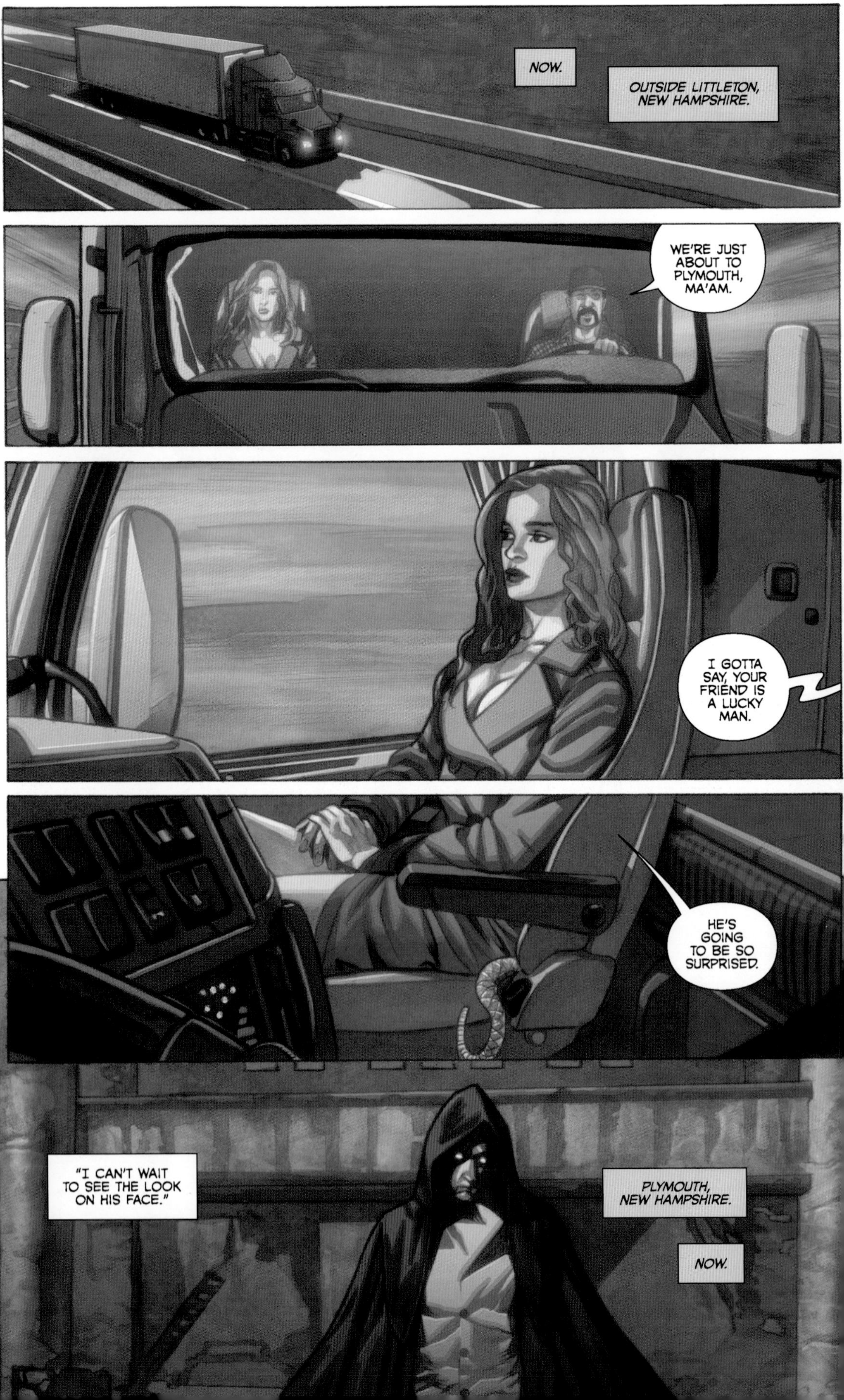
NOW.
OUTSIDE LITTLETON, NEW HAMPSHIRE.
WE'RE JUST ABOUT TO PLYMOUTH, MA'AM.
I GOTTA SAY, YOUR FRIEND IS A LUCKY MAN.
HE'S GOING TO BE SO SURPRISED.
"I CAN'T WAIT TO SEE THE LOOK ON HIS FACE."
PLYMOUTH, NEW HAMPSHIRE.
NOW.

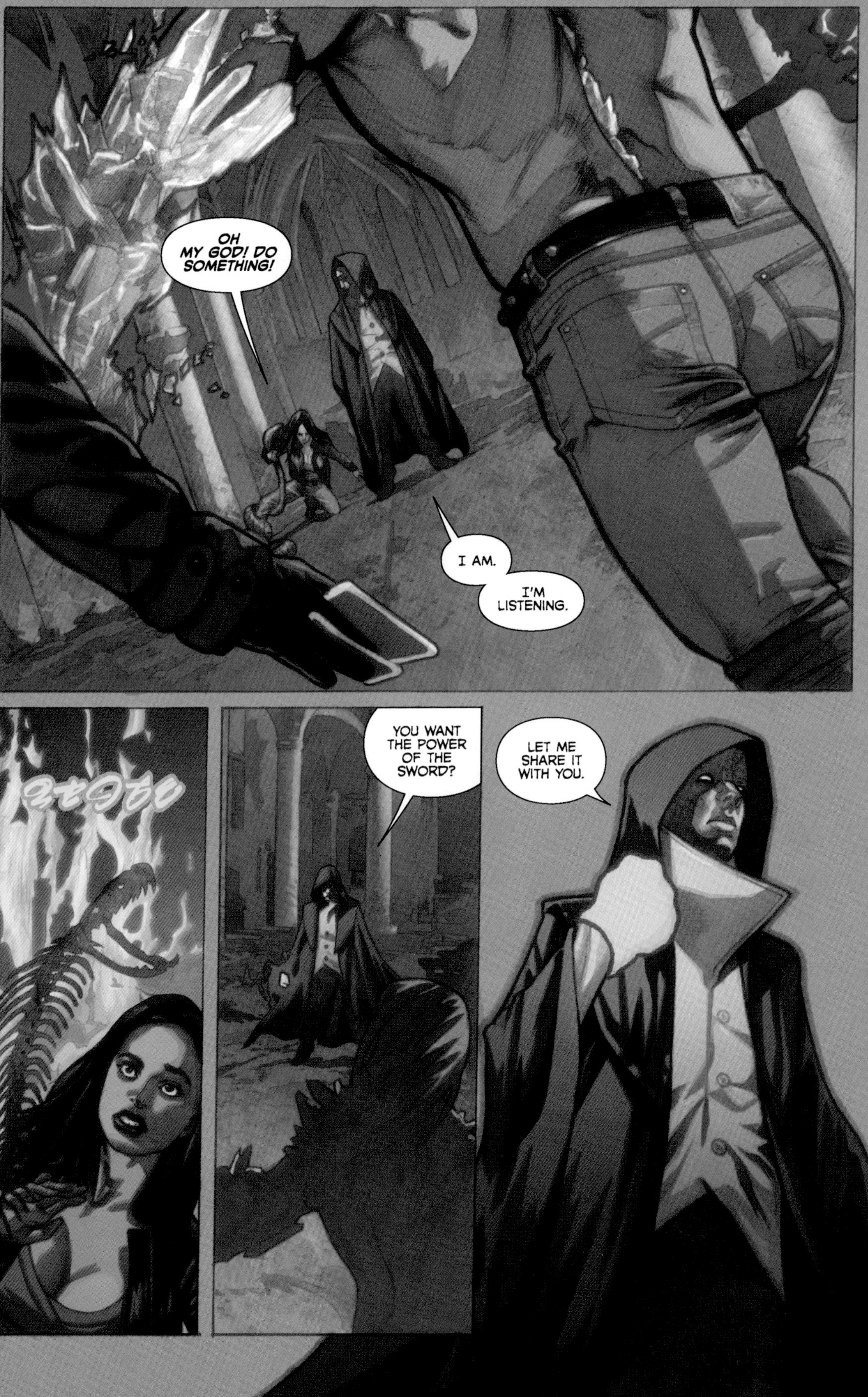
OH MY GOD! DO SOMETHING!
I AM.
I'M LISTENING.
YOU WANT THE POWER OF THE SWORD?
LET ME SHARE IT WITH YOU.

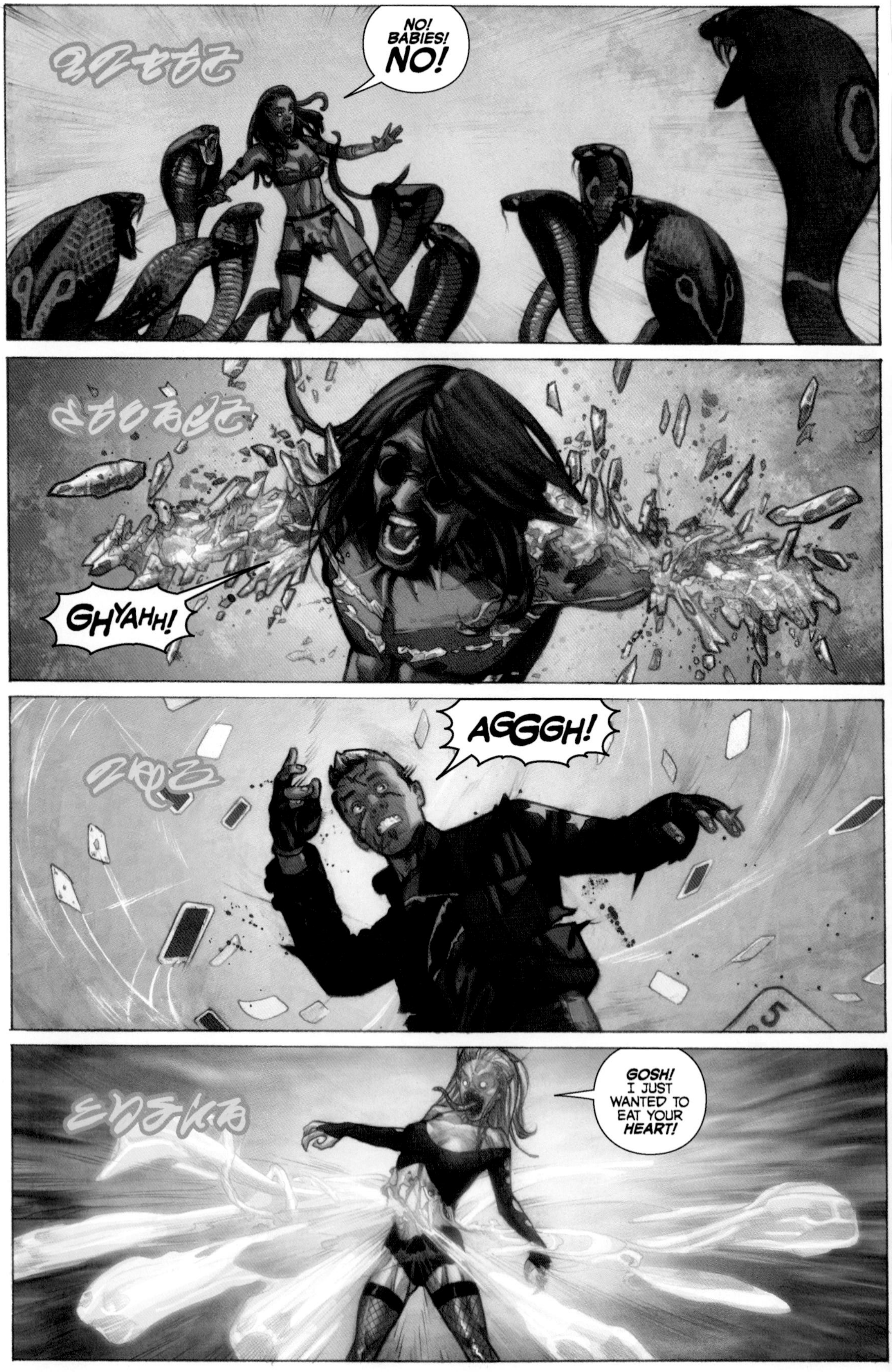
NO! BABIES! NO!
GHYAHH!
AGGGH!
GOSH! I JUST WANTED TO EAT YOUR HEART!

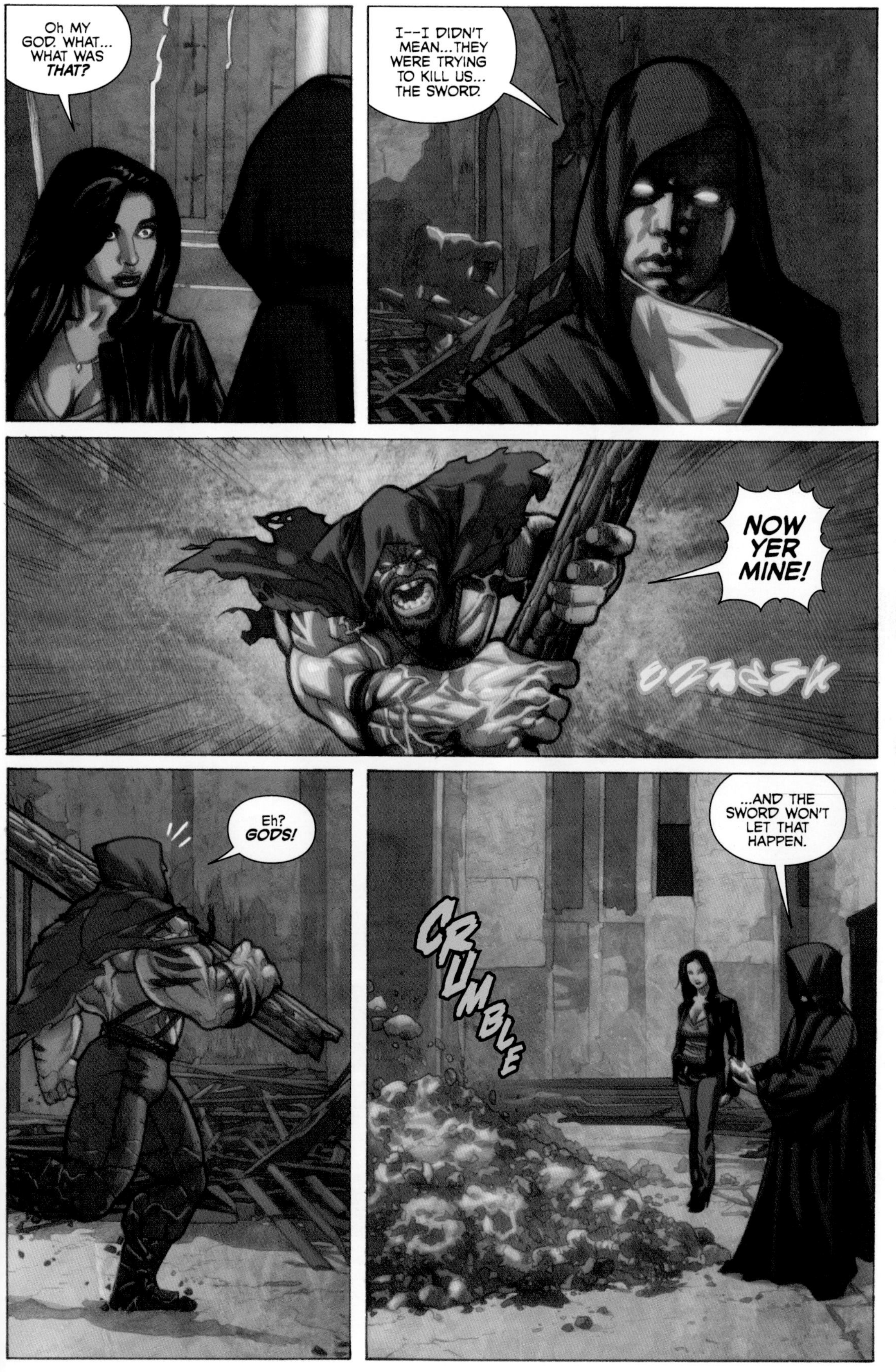
Oh MY GOD. WHAT... WHAT WAS *THAT?*
I--I DIDN'T MEAN...THEY WERE TRYING TO KILL US... THE SWORD.
NOW YER MINE!
Eh? *GODS!*
CRUMBLE
...AND THE SWORD WON'T LET THAT HAPPEN.

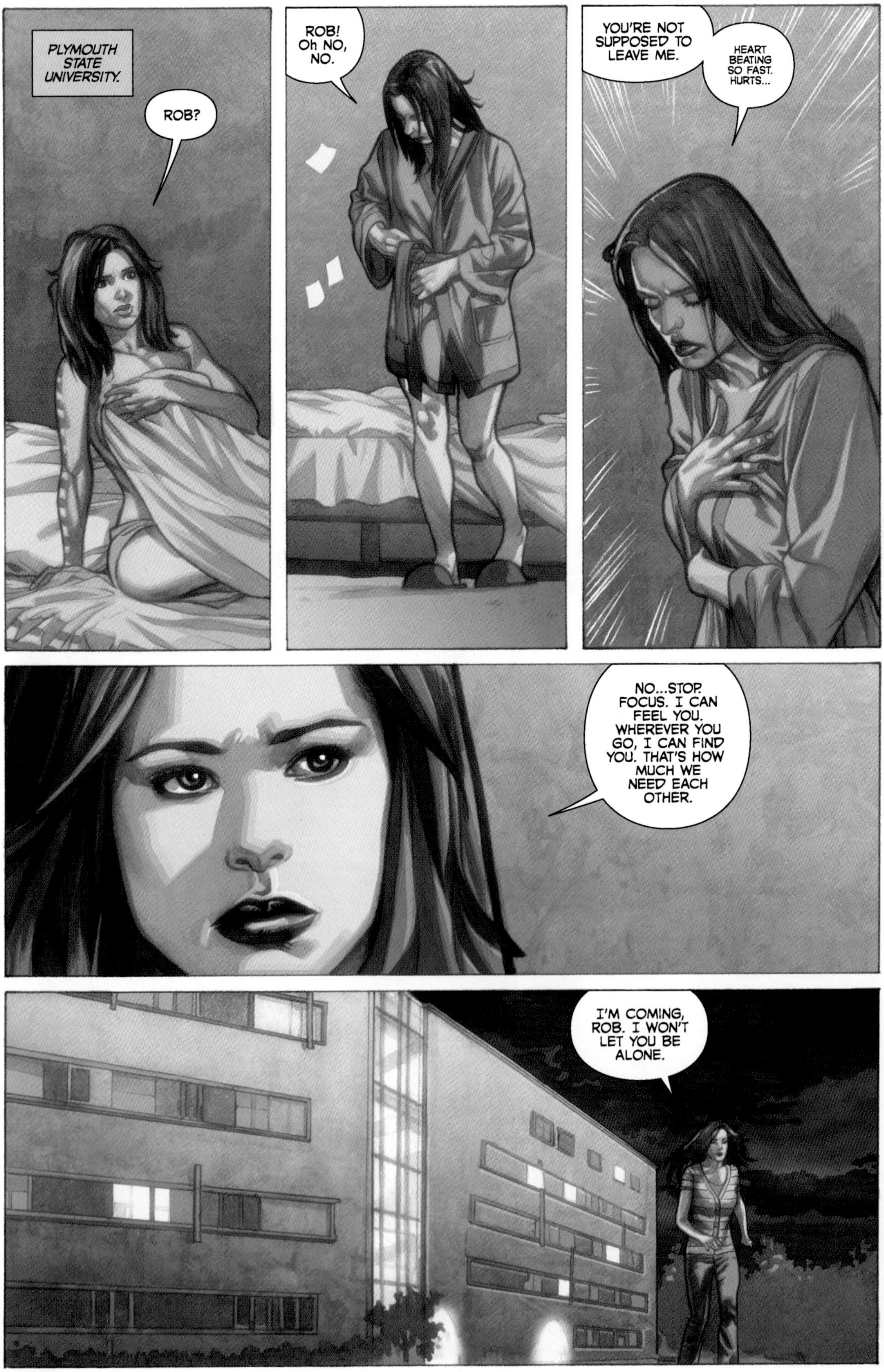
PLYMOUTH STATE UNIVERSITY.
ROB?
ROB! Oh NO, NO.
YOU'RE NOT SUPPOSED TO LEAVE ME.
HEART BEATING SO FAST. HURTS...
NO...STOP. FOCUS. I CAN FEEL YOU. WHEREVER YOU GO, I CAN FIND YOU. THAT'S HOW MUCH WE NEED EACH OTHER.
I'M COMING, ROB. I WON'T LET YOU BE ALONE.

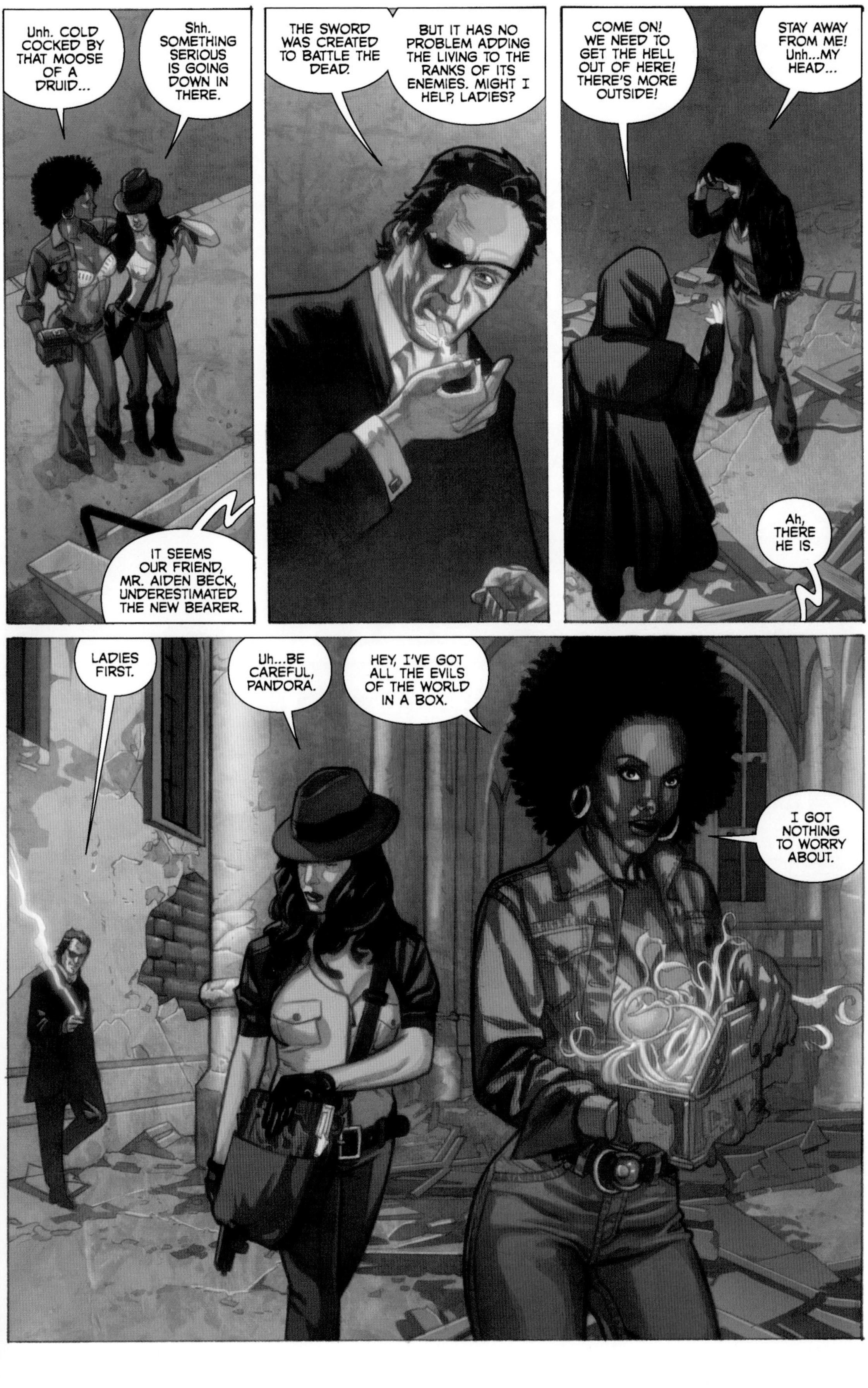
Unh. COLD COCKED BY THAT MOOSE OF A DRUID...
Shh. SOMETHING SERIOUS IS GOING DOWN IN THERE.
IT SEEMS OUR FRIEND, MR. AIDEN BECK, UNDERESTIMATED THE NEW BEARER.
THE SWORD WAS CREATED TO BATTLE THE DEAD.
BUT IT HAS NO PROBLEM ADDING THE LIVING TO THE RANKS OF ITS ENEMIES. MIGHT I HELP, LADIES?
COME ON! WE NEED TO GET THE HELL OUT OF HERE! THERE'S MORE OUTSIDE!
STAY AWAY FROM ME! Unh...MY HEAD...
Ah, THERE HE IS.
LADIES FIRST.
Uh...BE CAREFUL, PANDORA.
HEY, I'VE GOT ALL THE EVILS OF THE WORLD IN A BOX.
I GOT NOTHING TO WORRY ABOUT.

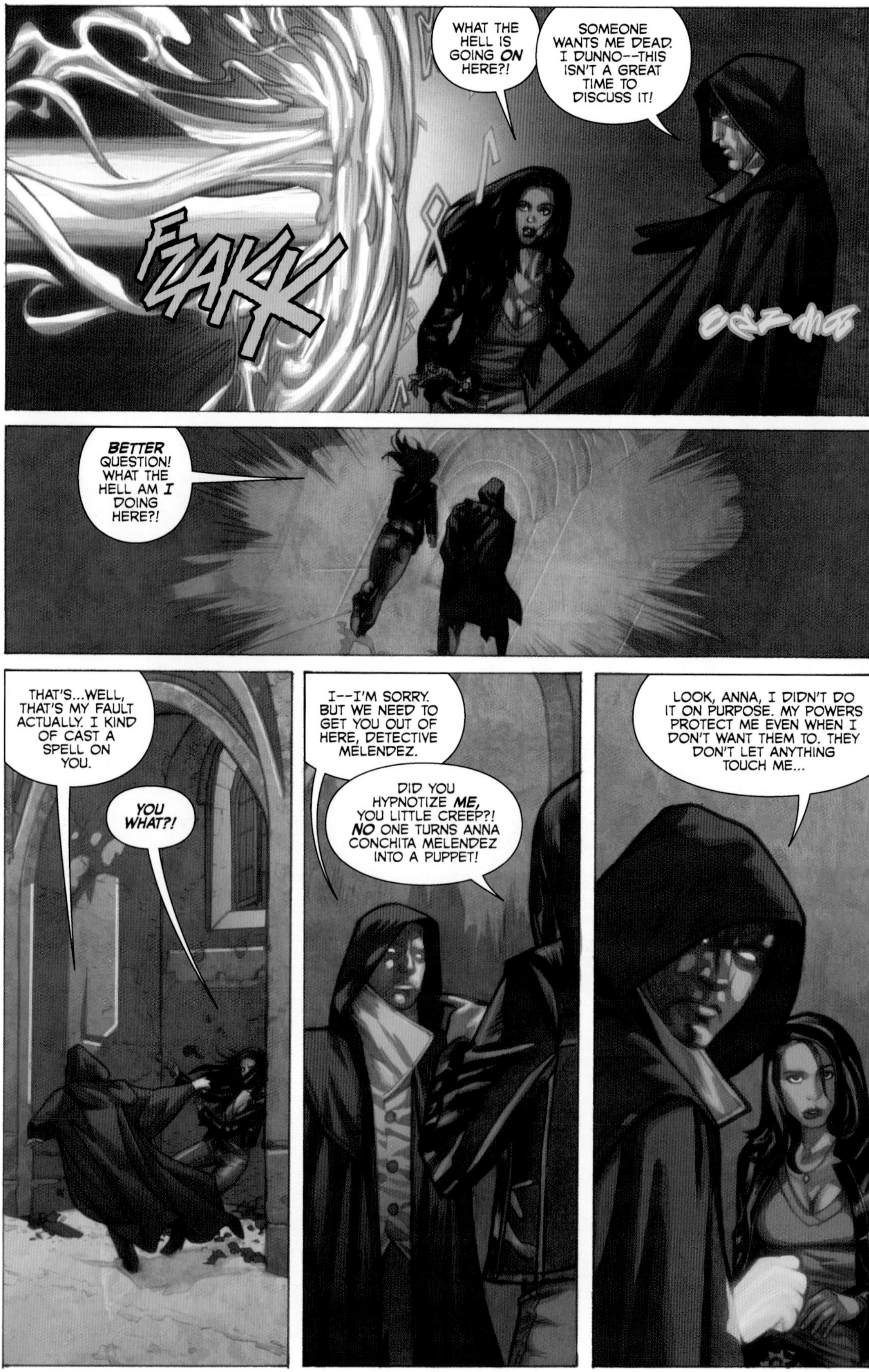
WHAT THE HELL IS GOING ON HERE?!
SOMEONE WANTS ME DEAD. I DUNNO--THIS ISN'T A GREAT TIME TO DISCUSS IT!
FZAKK
BETTER QUESTION! WHAT THE HELL AM I DOING HERE?!
THAT'S...WELL, THAT'S MY FAULT ACTUALLY. I KIND OF CAST A SPELL ON YOU.
YOU WHAT?!
I--I'M SORRY. BUT WE NEED TO GET YOU OUT OF HERE, DETECTIVE MELENDEZ.
DID YOU HYPNOTIZE ME, YOU LITTLE CREEP?! NO ONE TURNS ANNA CONCHITA MELENDEZ INTO A PUPPET!
LOOK, ANNA, I DIDN'T DO IT ON PURPOSE. MY POWERS PROTECT ME EVEN WHEN I DON'T WANT THEM TO. THEY DON'T LET ANYTHING TOUCH ME...

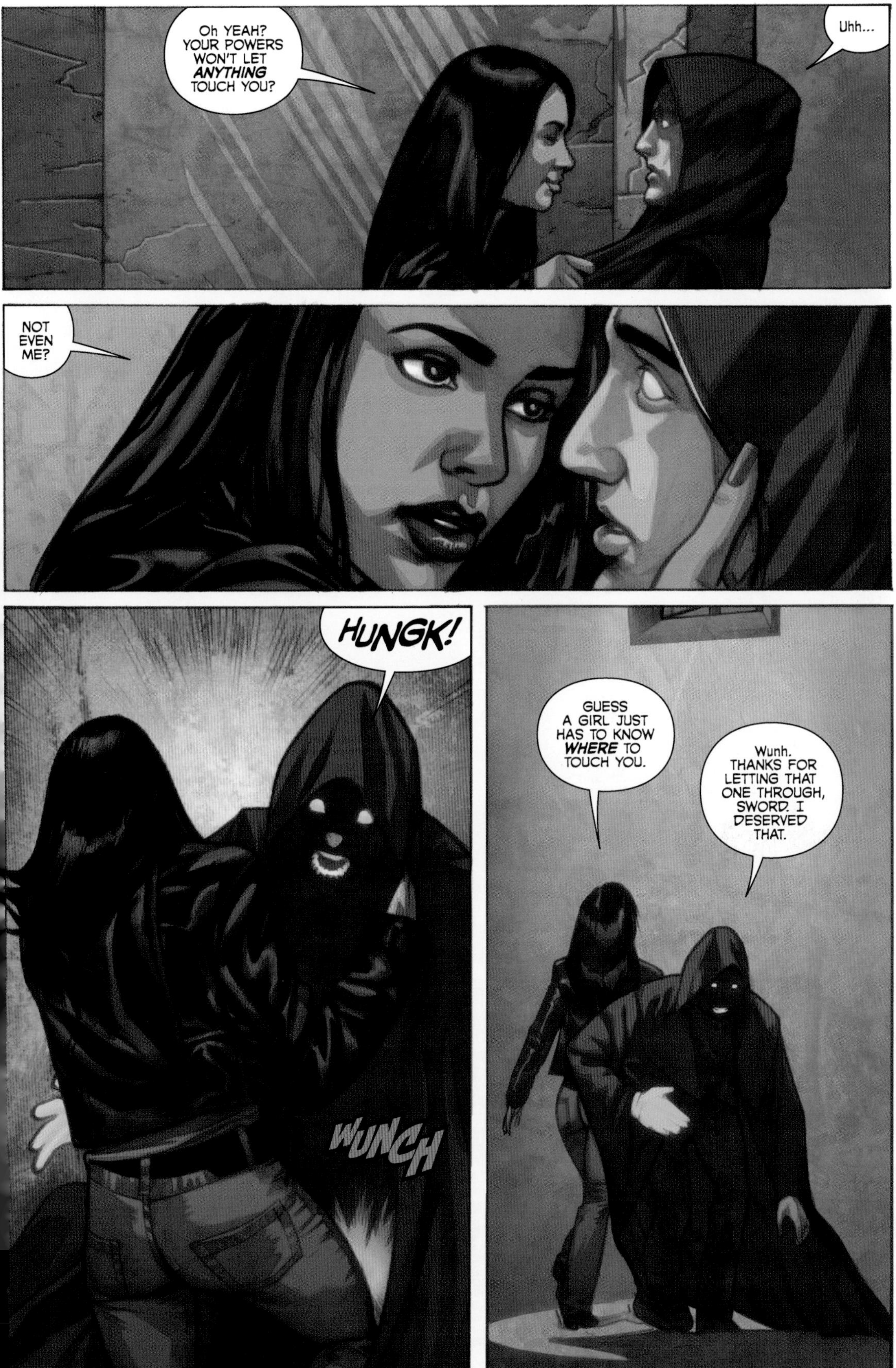
Oh YEAH? YOUR POWERS WON'T LET ANYTHING TOUCH YOU?
Uhh...
NOT EVEN ME?
HUNGK!
WUNCH
GUESS A GIRL JUST HAS TO KNOW WHERE TO TOUCH YOU.
Wunh. THANKS FOR LETTING THAT ONE THROUGH, SWORD. I DESERVED THAT.

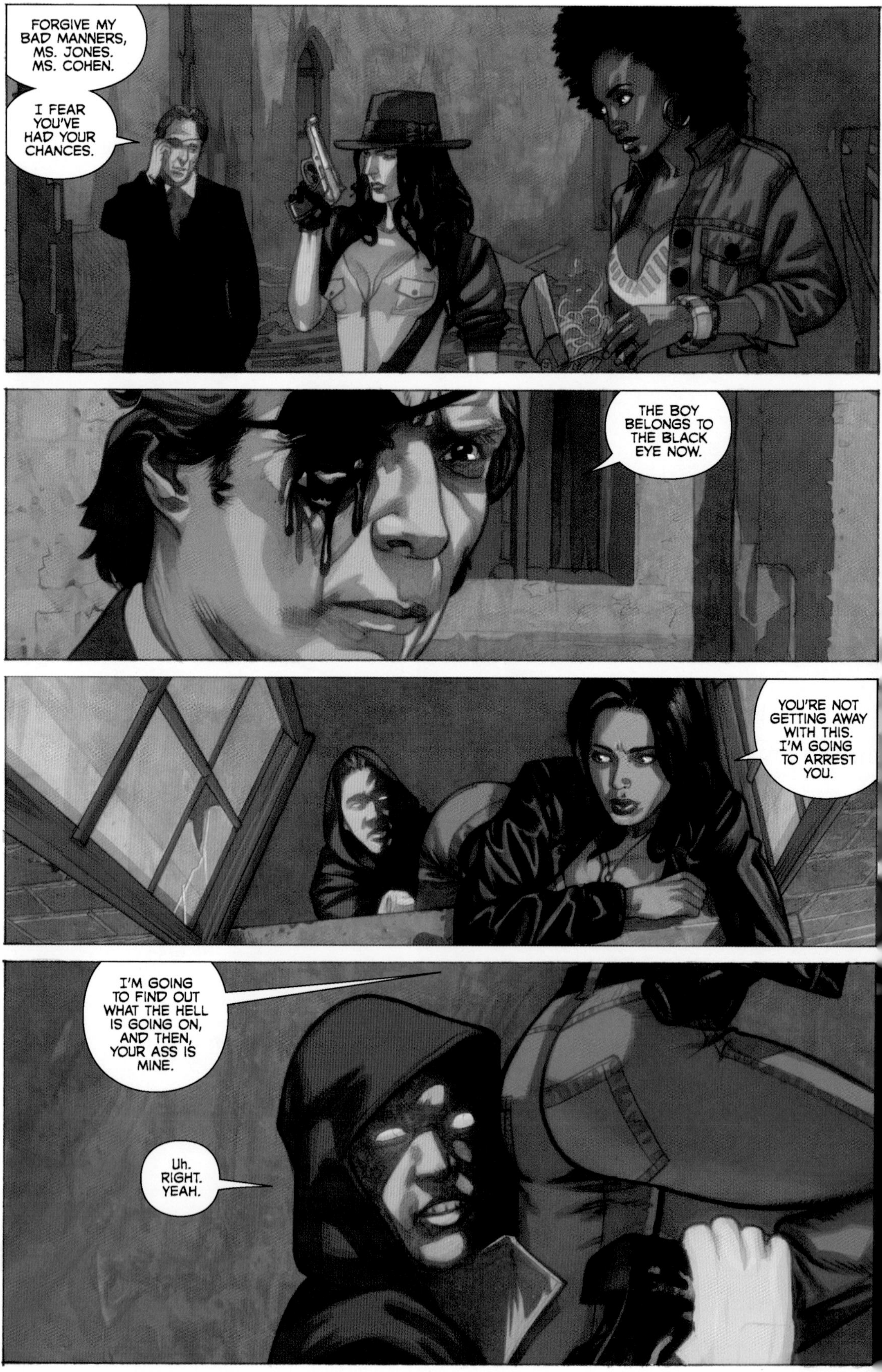
FORGIVE MY BAD MANNERS, MS. JONES. MS. COHEN.
I FEAR YOU'VE HAD YOUR CHANCES.
THE BOY BELONGS TO THE BLACK EYE NOW.
YOU'RE NOT GETTING AWAY WITH THIS. I'M GOING TO ARREST YOU.
I'M GOING TO FIND OUT WHAT THE HELL IS GOING ON, AND THEN, YOUR ASS IS MINE.
Uh. RIGHT. YEAH.

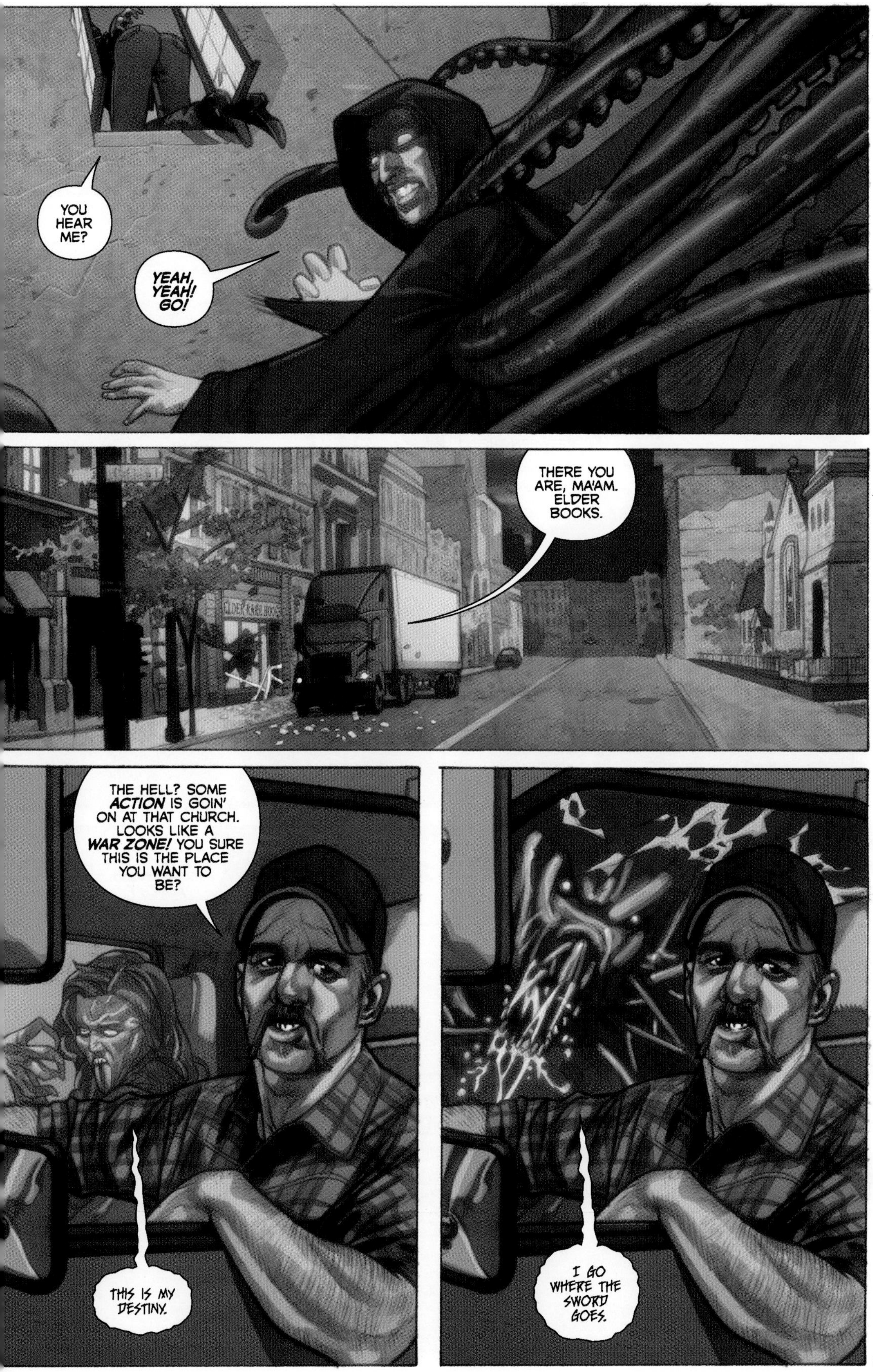
YOU HEAR ME?
YEAH, YEAH! GO!
THERE YOU ARE, MA'AM. ELDER BOOKS.
ELDER RARE BOOKS
THE HELL? SOME ACTION IS GOIN' ON AT THAT CHURCH. LOOKS LIKE A WAR ZONE! YOU SURE THIS IS THE PLACE YOU WANT TO BE?
THIS IS MY DESTINY.
I GO WHERE THE SWORD GOES.

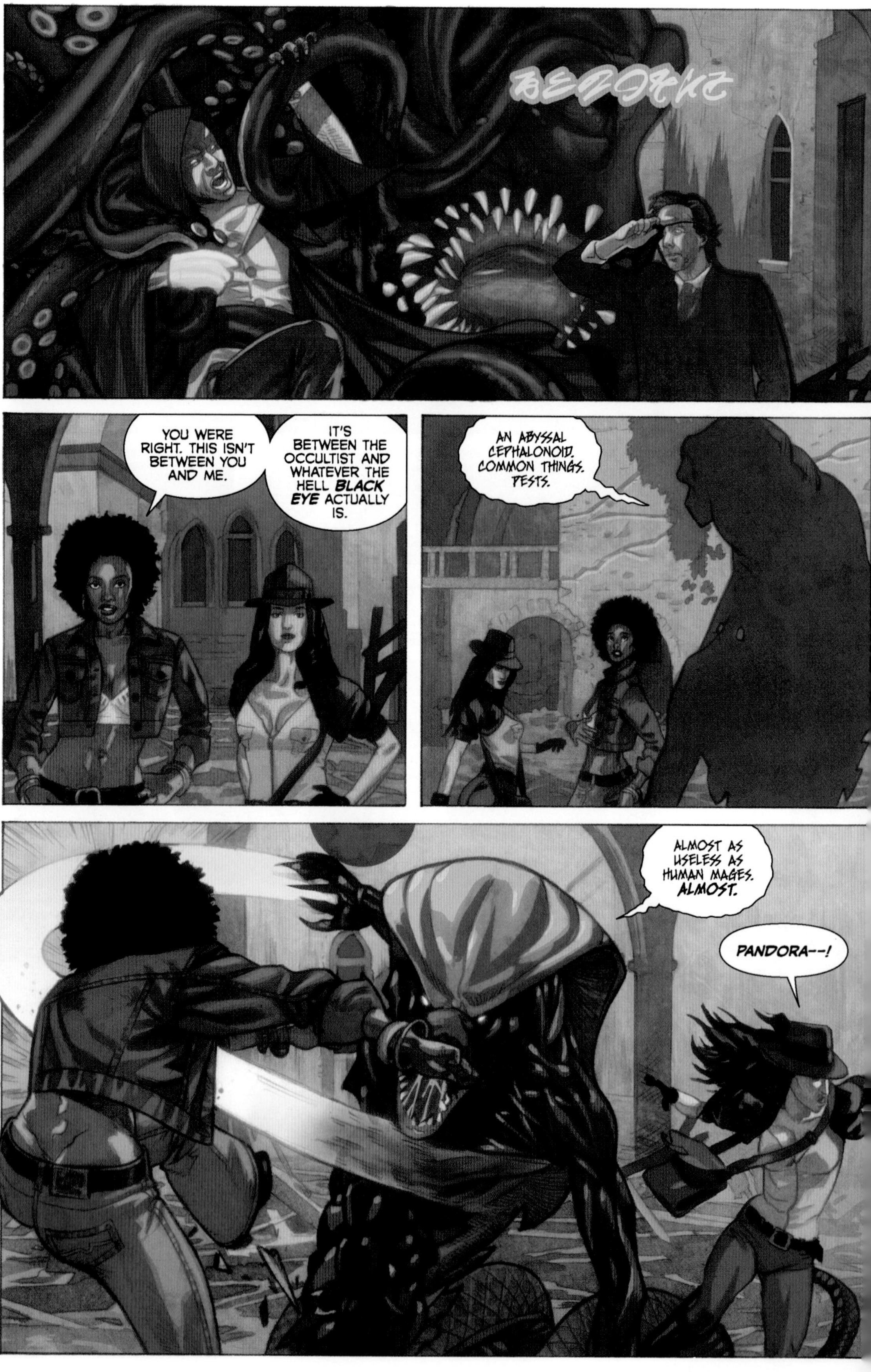
YOU WERE RIGHT. THIS ISN'T BETWEEN YOU AND ME.
IT'S BETWEEN THE OCCULTIST AND WHATEVER THE HELL BLACK EYE ACTUALLY IS.
AN ABYSSAL CEPHALONOID. COMMON THINGS. PESTS.
ALMOST AS USELESS AS HUMAN MAGES. ALMOST.
PANDORA--!

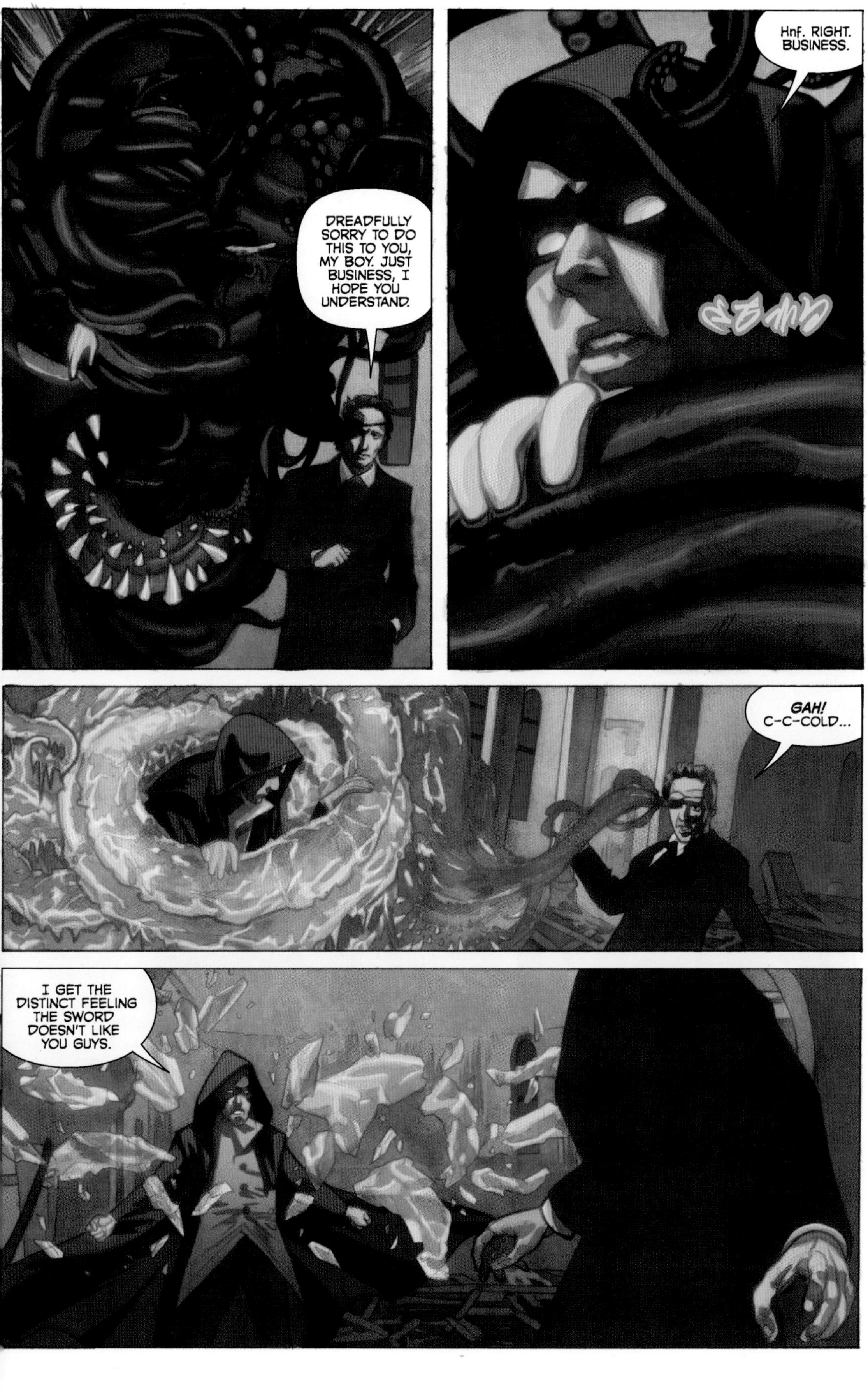
DREADFULLY SORRY TO DO THIS TO YOU, MY BOY. JUST BUSINESS, I HOPE YOU UNDERSTAND.
Hnf. RIGHT. BUSINESS.
GAH! C-C-COLD...
I GET THE DISTINCT FEELING THE SWORD DOESN'T LIKE YOU GUYS.

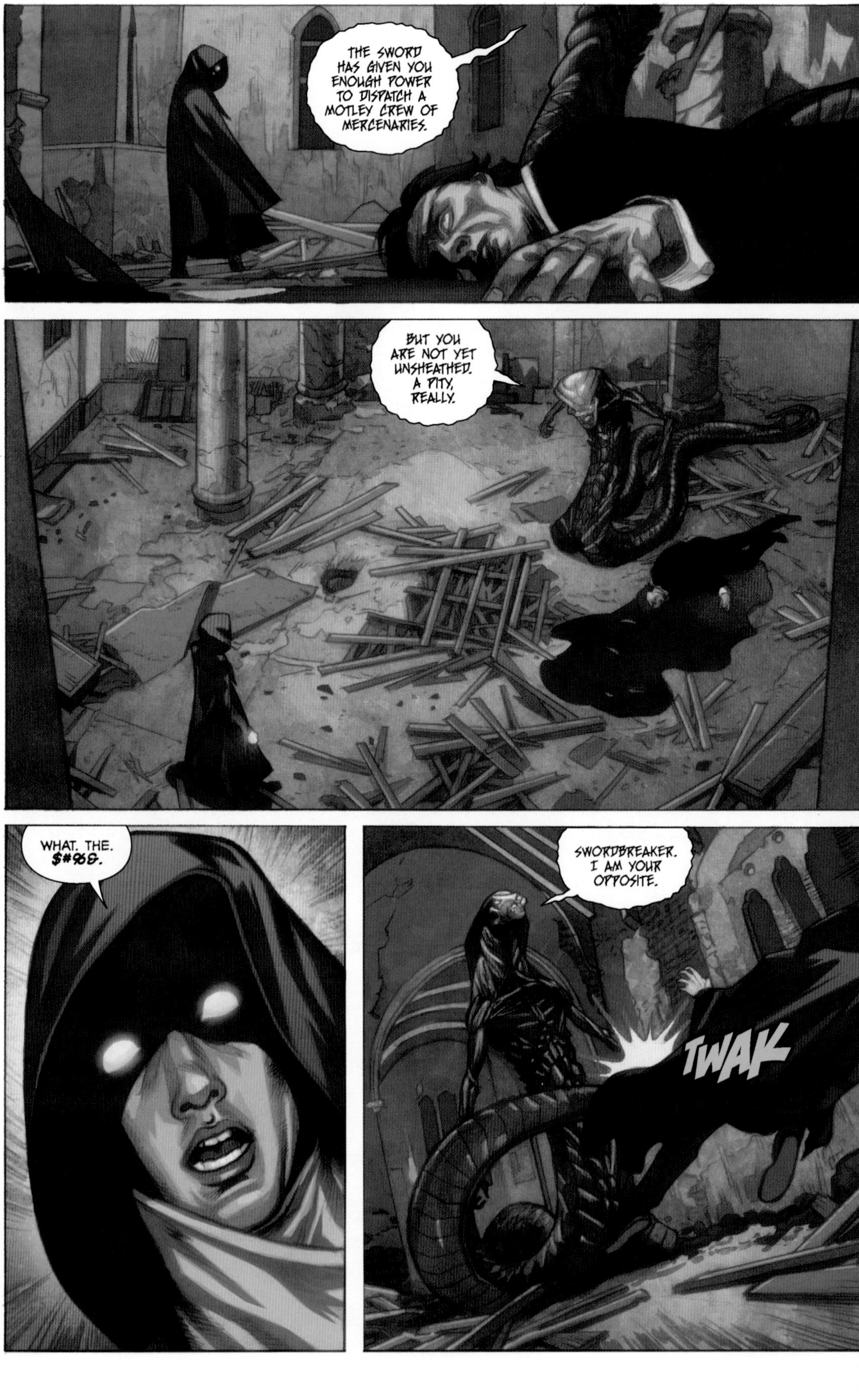

THE SWORD HAS GIVEN YOU ENOUGH POWER TO DISPATCH A MOTLEY CREW OF MERCENARIES.
BUT YOU ARE NOT YET UNSHEATHED. A PITY, REALLY.
WHAT. THE. $#%&.
SWORDBREAKER. I AM YOUR OPPOSITE.
TWAK

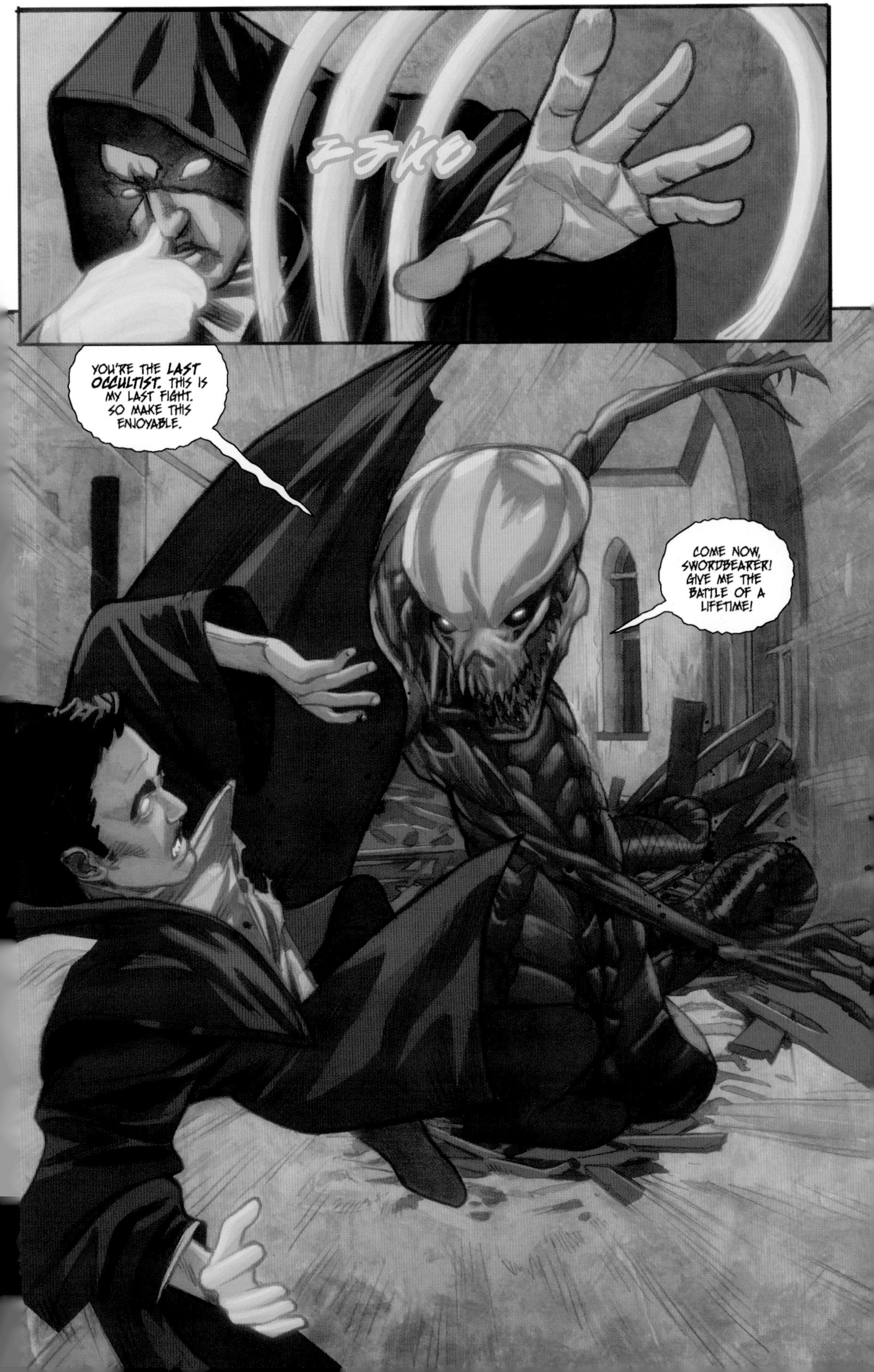
YOU'RE THE LAST OCCULTIST. THIS IS MY LAST FIGHT. SO MAKE THIS ENJOYABLE.
COME NOW, SWORDBEARER! GIVE ME THE BATTLE OF A LIFETIME!

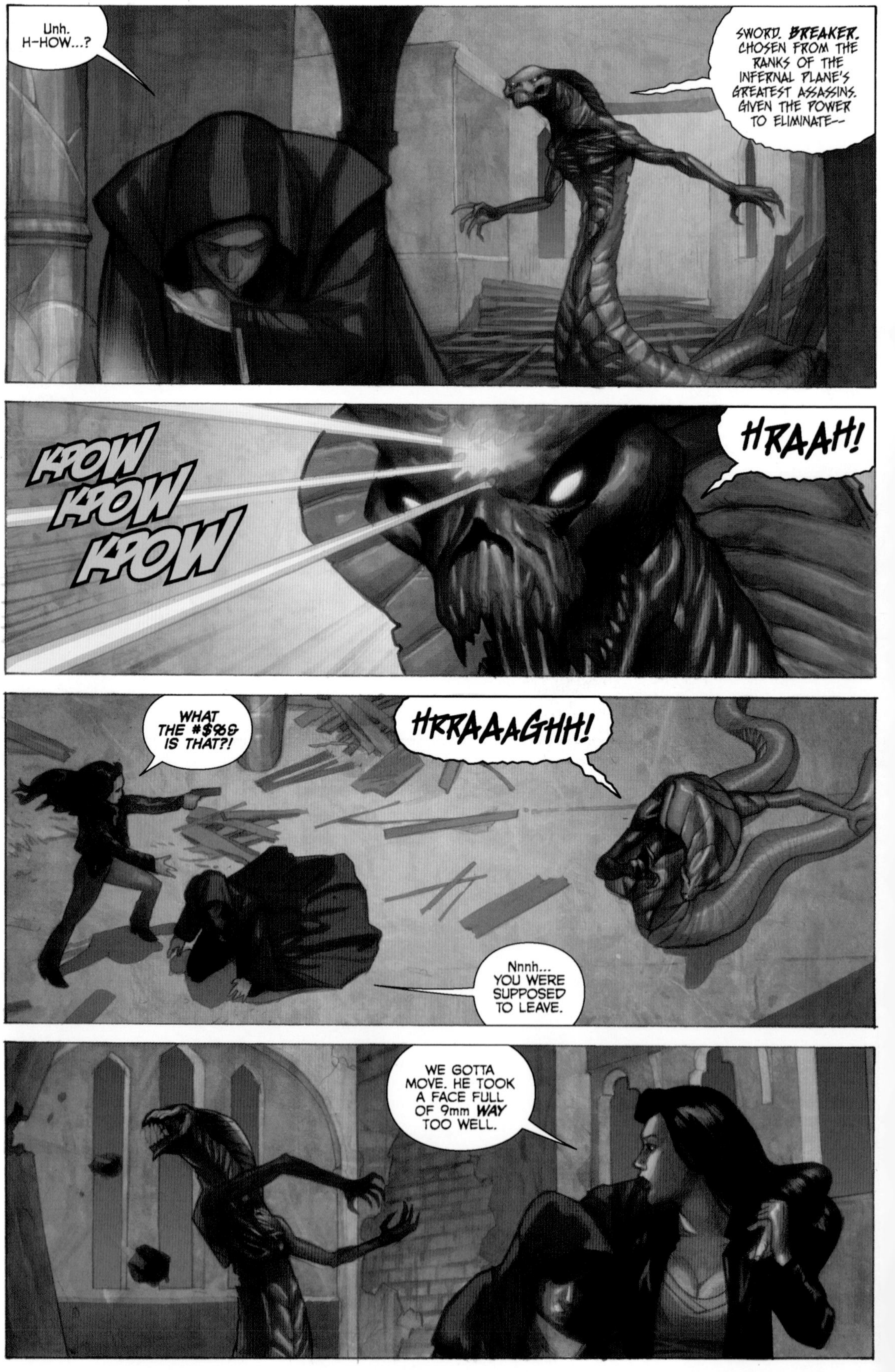
Unh. H-HOW...?
SWORD. BREAKER. CHOSEN FROM THE RANKS OF THE INFERNAL PLANE'S GREATEST ASSASSINS. GIVEN THE POWER TO ELIMINATE--
KPOW KPOW KPOW
HRAAH!
WHAT THE #$%& IS THAT?!
HRRAAAGHH!
Nnnh... YOU WERE SUPPOSED TO LEAVE.
WE GOTTA MOVE. HE TOOK A FACE FULL OF 9mm WAY TOO WELL.

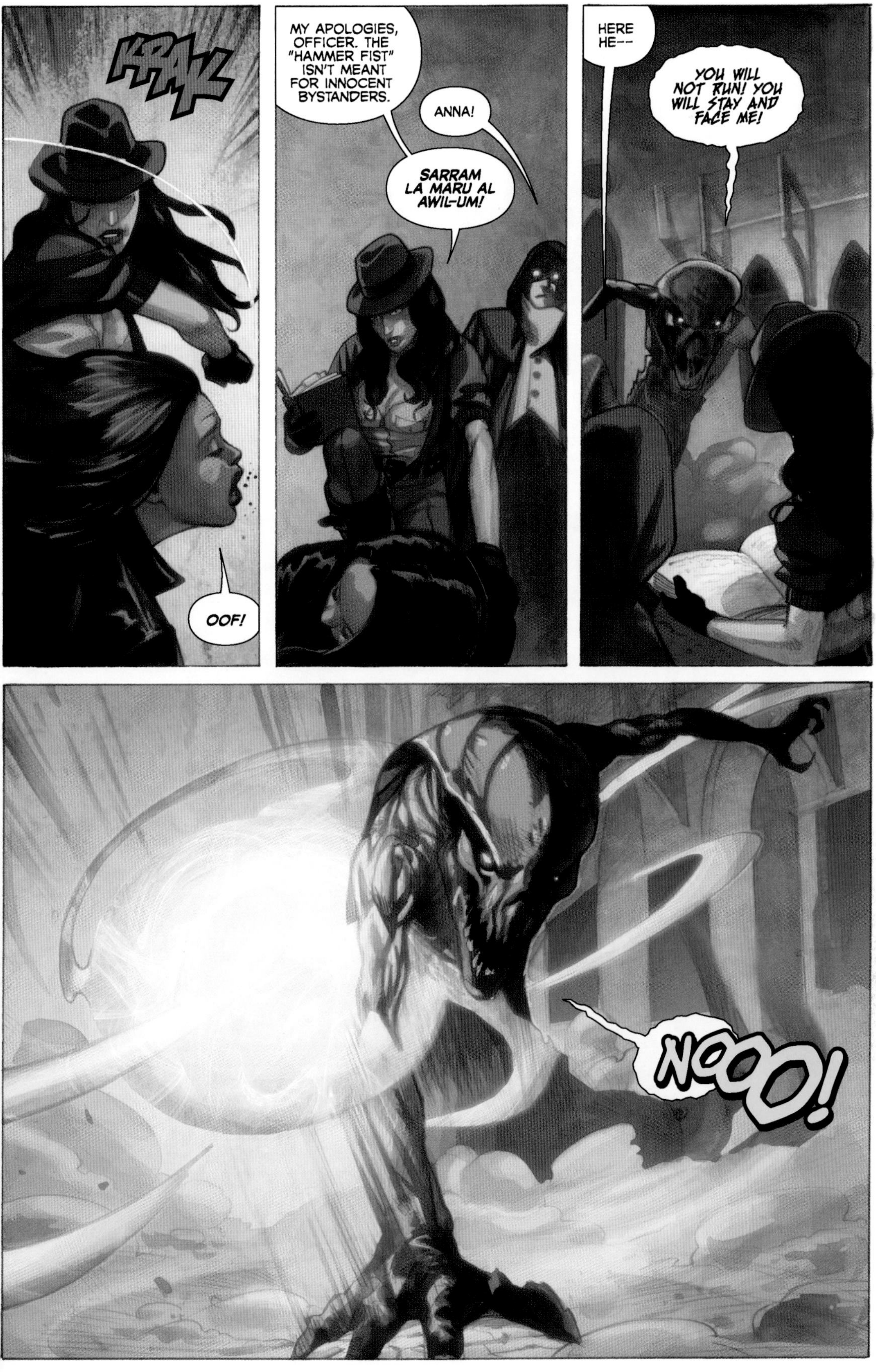
KRAK
OOF!
MY APOLOGIES, OFFICER. THE "HAMMER FIST" ISN'T MEANT FOR INNOCENT BYSTANDERS.
ANNA!
SARRAM LA MARU AL AWIL-UM!
HERE HE--
YOU WILL NOT RUN! YOU WILL STAY AND FACE ME!
NOOO!

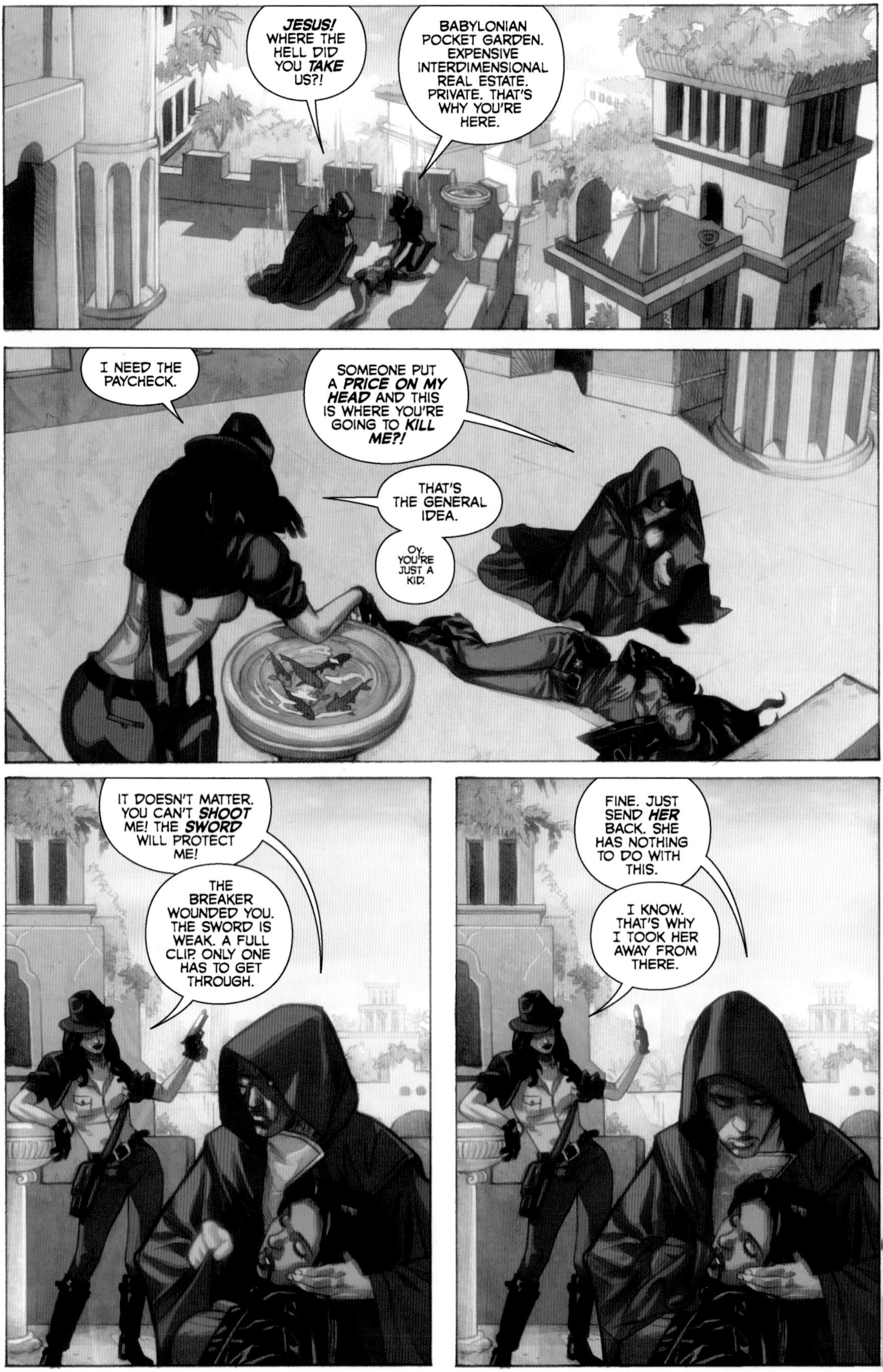
JESUS! WHERE THE HELL DID YOU TAKE US?!
BABYLONIAN POCKET GARDEN. EXPENSIVE INTERDIMENSIONAL REAL ESTATE. PRIVATE. THAT'S WHY YOU'RE HERE.
I NEED THE PAYCHECK.
SOMEONE PUT A PRICE ON MY HEAD AND THIS IS WHERE YOU'RE GOING TO KILL ME?!
THAT'S THE GENERAL IDEA.
OY. YOU'RE JUST A KID.
IT DOESN'T MATTER. YOU CAN'T SHOOT ME! THE SWORD WILL PROTECT ME!
THE BREAKER WOUNDED YOU. THE SWORD IS WEAK. A FULL CLIP. ONLY ONE HAS TO GET THROUGH.
FINE. JUST SEND HER BACK. SHE HAS NOTHING TO DO WITH THIS.
I KNOW. THAT'S WHY I TOOK HER AWAY FROM THERE.

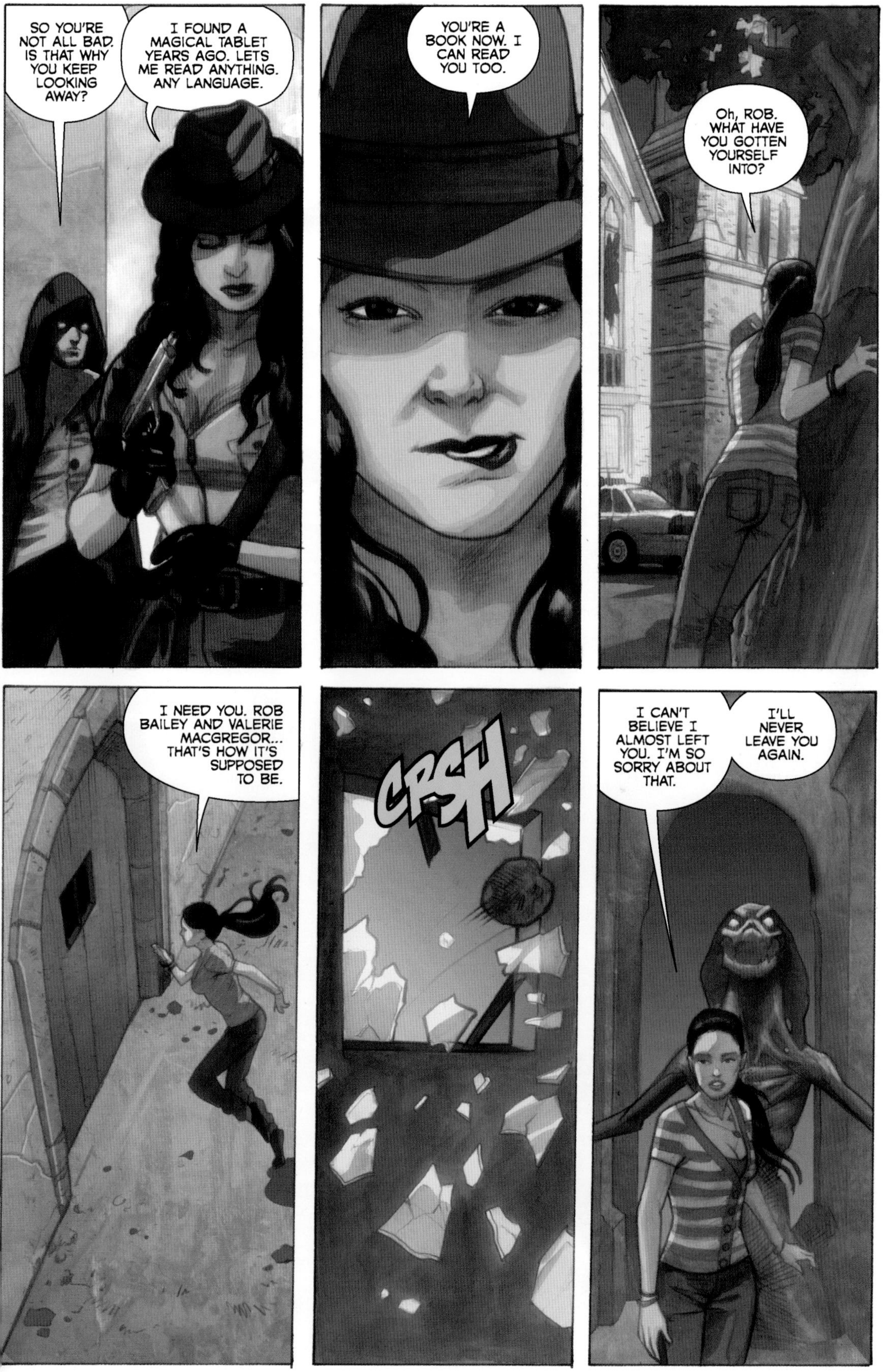
SO YOU'RE NOT ALL BAD. IS THAT WHY YOU KEEP LOOKING AWAY?
I FOUND A MAGICAL TABLET YEARS AGO. LETS ME READ ANYTHING. ANY LANGUAGE.
YOU'RE A BOOK NOW. I CAN READ YOU TOO.
Oh, ROB. WHAT HAVE YOU GOTTEN YOURSELF INTO?
I NEED YOU. ROB BAILEY AND VALERIE MACGREGOR... THAT'S HOW IT'S SUPPOSED TO BE.
CRSH
I CAN'T BELIEVE I ALMOST LEFT YOU. I'M SO SORRY ABOUT THAT.
I'LL NEVER LEAVE YOU AGAIN.

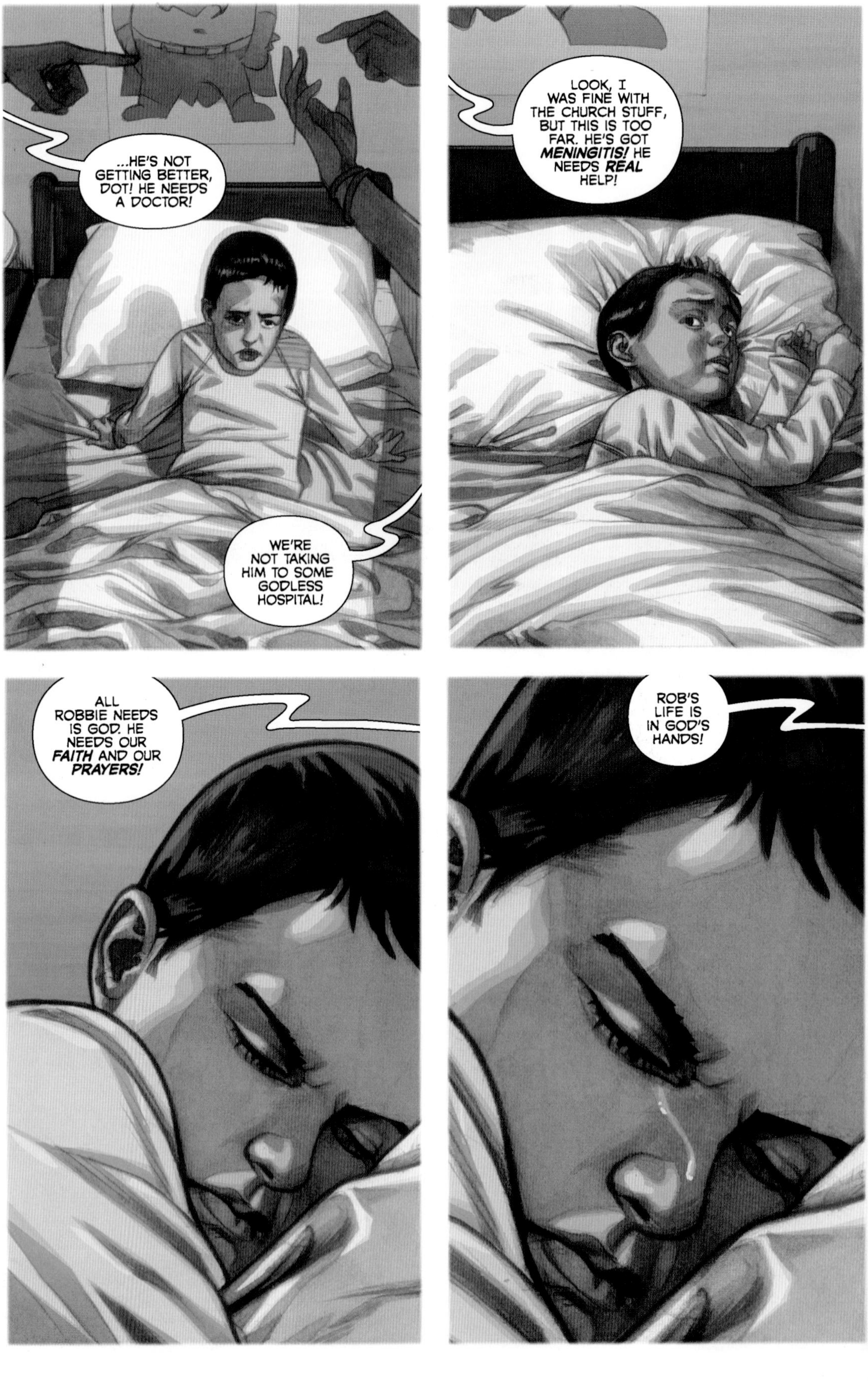
...HE'S NOT GETTING BETTER, DOT! HE NEEDS A DOCTOR!
WE'RE NOT TAKING HIM TO SOME GODLESS HOSPITAL!
LOOK, I WAS FINE WITH THE CHURCH STUFF, BUT THIS IS TOO FAR. HE'S GOT *MENINGITIS!* HE NEEDS *REAL* HELP!
ALL ROBBIE NEEDS IS GOD. HE NEEDS OUR *FAITH* AND OUR *PRAYERS!*
ROB'S LIFE IS IN GOD'S HANDS!

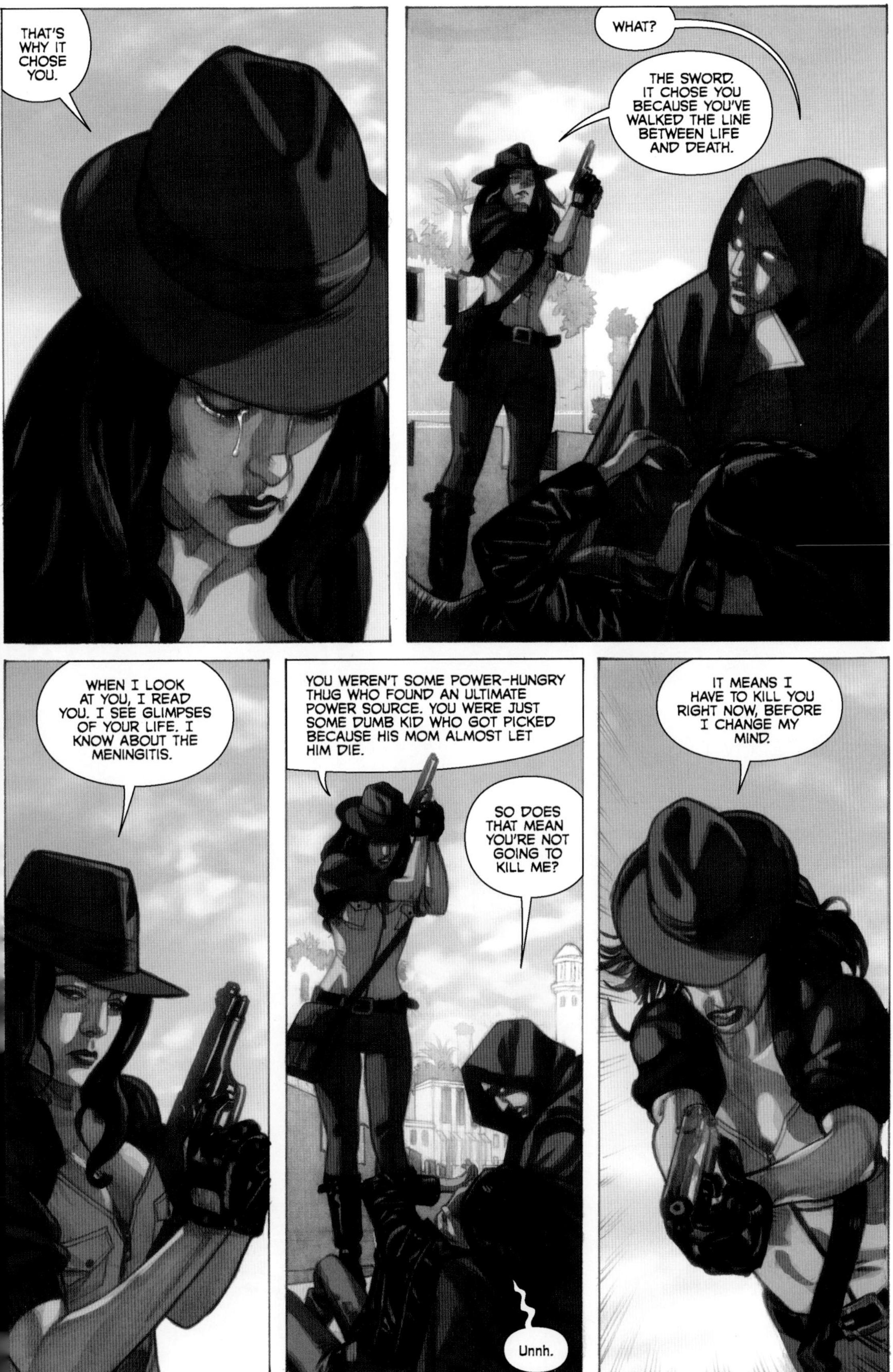
THAT'S WHY IT CHOSE YOU.
WHAT?
THE SWORD. IT CHOSE YOU BECAUSE YOU'VE WALKED THE LINE BETWEEN LIFE AND DEATH.
WHEN I LOOK AT YOU, I READ YOU. I SEE GLIMPSES OF YOUR LIFE. I KNOW ABOUT THE MENINGITIS.
YOU WEREN'T SOME POWER-HUNGRY THUG WHO FOUND AN ULTIMATE POWER SOURCE. YOU WERE JUST SOME DUMB KID WHO GOT PICKED BECAUSE HIS MOM ALMOST LET HIM DIE.
SO DOES THAT MEAN YOU'RE NOT GOING TO KILL ME?
Unnh.
IT MEANS I HAVE TO KILL YOU RIGHT NOW, BEFORE I CHANGE MY MIND.

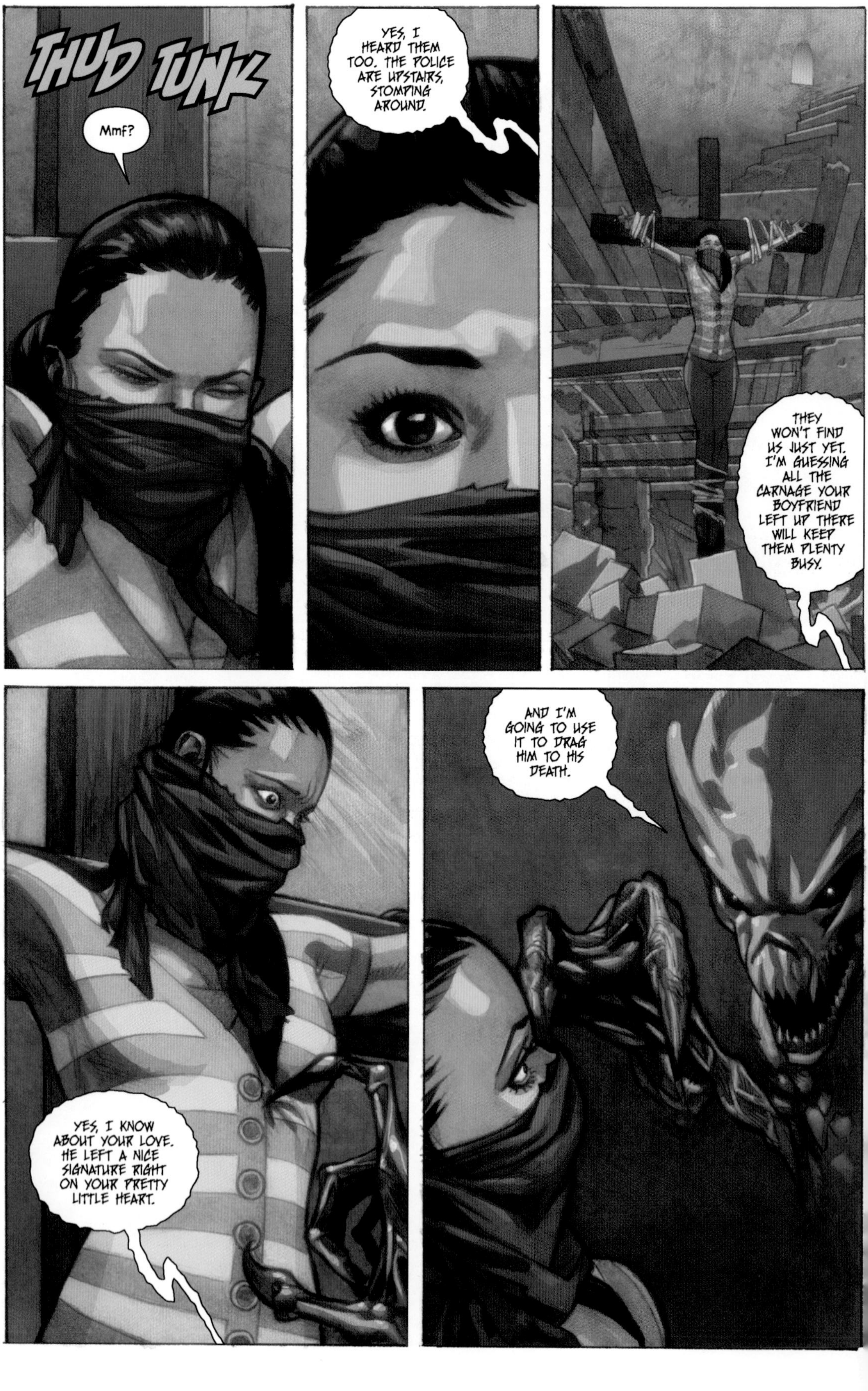
THUD TUNK
Mmf?
YES, I HEARD THEM TOO. THE POLICE ARE UPSTAIRS, STOMPING AROUND.
THEY WON'T FIND US JUST YET. I'M GUESSING ALL THE CARNAGE YOUR BOYFRIEND LEFT UP THERE WILL KEEP THEM PLENTY BUSY.
YES, I KNOW ABOUT YOUR LOVE. HE LEFT A NICE SIGNATURE RIGHT ON YOUR PRETTY LITTLE HEART.
AND I'M GOING TO USE IT TO DRAG HIM TO HIS DEATH.

CHAPTER FOUR

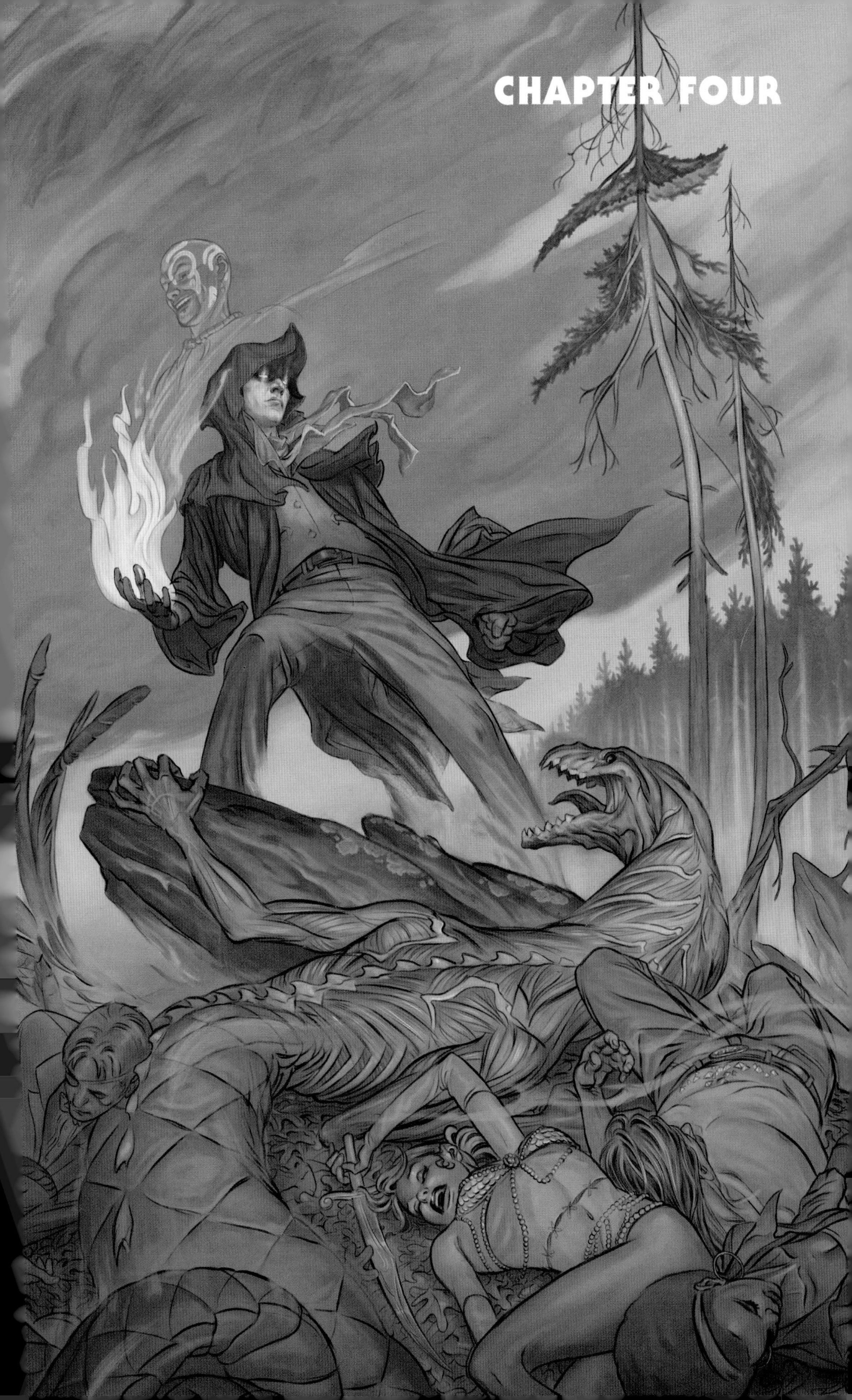

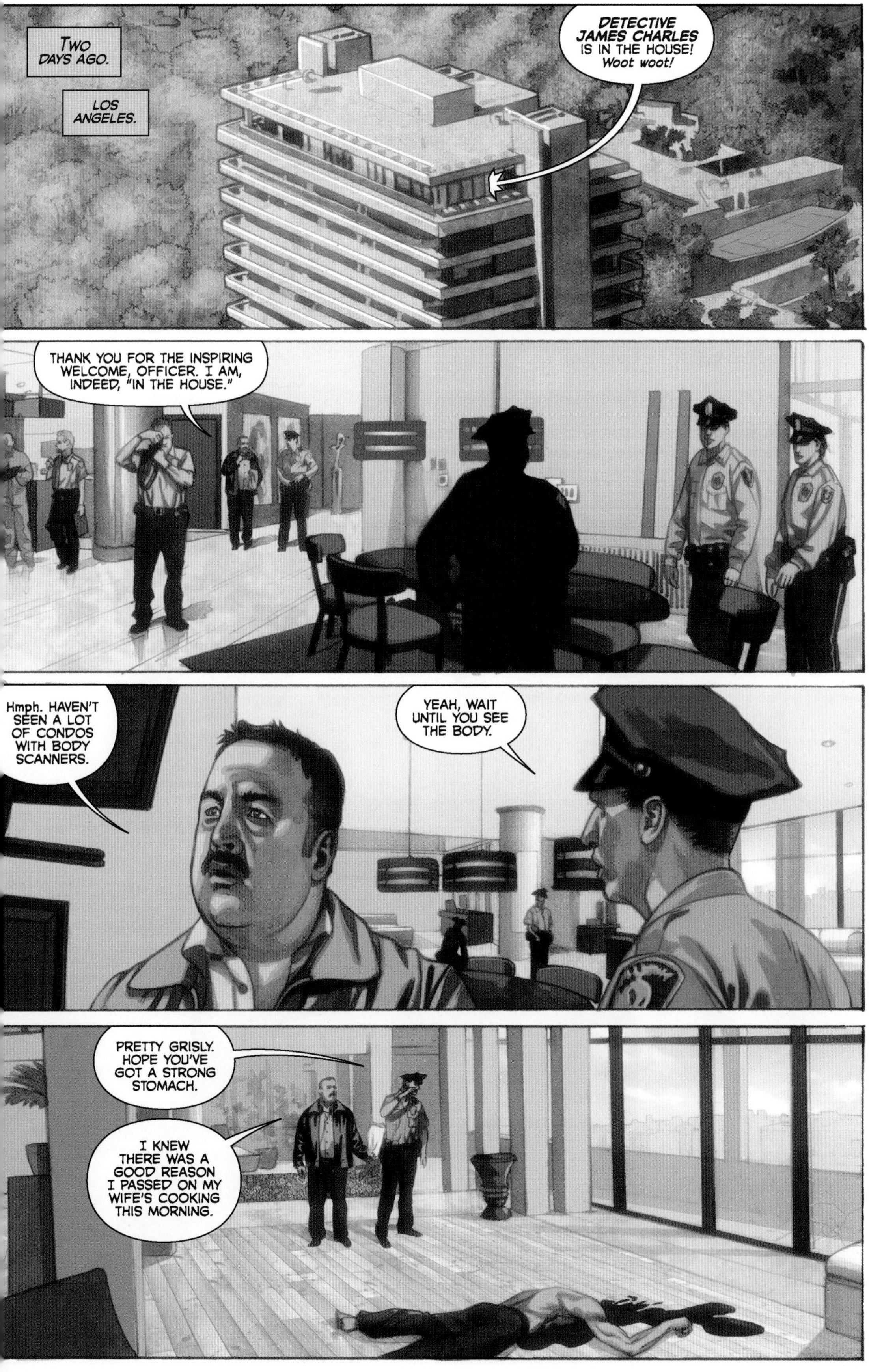
TWO DAYS AGO.
LOS ANGELES.
DETECTIVE JAMES CHARLES IS IN THE HOUSE! Woot woot!
THANK YOU FOR THE INSPIRING WELCOME, OFFICER. I AM, INDEED, "IN THE HOUSE."
Hmph. HAVEN'T SEEN A LOT OF CONDOS WITH BODY SCANNERS.
YEAH, WAIT UNTIL YOU SEE THE BODY.
PRETTY GRISLY. HOPE YOU'VE GOT A STRONG STOMACH.
I KNEW THERE WAS A GOOD REASON I PASSED ON MY WIFE'S COOKING THIS MORNING.

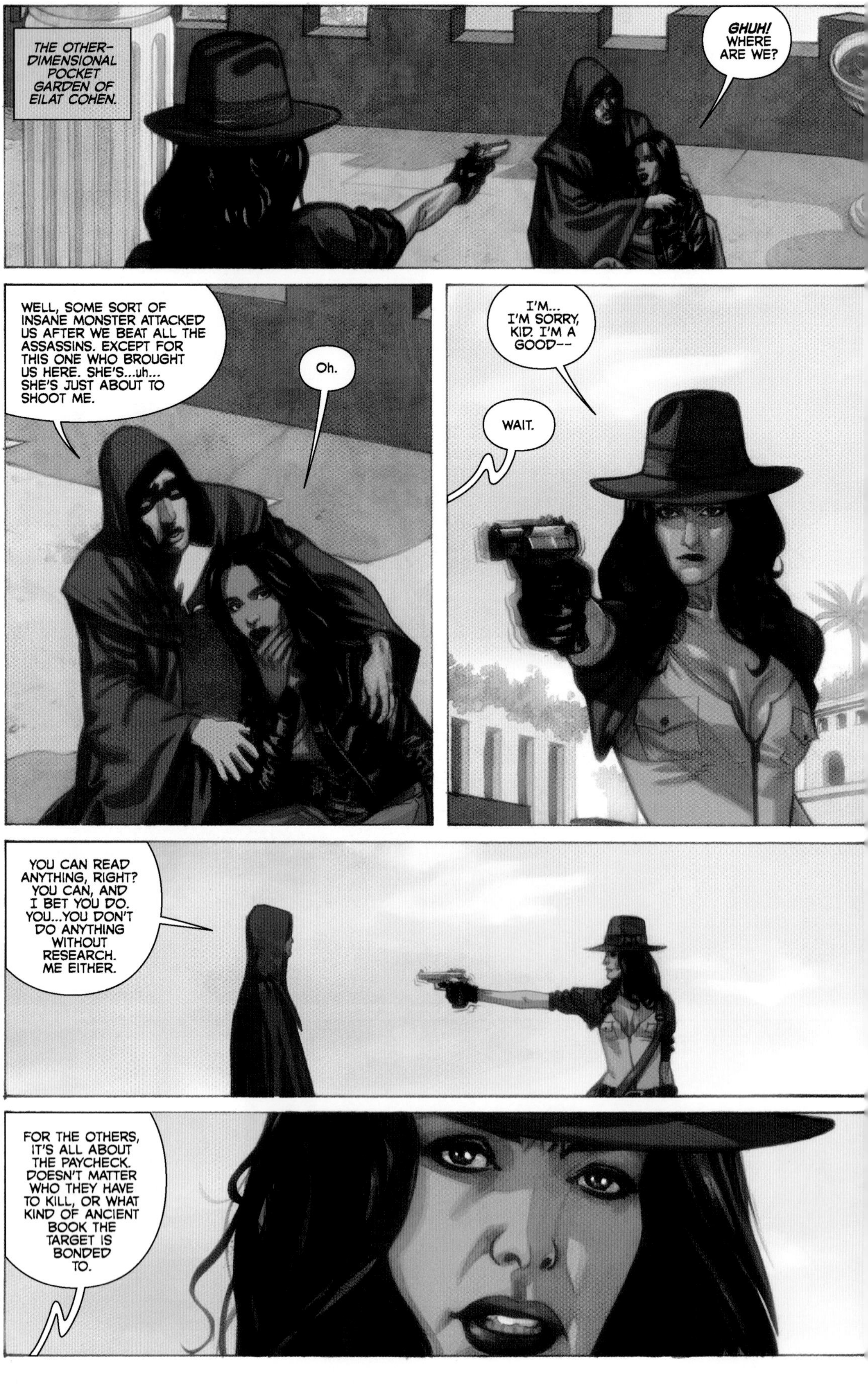

THE OTHER-DIMENSIONAL POCKET GARDEN OF EILAT COHEN.
GHUH! WHERE ARE WE?
WELL, SOME SORT OF INSANE MONSTER ATTACKED US AFTER WE BEAT ALL THE ASSASSINS. EXCEPT FOR THIS ONE WHO BROUGHT US HERE. SHE'S...uh... SHE'S JUST ABOUT TO SHOOT ME.
Oh.
I'M... I'M SORRY, KID. I'M A GOOD--
WAIT.
YOU CAN READ ANYTHING, RIGHT? YOU CAN, AND I BET YOU DO. YOU...YOU DON'T DO ANYTHING WITHOUT RESEARCH. ME EITHER.
FOR THE OTHERS, IT'S ALL ABOUT THE PAYCHECK. DOESN'T MATTER WHO THEY HAVE TO KILL, OR WHAT KIND OF ANCIENT BOOK THE TARGET IS BONDED TO.

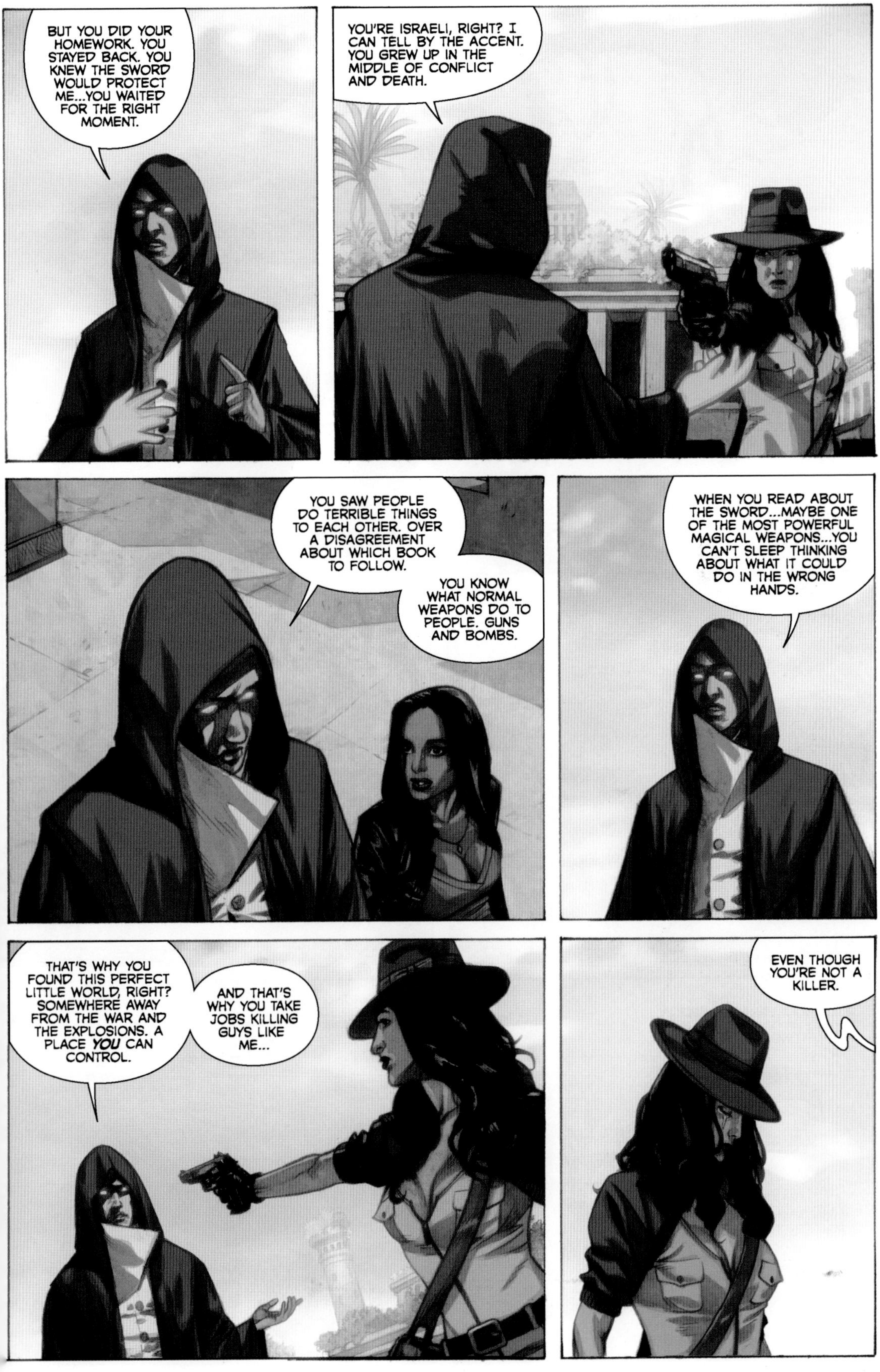
BUT YOU DID YOUR HOMEWORK. YOU STAYED BACK. YOU KNEW THE SWORD WOULD PROTECT ME...YOU WAITED FOR THE RIGHT MOMENT.
YOU'RE ISRAELI, RIGHT? I CAN TELL BY THE ACCENT. YOU GREW UP IN THE MIDDLE OF CONFLICT AND DEATH.
YOU SAW PEOPLE DO TERRIBLE THINGS TO EACH OTHER. OVER A DISAGREEMENT ABOUT WHICH BOOK TO FOLLOW.
YOU KNOW WHAT NORMAL WEAPONS DO TO PEOPLE. GUNS AND BOMBS.
WHEN YOU READ ABOUT THE SWORD...MAYBE ONE OF THE MOST POWERFUL MAGICAL WEAPONS...YOU CAN'T SLEEP THINKING ABOUT WHAT IT COULD DO IN THE WRONG HANDS.
THAT'S WHY YOU FOUND THIS PERFECT LITTLE WORLD, RIGHT? SOMEWHERE AWAY FROM THE WAR AND THE EXPLOSIONS. A PLACE *YOU* CAN CONTROL.
AND THAT'S WHY YOU TAKE JOBS KILLING GUYS LIKE ME...
EVEN THOUGH YOU'RE NOT A KILLER.

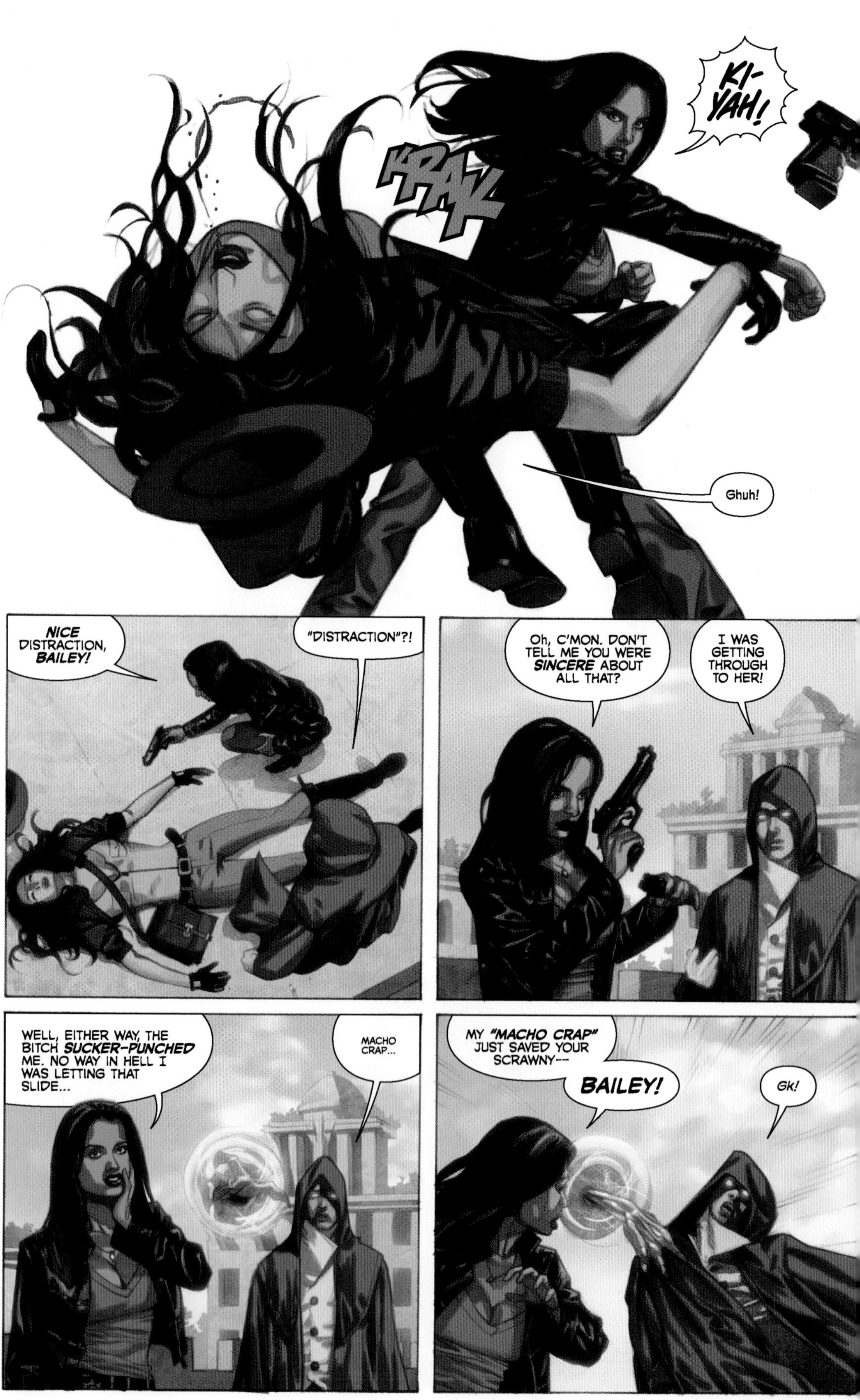
KI-YAH!
KRAK
Ghuh!
NICE DISTRACTION, BAILEY!
"DISTRACTION"?!
Oh, C'MON. DON'T TELL ME YOU WERE SINCERE ABOUT ALL THAT?
I WAS GETTING THROUGH TO HER!
WELL, EITHER WAY, THE BITCH SUCKER-PUNCHED ME. NO WAY IN HELL I WAS LETTING THAT SLIDE...
MACHO CRAP...
MY "MACHO CRAP" JUST SAVED YOUR SCRAWNY--
BAILEY!
Gk!

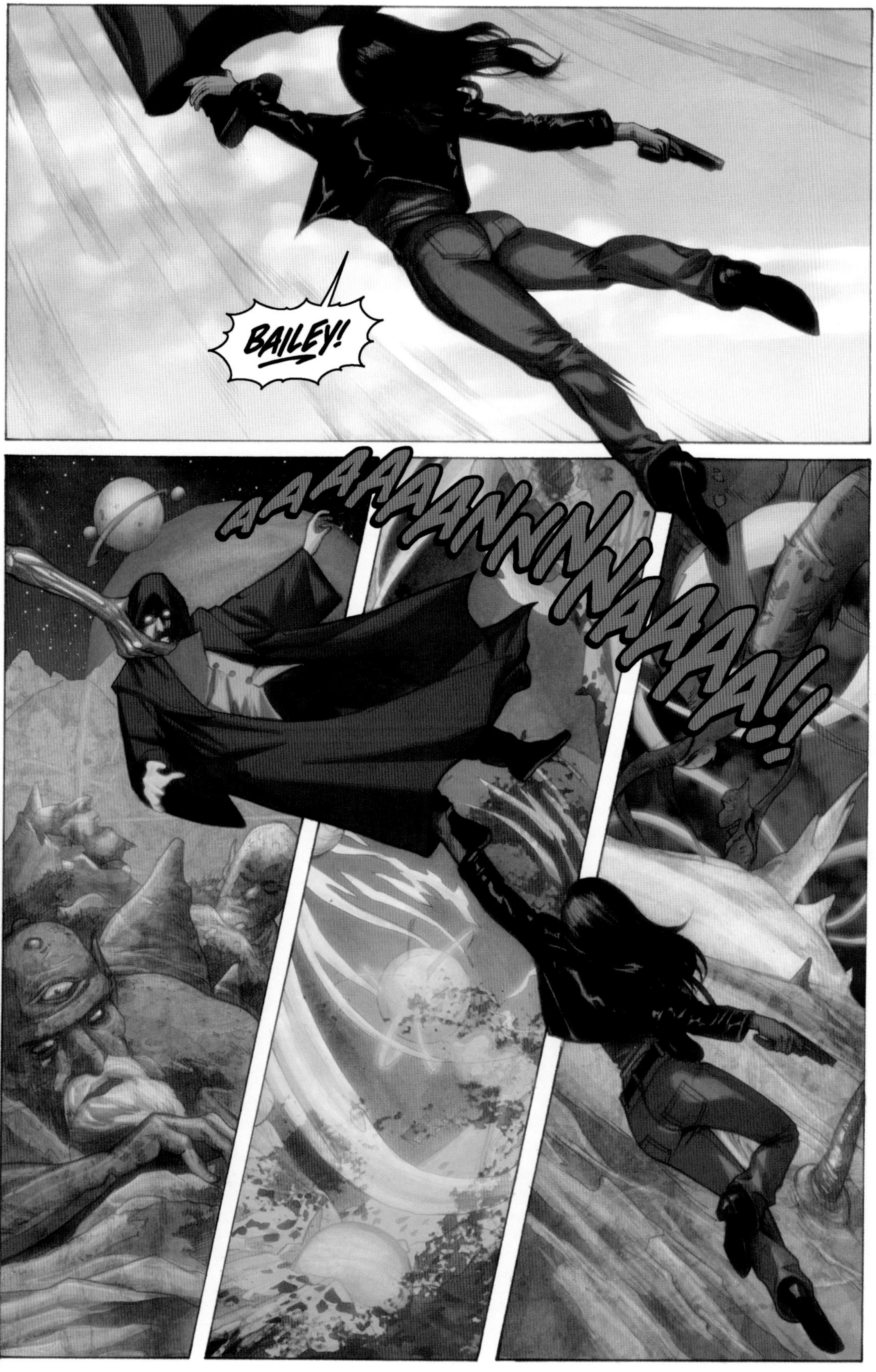
BAILEY!
AAAAAANNNNNAAAA!!

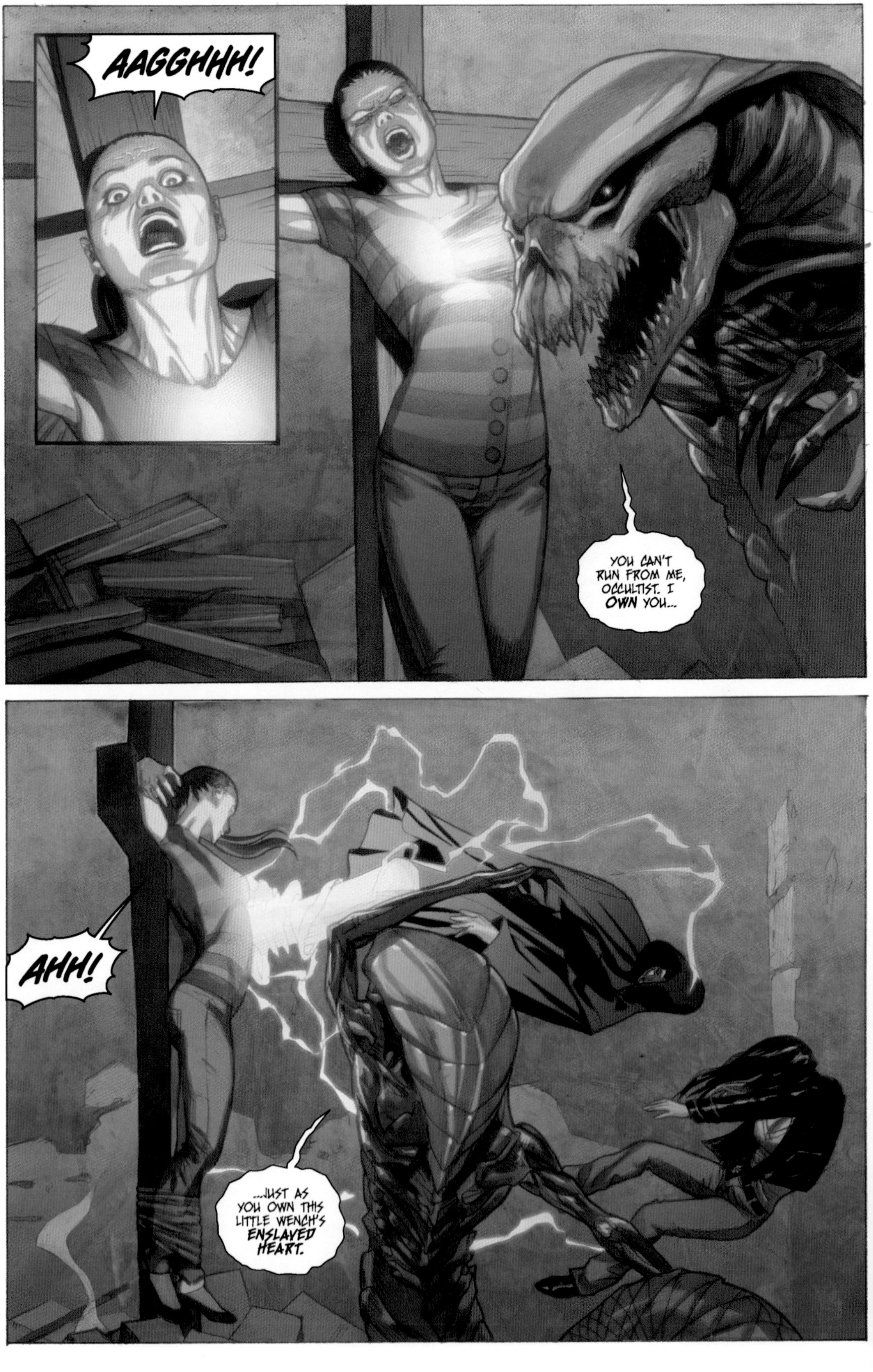
AAGGHHH!
YOU CAN'T RUN FROM ME, OCCULTIST. I OWN YOU...
AHH!
...JUST AS YOU OWN THIS LITTLE WENCH'S ENSLAVED HEART.

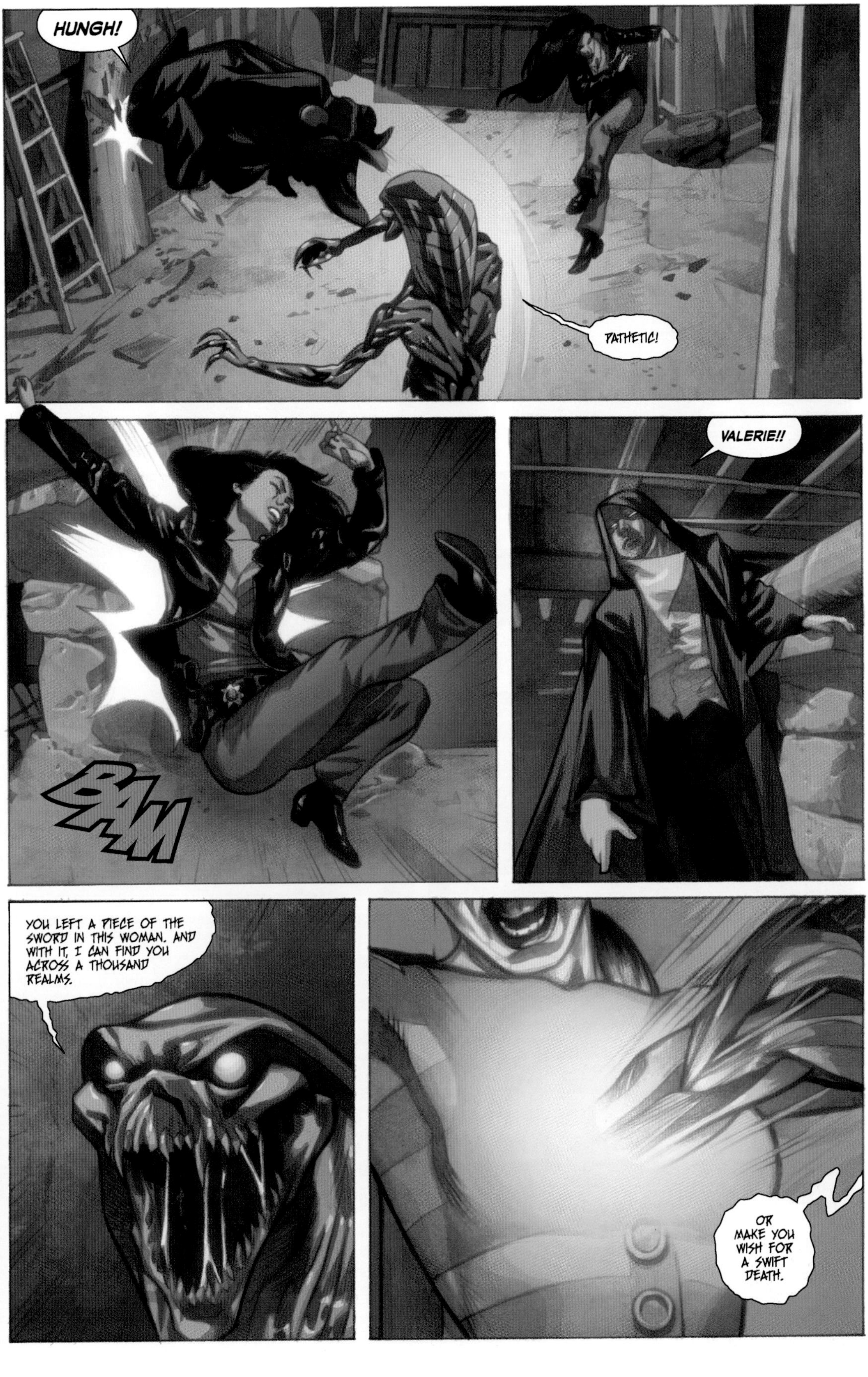
HUNGH!
PATHETIC!
BAM
VALERIE!!
YOU LEFT A PIECE OF THE SWORD IN THIS WOMAN. AND WITH IT, I CAN FIND YOU ACROSS A THOUSAND REALMS.
OR MAKE YOU WISH FOR A SWIFT DEATH.

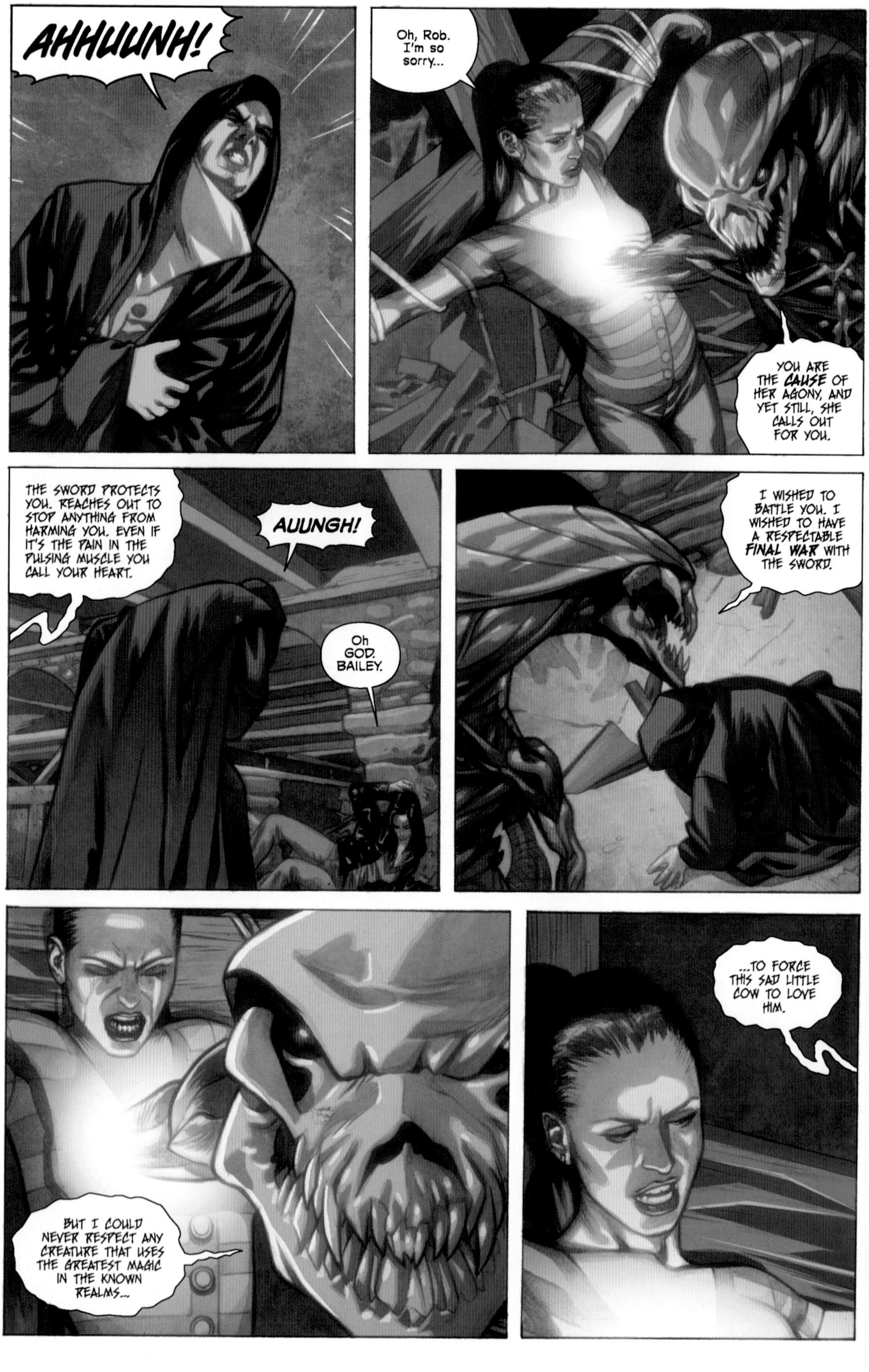
AHHUUNH!
Oh, Rob. I'm so sorry...
YOU ARE THE CAUSE OF HER AGONY, AND YET STILL, SHE CALLS OUT FOR YOU.
THE SWORD PROTECTS YOU. REACHES OUT TO STOP ANYTHING FROM HARMING YOU. EVEN IF IT'S THE PAIN IN THE PULSING MUSCLE YOU CALL YOUR HEART.
AUUNGH!
Oh GOD. BAILEY.
I WISHED TO BATTLE YOU. I WISHED TO HAVE A RESPECTABLE FINAL WAR WITH THE SWORD.
BUT I COULD NEVER RESPECT ANY CREATURE THAT USES THE GREATEST MAGIC IN THE KNOWN REALMS...
...TO FORCE THIS SAD LITTLE COW TO LOVE HIM.

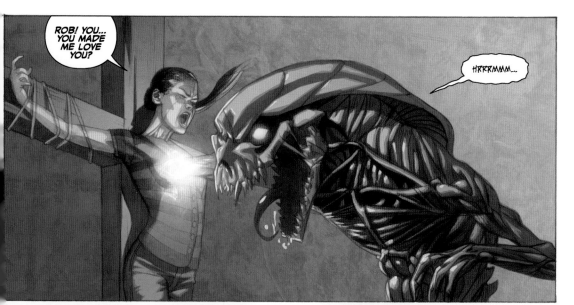

ROB! YOU... YOU MADE ME LOVE YOU?

HRRRMMM...

NO! RELEASE ME!!!

VALERIE! VAL! I'M SO SORRY!

NYYAGH!

YOU COULDN'T LET ME *GO!?* ALL I WANTED WAS A *CHANCE,* AND YOU TOOK IT *AWAY* FROM ME!

TELL ME HOW TO HELP YOU!

THE SPELL IS ALMOST BROKEN-- SHE'S ALMOST FREE...IT'S JUST NOT ENOUGH...

WHAT'S NOT ENOUGH?!

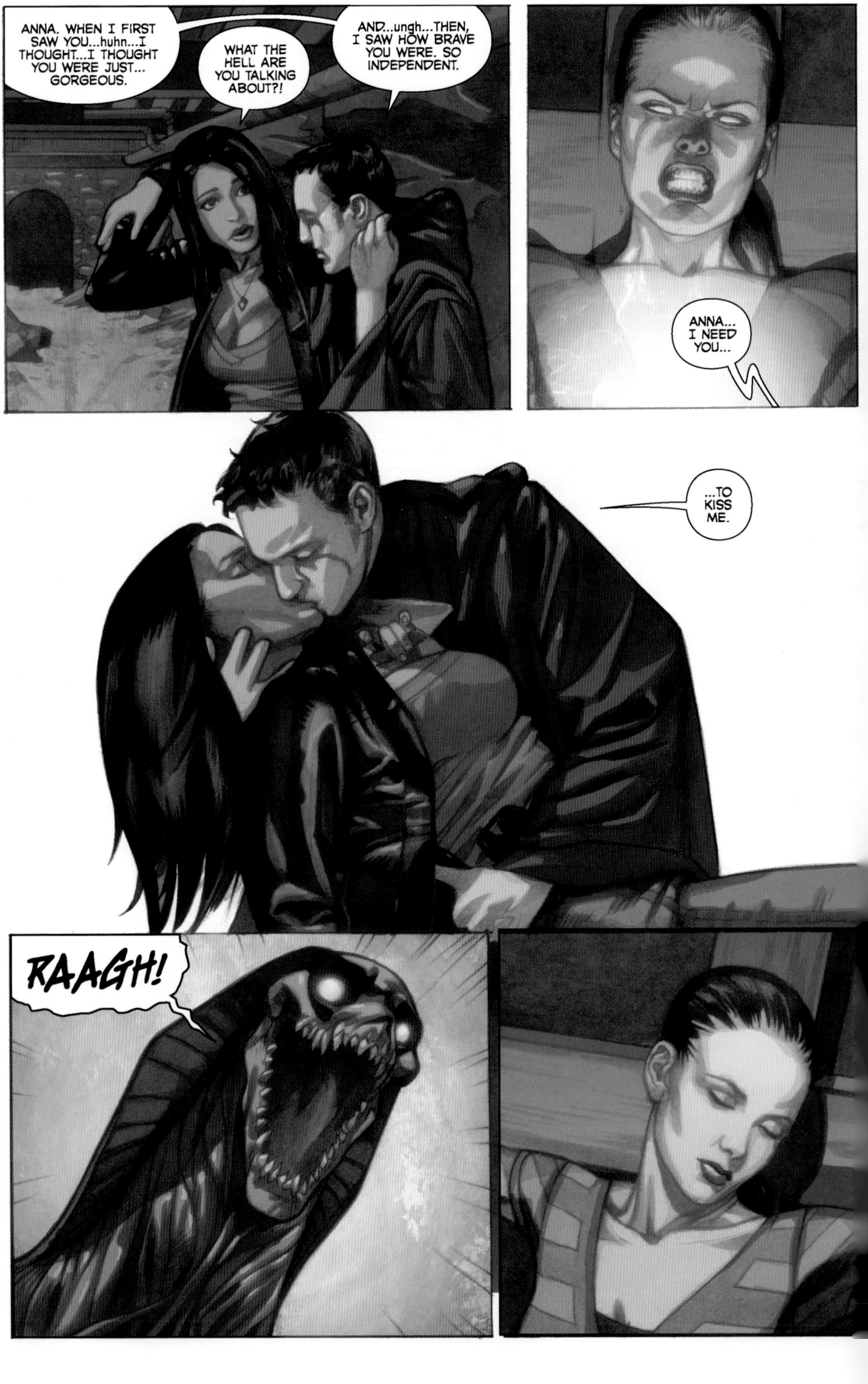

ANNA. WHEN I FIRST SAW YOU...huhn...I THOUGHT...I THOUGHT YOU WERE JUST... GORGEOUS.
WHAT THE HELL ARE YOU TALKING ABOUT?!
AND...ungh...THEN, I SAW HOW BRAVE YOU WERE. SO INDEPENDENT.
ANNA... I NEED YOU...
...TO KISS ME.
RAAGH!

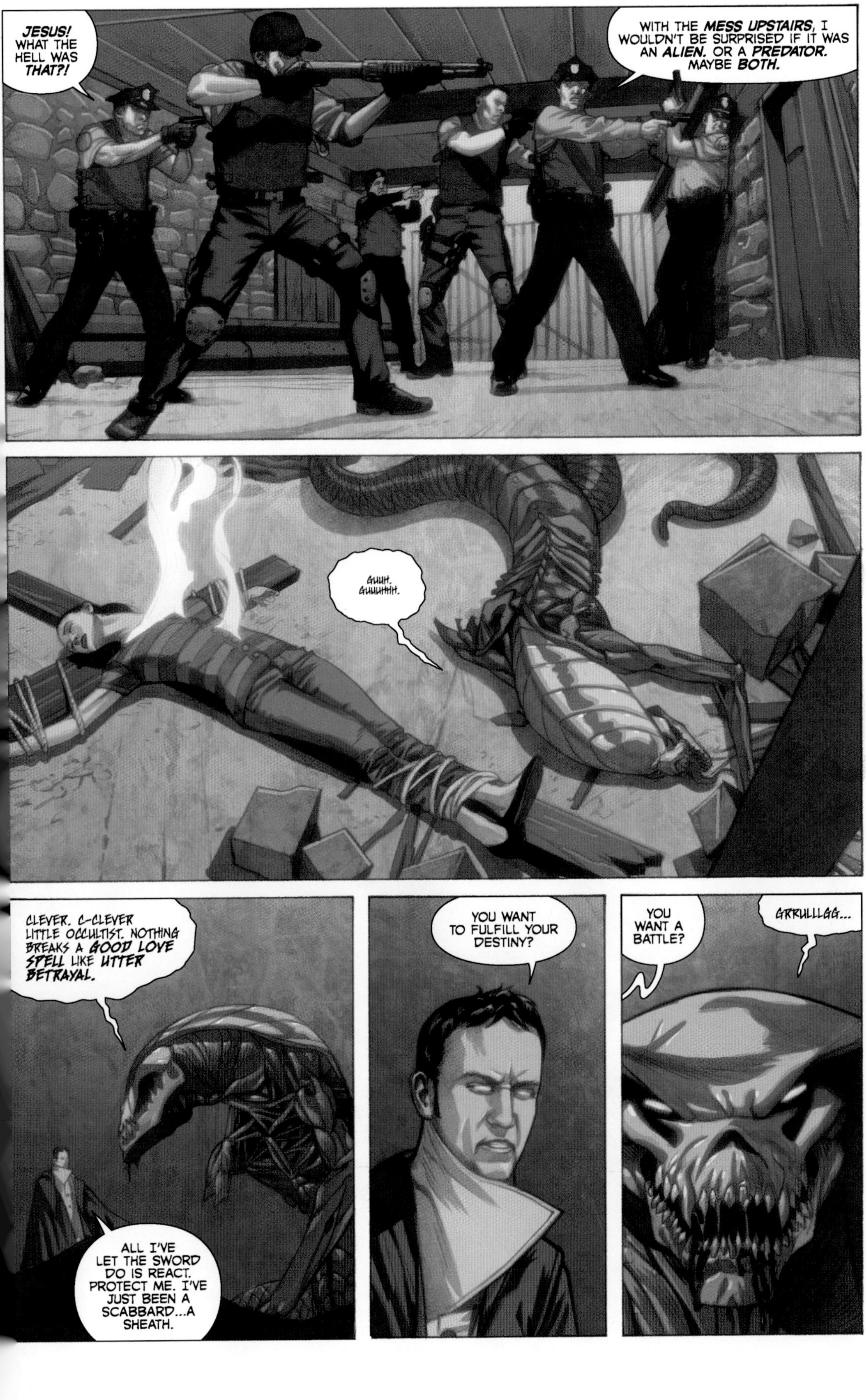
JESUS! WHAT THE HELL WAS THAT?!
WITH THE MESS UPSTAIRS, I WOULDN'T BE SURPRISED IF IT WAS AN ALIEN. OR A PREDATOR. MAYBE BOTH.
GUUH. GUUUHHH.
CLEVER. C-CLEVER LITTLE OCCULTIST. NOTHING BREAKS A GOOD LOVE SPELL LIKE UTTER BETRAYAL.
ALL I'VE LET THE SWORD DO IS REACT. PROTECT ME. I'VE JUST BEEN A SCABBARD...A SHEATH.
YOU WANT TO FULFILL YOUR DESTINY?
YOU WANT A BATTLE?
GRRULLLGG...

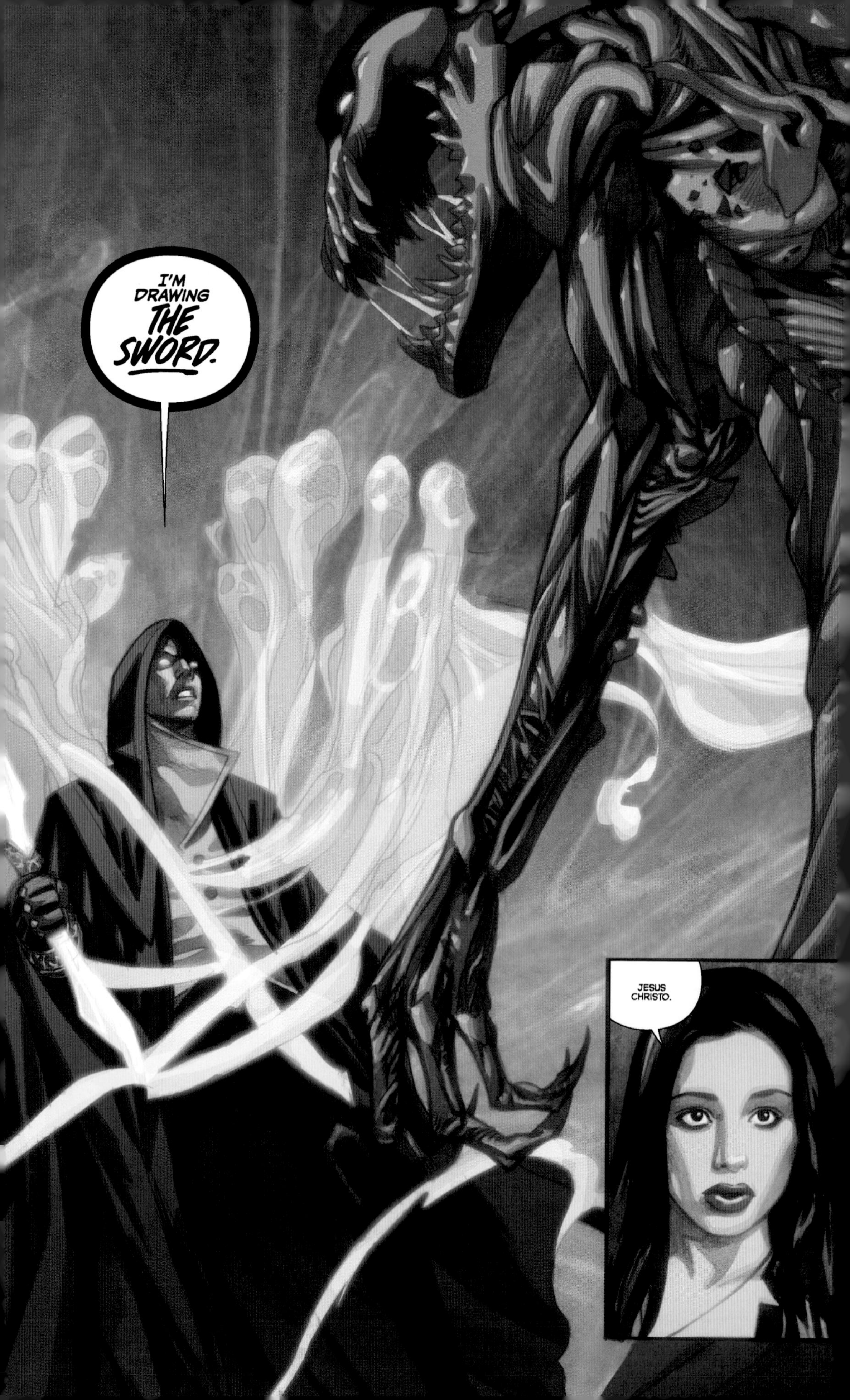
I'M DRAWING THE SWORD.
JESUS CHRISTO.

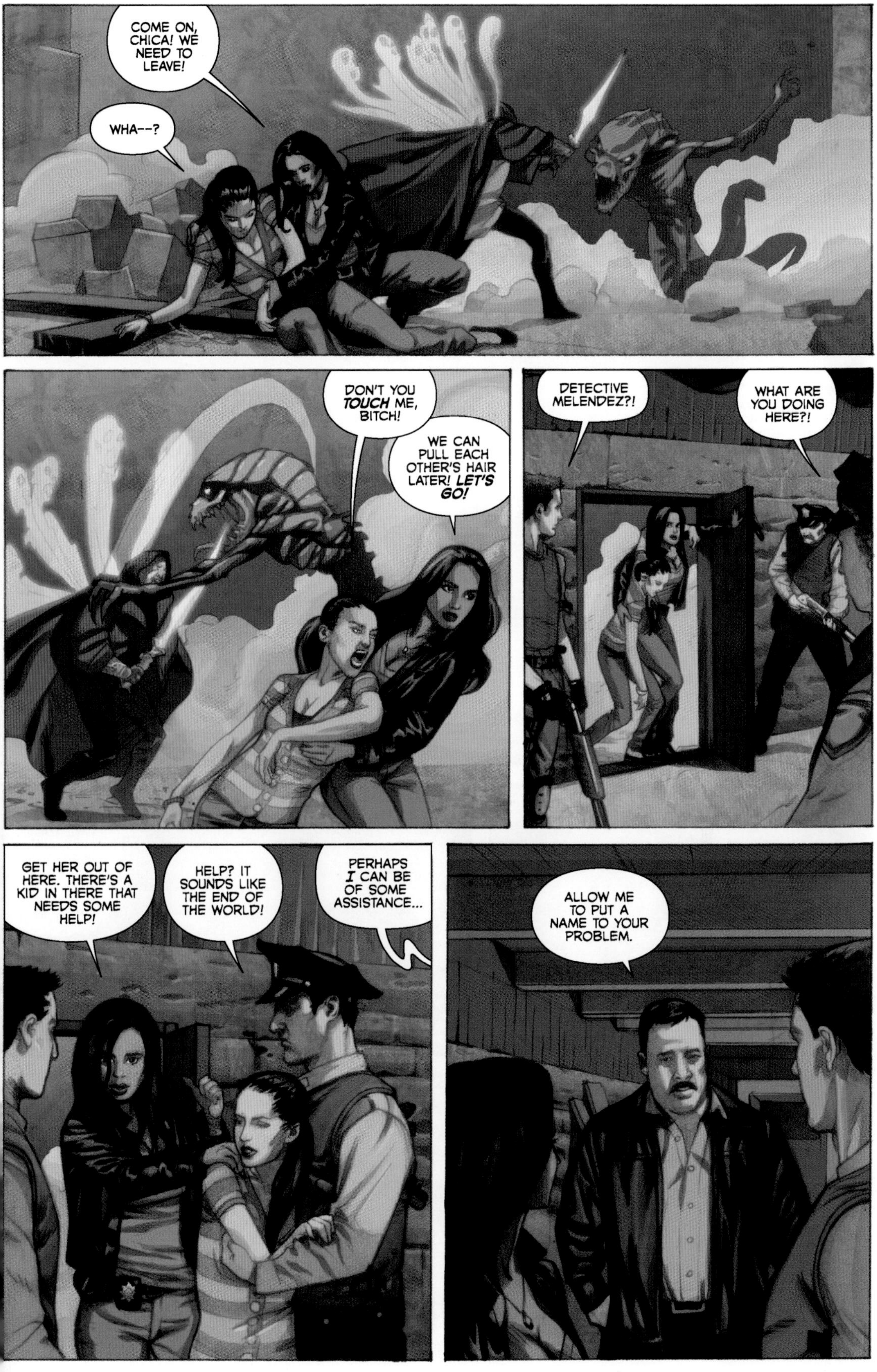
COME ON, CHICA! WE NEED TO LEAVE!
WHA--?
DON'T YOU *TOUCH* ME, BITCH!
WE CAN PULL EACH OTHER'S HAIR LATER! *LET'S GO!*
DETECTIVE MELENDEZ?!
WHAT ARE YOU DOING HERE?!
GET HER OUT OF HERE. THERE'S A KID IN THERE THAT NEEDS SOME HELP!
HELP? IT SOUNDS LIKE THE END OF THE WORLD!
PERHAPS *I* CAN BE OF SOME ASSISTANCE...
ALLOW ME TO PUT A NAME TO YOUR PROBLEM.

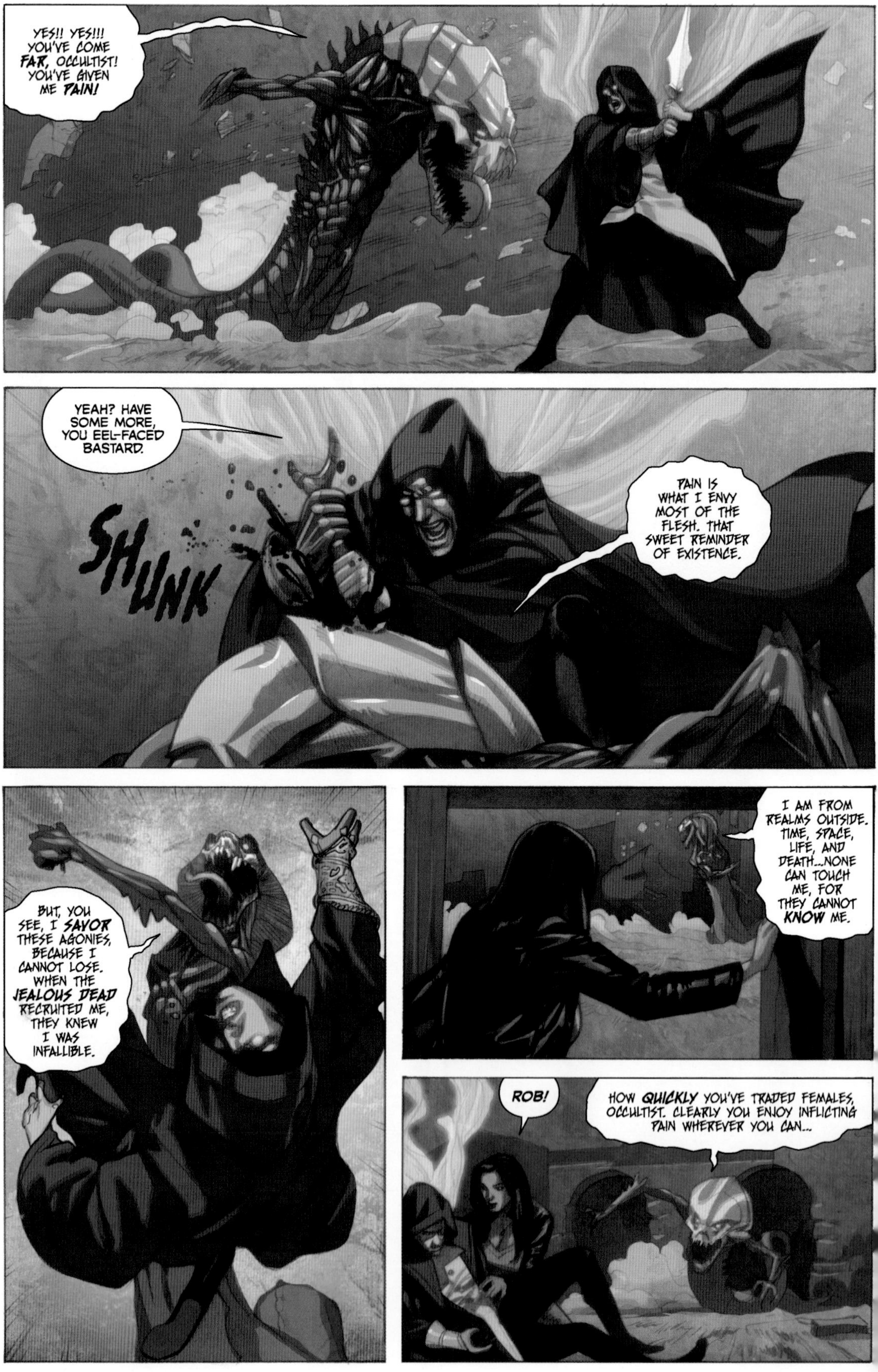
YES!! YES!!! YOU'VE COME FAR, OCCULTIST! YOU'VE GIVEN ME PAIN!
YEAH? HAVE SOME MORE, YOU EEL-FACED BASTARD.
SHUNK
PAIN IS WHAT I ENVY MOST OF THE FLESH. THAT SWEET REMINDER OF EXISTENCE.
BUT, YOU SEE, I SAVOR THESE AGONIES, BECAUSE I CANNOT LOSE. WHEN THE JEALOUS DEAD RECRUITED ME, THEY KNEW I WAS INFALLIBLE.
I AM FROM REALMS OUTSIDE. TIME, SPACE, LIFE, AND DEATH...NONE CAN TOUCH ME, FOR THEY CANNOT KNOW ME.
ROB!
HOW QUICKLY YOU'VE TRADED FEMALES, OCCULTIST. CLEARLY YOU ENJOY INFLICTING PAIN WHEREVER YOU CAN...

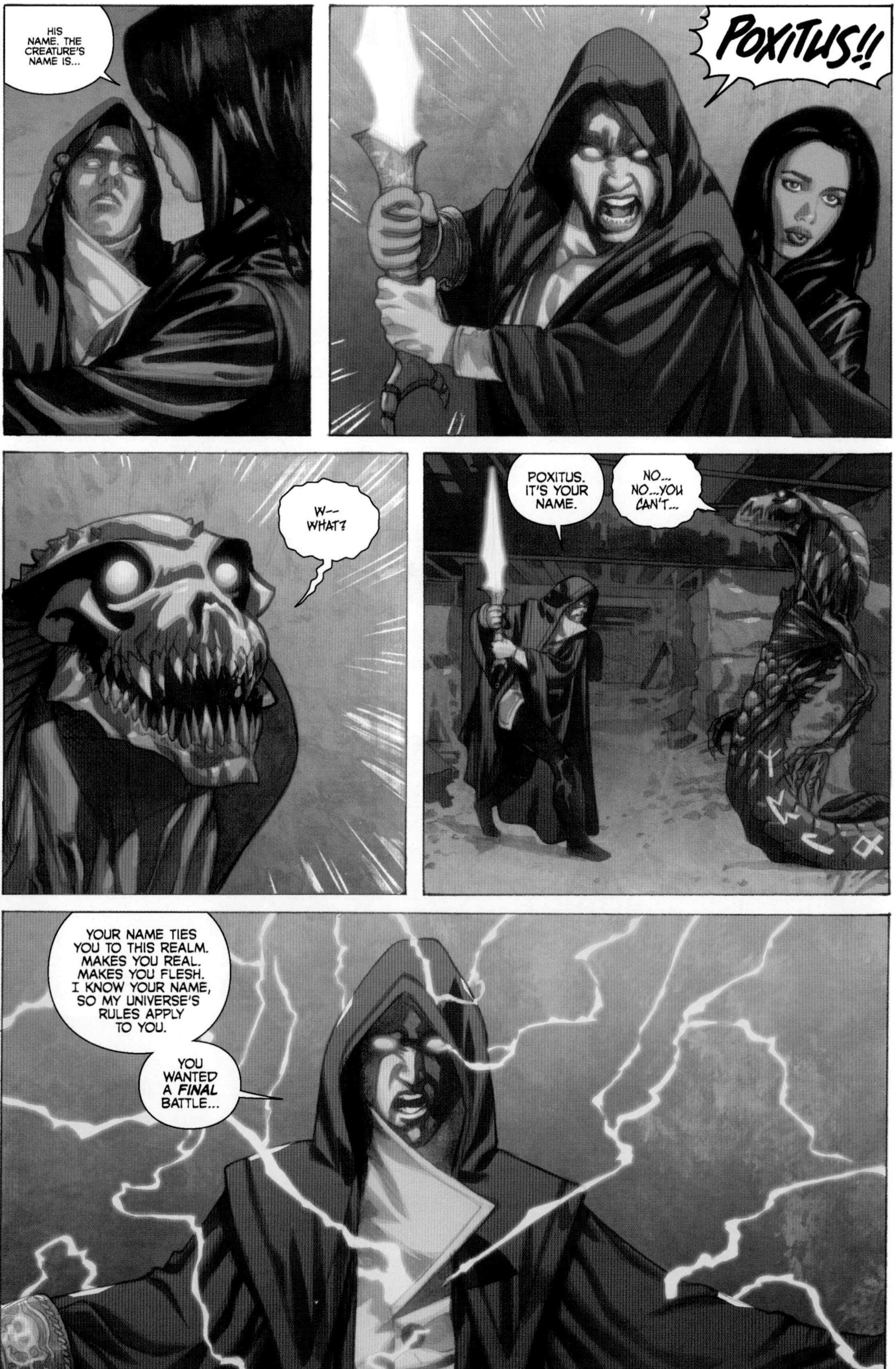
HIS NAME. THE CREATURE'S NAME IS...
POXITUS!!
W-- WHAT?
POXITUS. IT'S YOUR NAME.
NO... NO...YOU CAN'T...
YOUR NAME TIES YOU TO THIS REALM. MAKES YOU REAL. MAKES YOU FLESH. I KNOW YOUR NAME, SO MY UNIVERSE'S RULES APPLY TO YOU.
YOU WANTED A *FINAL* BATTLE...

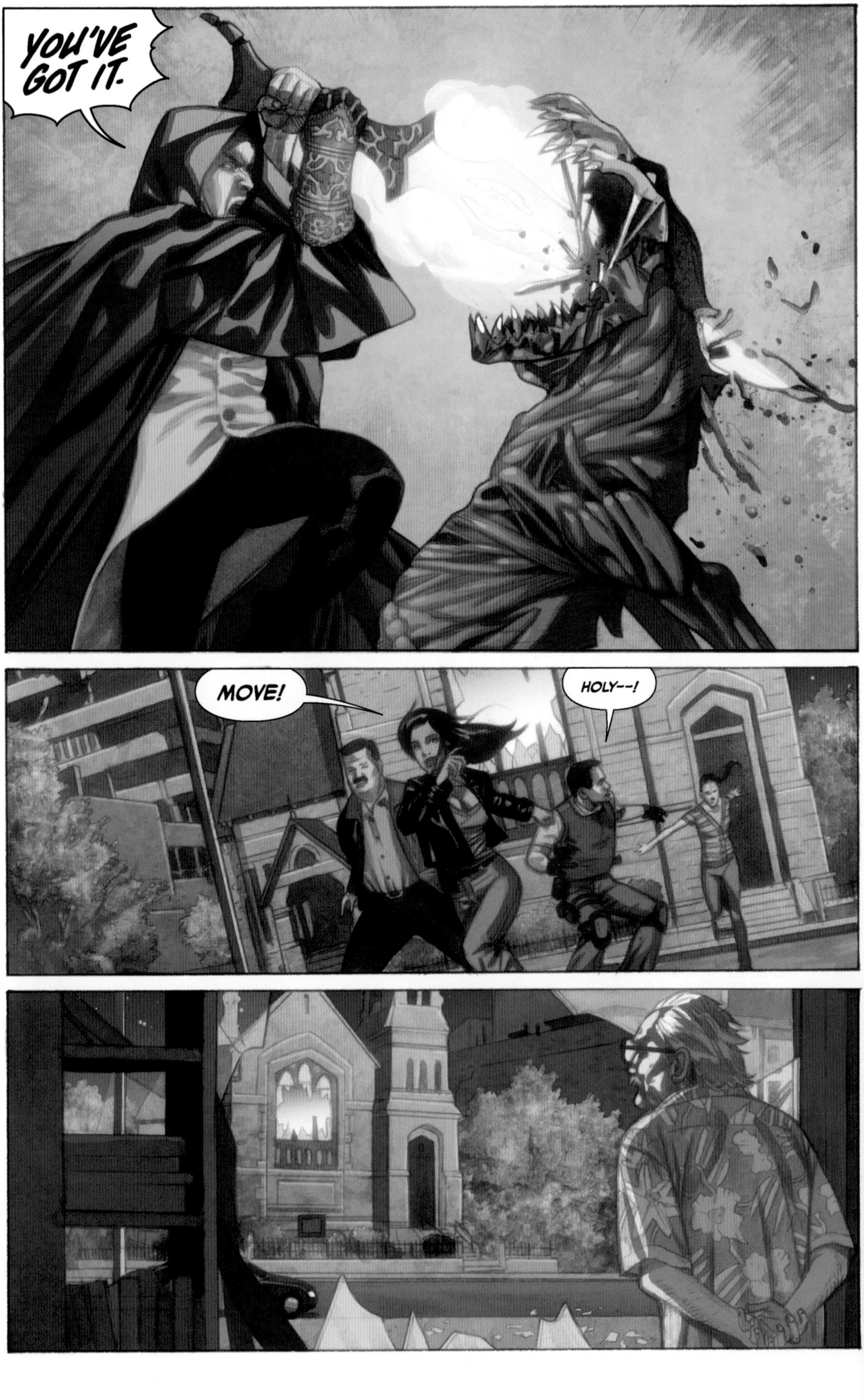
YOU'VE GOT IT.
MOVE!
HOLY--!

MORNING.

Uh...I HAD THE STRANGEST DREAM. SOME KIND OF SNAKE, AND...IT WAS WEIRD. AND YOU...

YOU...

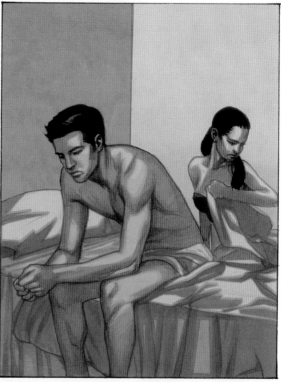

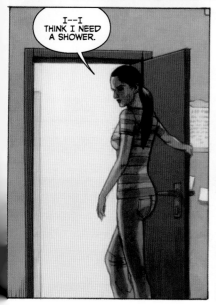

I--I THINK I NEED A SHOWER.

GOODBYE, VAL.

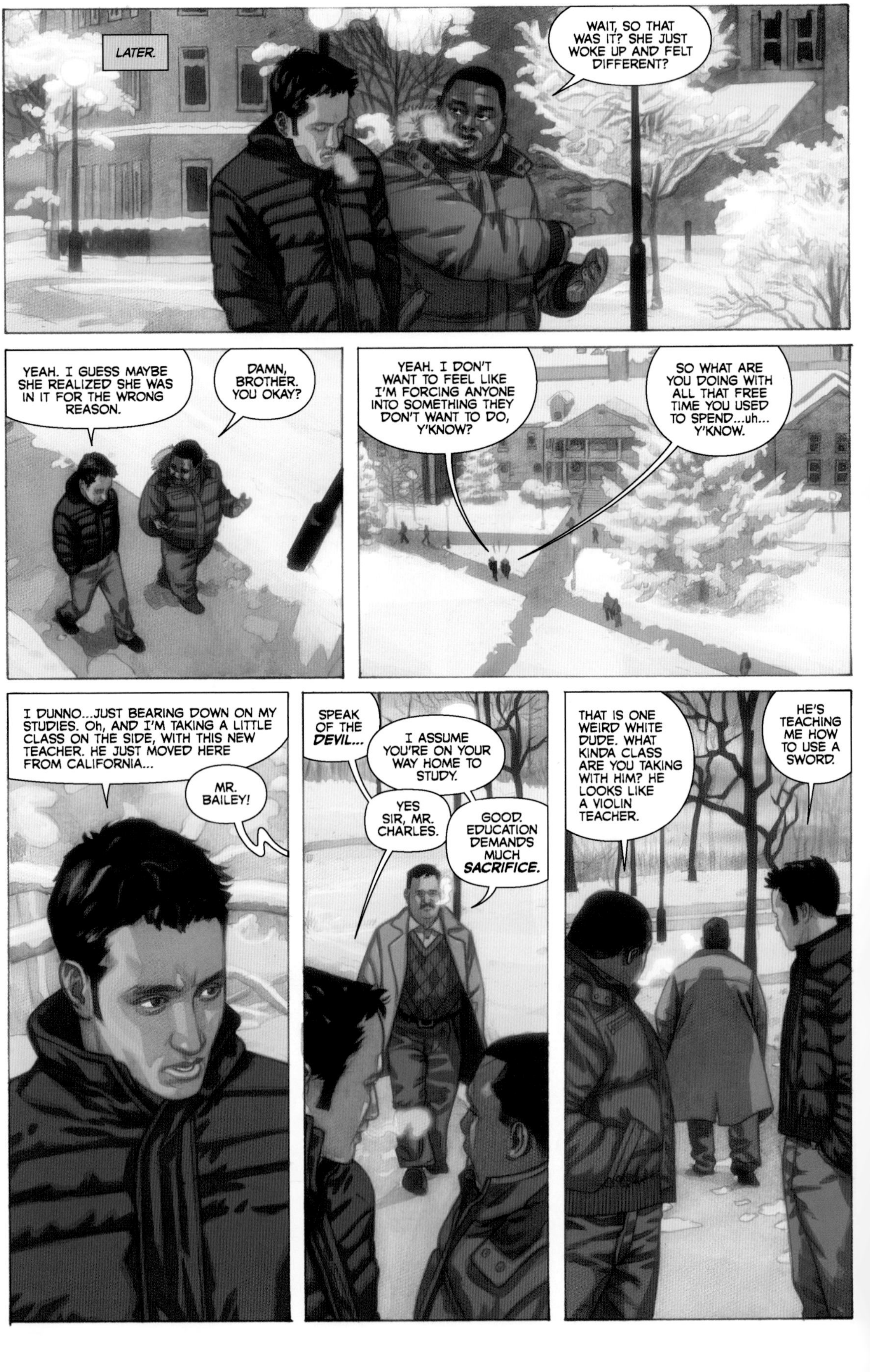
LATER.
WAIT, SO THAT WAS IT? SHE JUST WOKE UP AND FELT DIFFERENT?
YEAH. I GUESS MAYBE SHE REALIZED SHE WAS IN IT FOR THE WRONG REASON.
DAMN, BROTHER. YOU OKAY?
YEAH. I DON'T WANT TO FEEL LIKE I'M FORCING ANYONE INTO SOMETHING THEY DON'T WANT TO DO, Y'KNOW?
SO WHAT ARE YOU DOING WITH ALL THAT FREE TIME YOU USED TO SPEND...uh... Y'KNOW.
I DUNNO...JUST BEARING DOWN ON MY STUDIES. Oh, AND I'M TAKING A LITTLE CLASS ON THE SIDE, WITH THIS NEW TEACHER. HE JUST MOVED HERE FROM CALIFORNIA...
MR. BAILEY!
SPEAK OF THE *DEVIL...*
I ASSUME YOU'RE ON YOUR WAY HOME TO STUDY.
YES SIR, MR. CHARLES.
GOOD. EDUCATION DEMANDS MUCH *SACRIFICE.*
THAT IS ONE WEIRD WHITE DUDE. WHAT KINDA CLASS ARE YOU TAKING WITH HIM? HE LOOKS LIKE A VIOLIN TEACHER.
HE'S TEACHING ME HOW TO USE A SWORD.

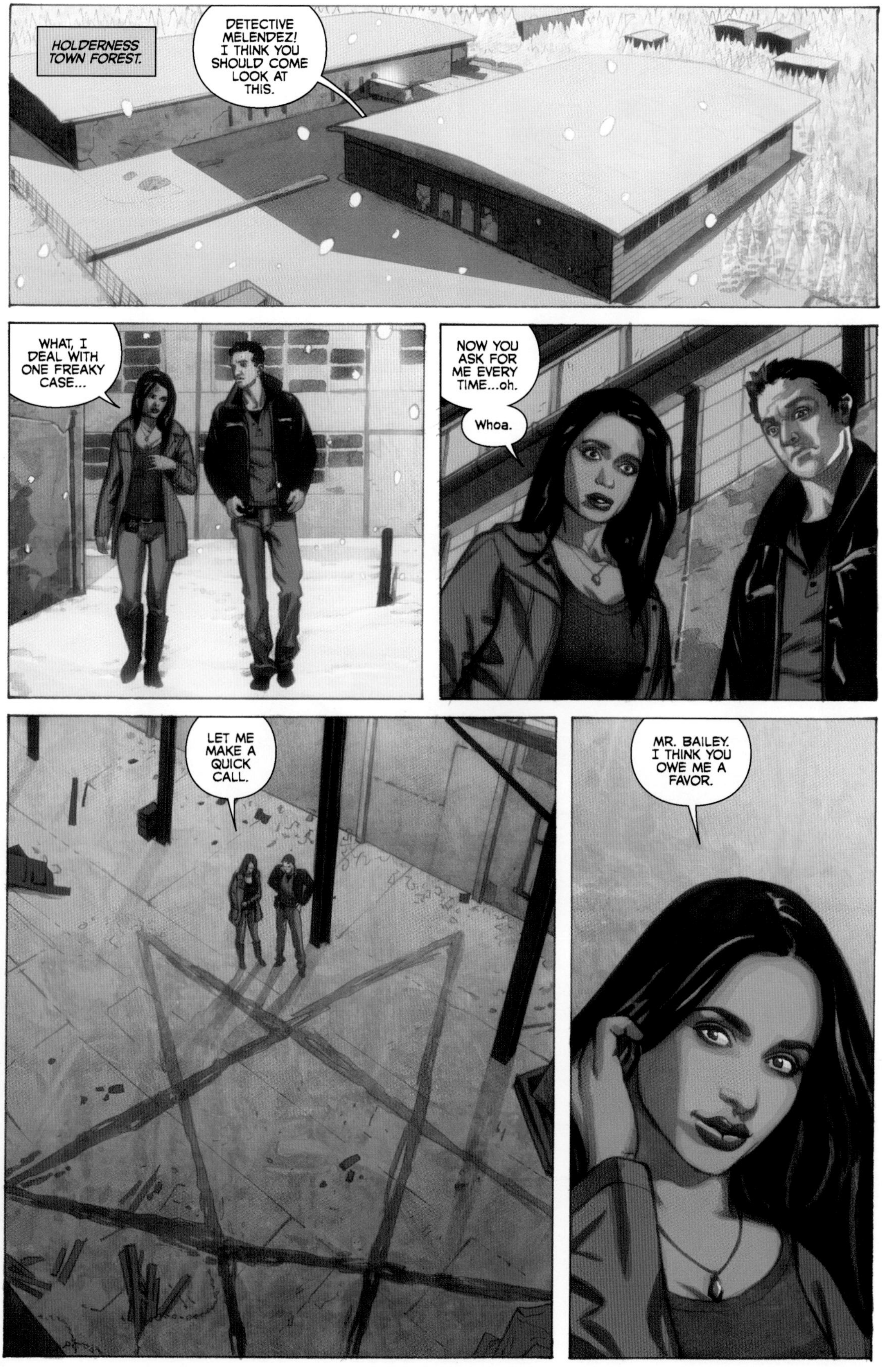
HOLDERNESS TOWN FOREST.
DETECTIVE MELENDEZ! I THINK YOU SHOULD COME LOOK AT THIS.
WHAT, I DEAL WITH ONE FREAKY CASE...
NOW YOU ASK FOR ME EVERY TIME...oh.
Whoa.
LET ME MAKE A QUICK CALL.
MR. BAILEY. I THINK YOU OWE ME A FAVOR.

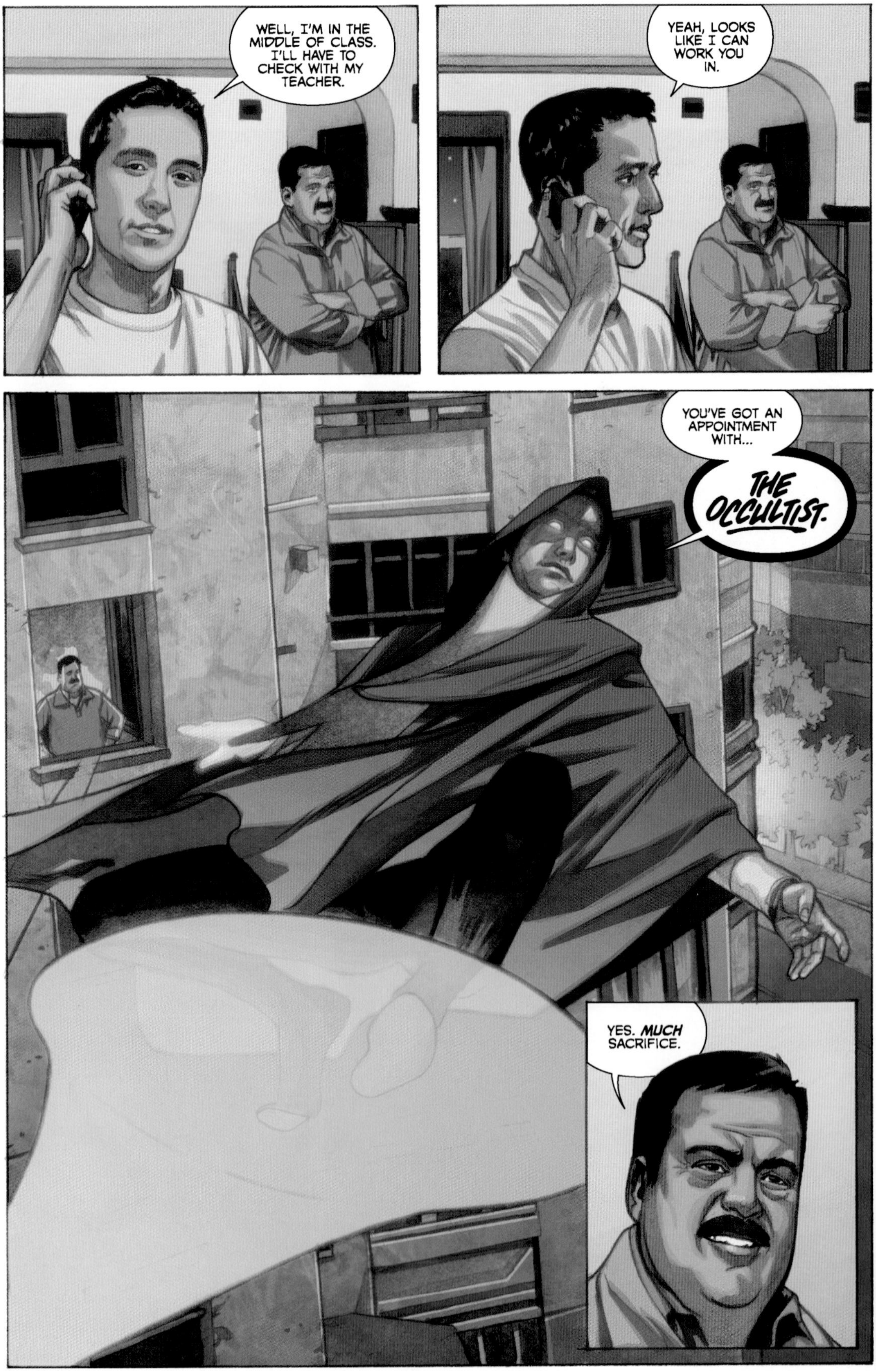
WELL, I'M IN THE MIDDLE OF CLASS. I'LL HAVE TO CHECK WITH MY TEACHER.
YEAH, LOOKS LIKE I CAN WORK YOU IN.
YOU'VE GOT AN APPOINTMENT WITH...
THE OCCULTIST.
YES. MUCH SACRIFICE.

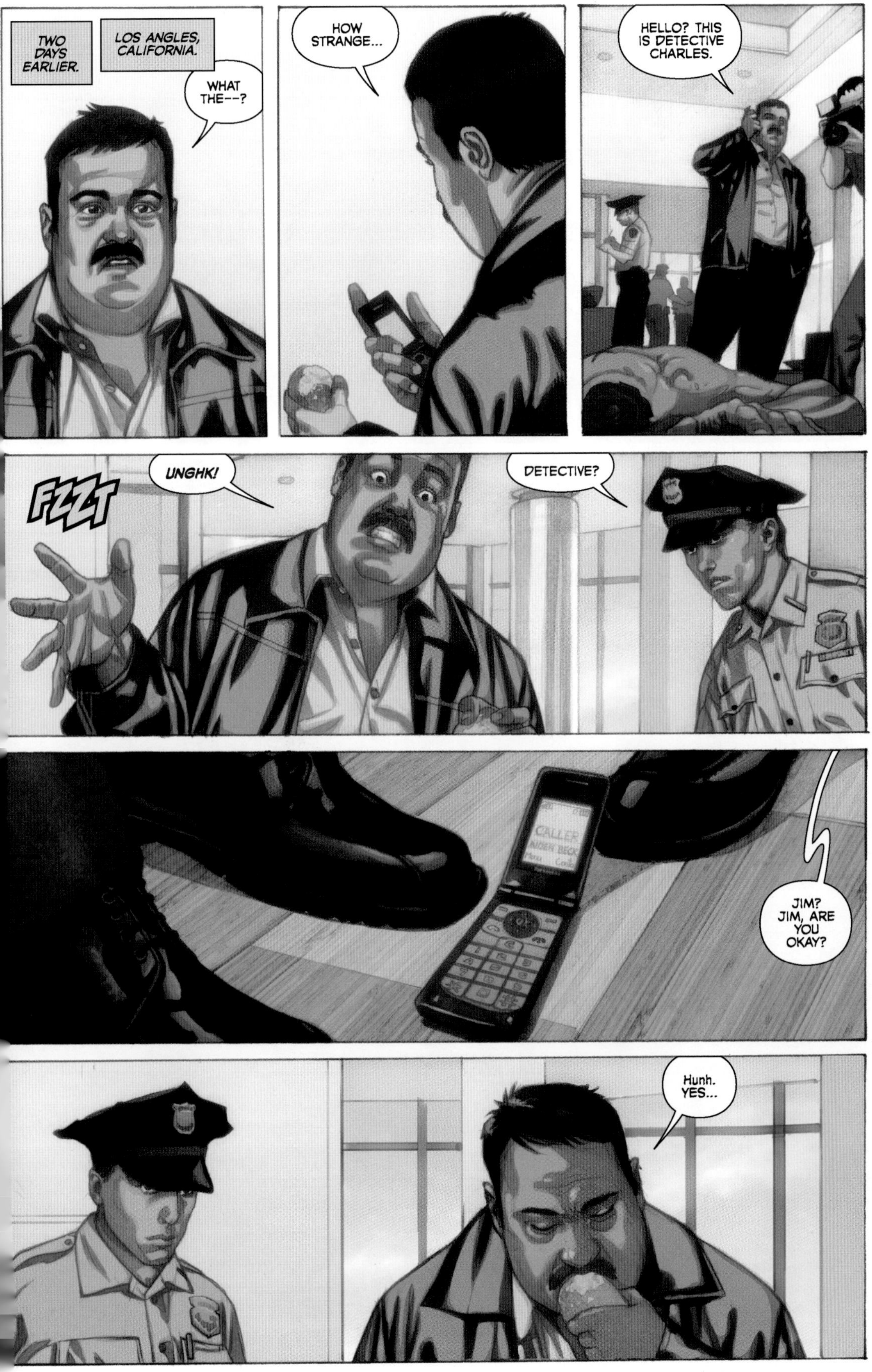
TWO DAYS EARLIER.
LOS ANGLES, CALIFORNIA.
WHAT THE--?
HOW STRANGE...
HELLO? THIS IS DETECTIVE CHARLES.
FZZT
UNGHK!
DETECTIVE?
CALLER
JIM? JIM, ARE YOU OKAY?
Hunh. YES...

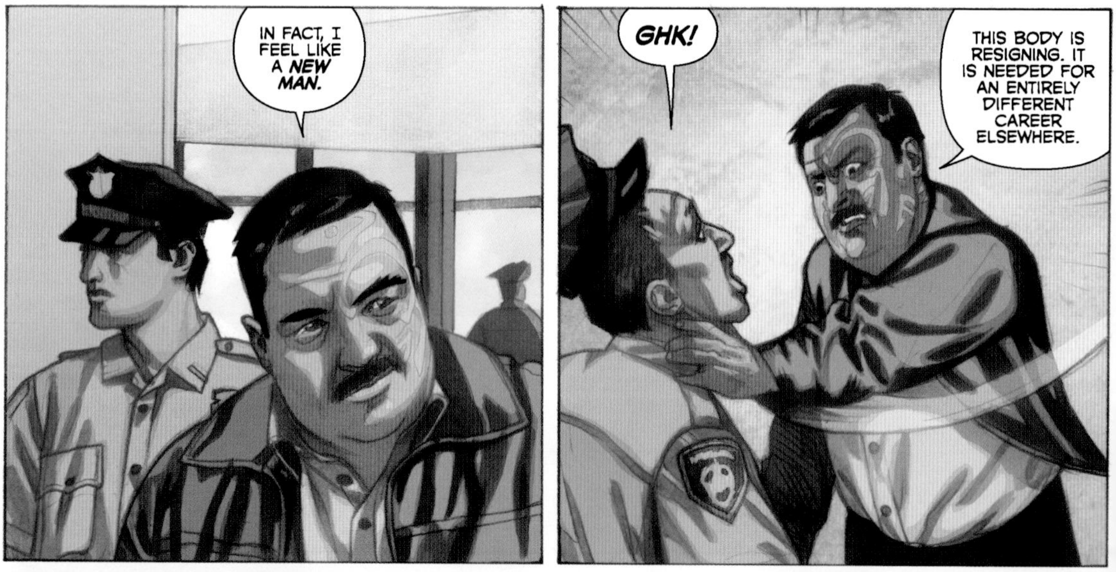
IN FACT, I FEEL LIKE A **NEW MAN.**
GHK!
THIS BODY IS RESIGNING. IT IS NEEDED FOR AN ENTIRELY DIFFERENT CAREER ELSEWHERE.

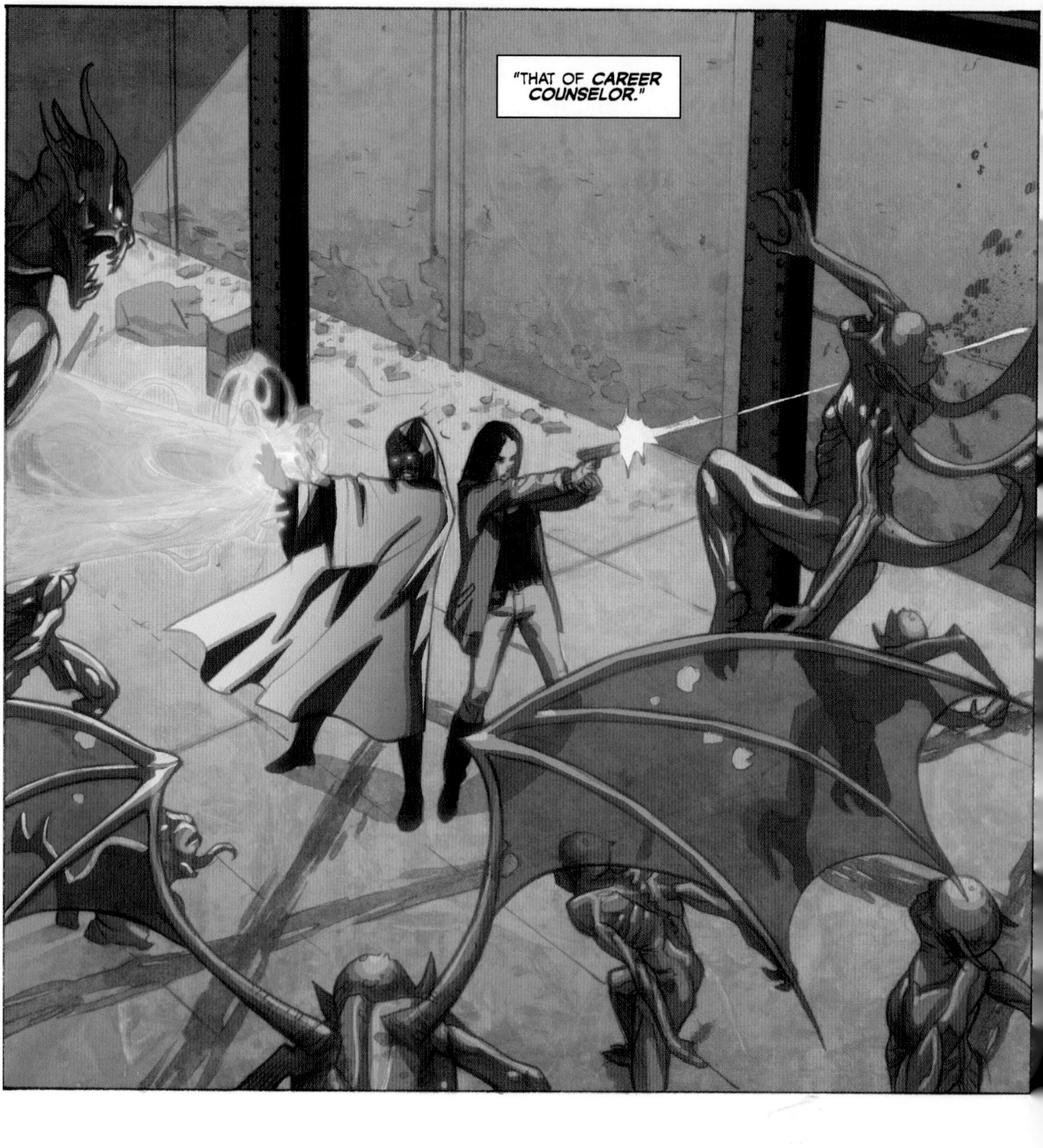
"THAT OF **CAREER COUNSELOR.**"

CHAPTER FIVE

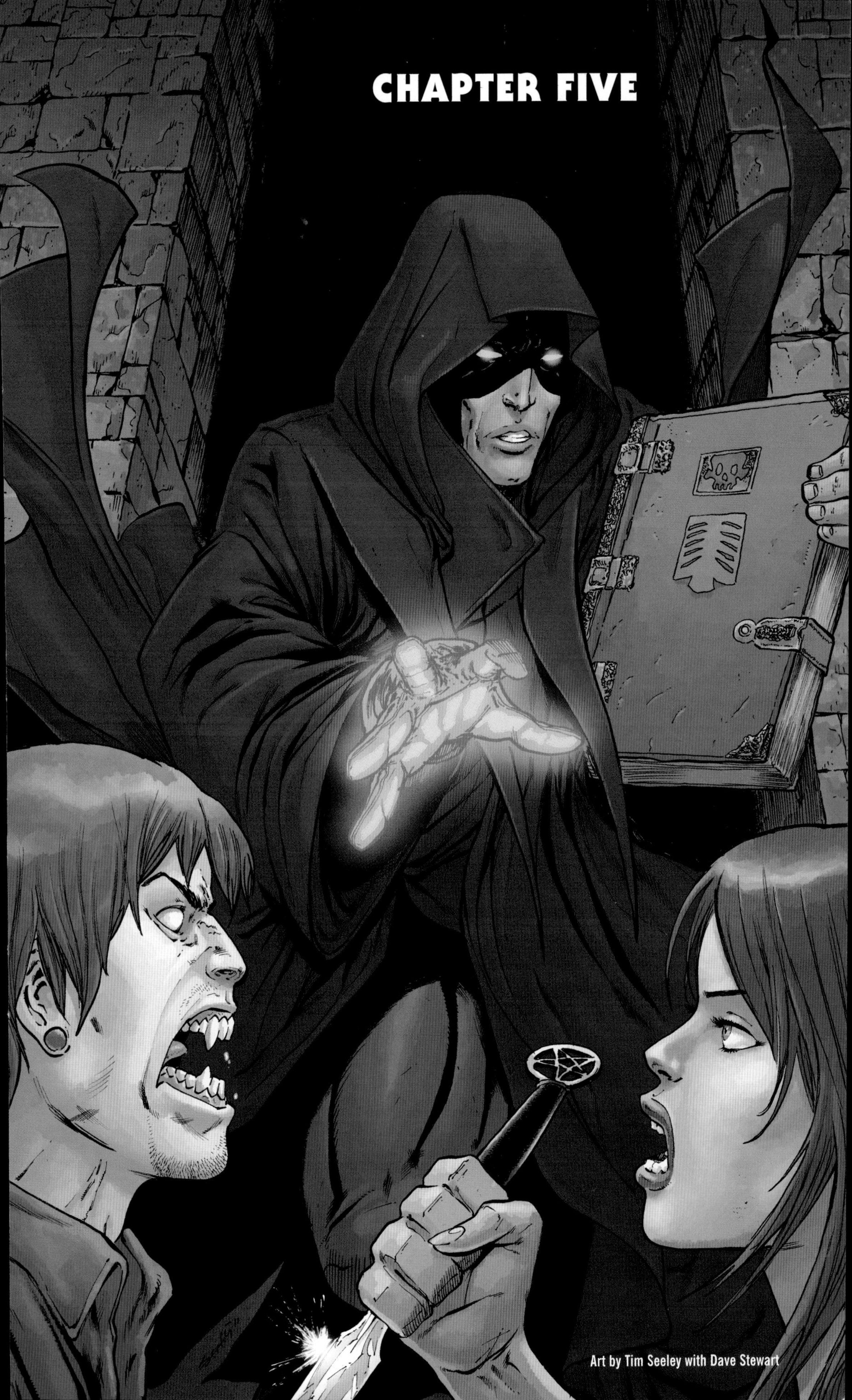

Art by Tim Seeley with Dave Stewart

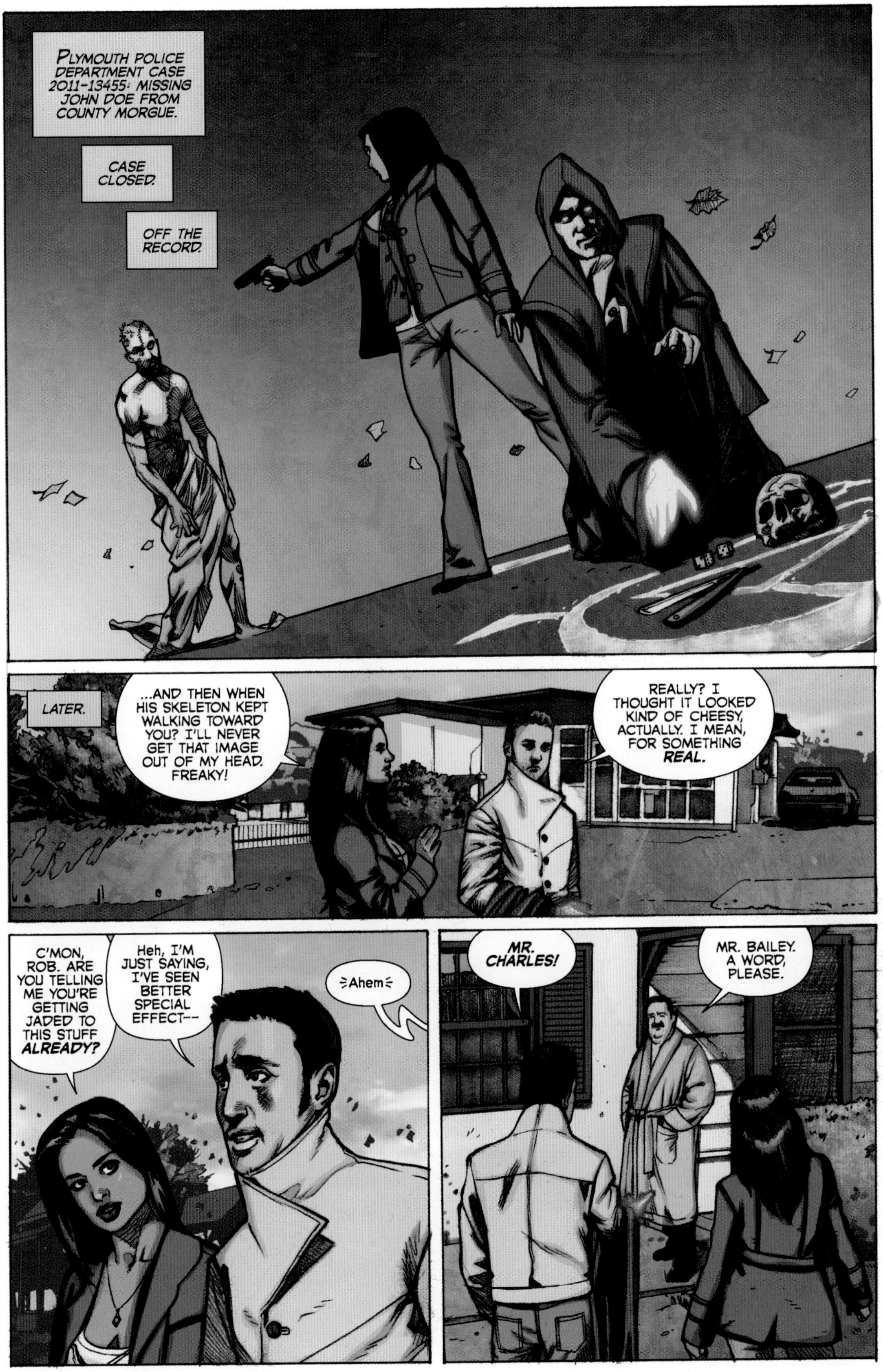
PLYMOUTH POLICE DEPARTMENT CASE 2011-13455: MISSING JOHN DOE FROM COUNTY MORGUE.
CASE CLOSED.
OFF THE RECORD.
LATER.
...AND THEN WHEN HIS SKELETON KEPT WALKING TOWARD YOU? I'LL NEVER GET THAT IMAGE OUT OF MY HEAD. FREAKY!
REALLY? I THOUGHT IT LOOKED KIND OF CHEESY, ACTUALLY. I MEAN, FOR SOMETHING REAL.
C'MON, ROB. ARE YOU TELLING ME YOU'RE GETTING JADED TO THIS STUFF ALREADY?
Heh, I'M JUST SAYING, I'VE SEEN BETTER SPECIAL EFFECT--
Ahem
MR. CHARLES!
MR. BAILEY. A WORD, PLEASE.

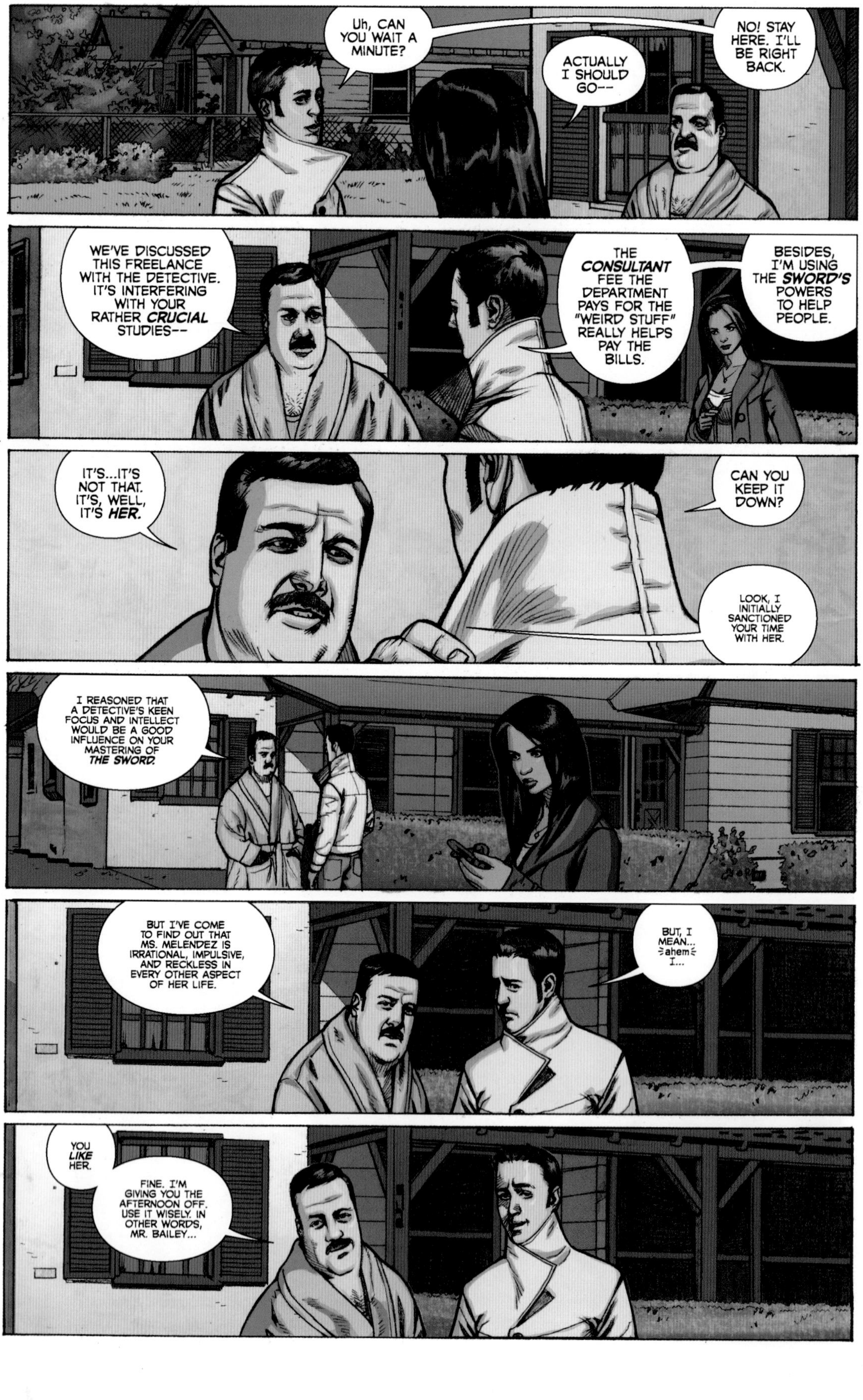
Uh, CAN YOU WAIT A MINUTE?
ACTUALLY I SHOULD GO--
NO! STAY HERE. I'LL BE RIGHT BACK.
WE'VE DISCUSSED THIS FREELANCE WITH THE DETECTIVE. IT'S INTERFERING WITH YOUR RATHER CRUCIAL STUDIES--
THE CONSULTANT FEE THE DEPARTMENT PAYS FOR THE "WEIRD STUFF" REALLY HELPS PAY THE BILLS.
BESIDES, I'M USING THE SWORD'S POWERS TO HELP PEOPLE.
IT'S...IT'S NOT THAT. IT'S, WELL, IT'S HER.
CAN YOU KEEP IT DOWN?
LOOK, I INITIALLY SANCTIONED YOUR TIME WITH HER.
I REASONED THAT A DETECTIVE'S KEEN FOCUS AND INTELLECT WOULD BE A GOOD INFLUENCE ON YOUR MASTERING OF THE SWORD.
BUT I'VE COME TO FIND OUT THAT MS. MELENDEZ IS IRRATIONAL, IMPULSIVE, AND RECKLESS IN EVERY OTHER ASPECT OF HER LIFE.
BUT, I MEAN... ahem I...
YOU LIKE HER.
FINE. I'M GIVING YOU THE AFTERNOON OFF. USE IT WISELY. IN OTHER WORDS, MR. BAILEY...

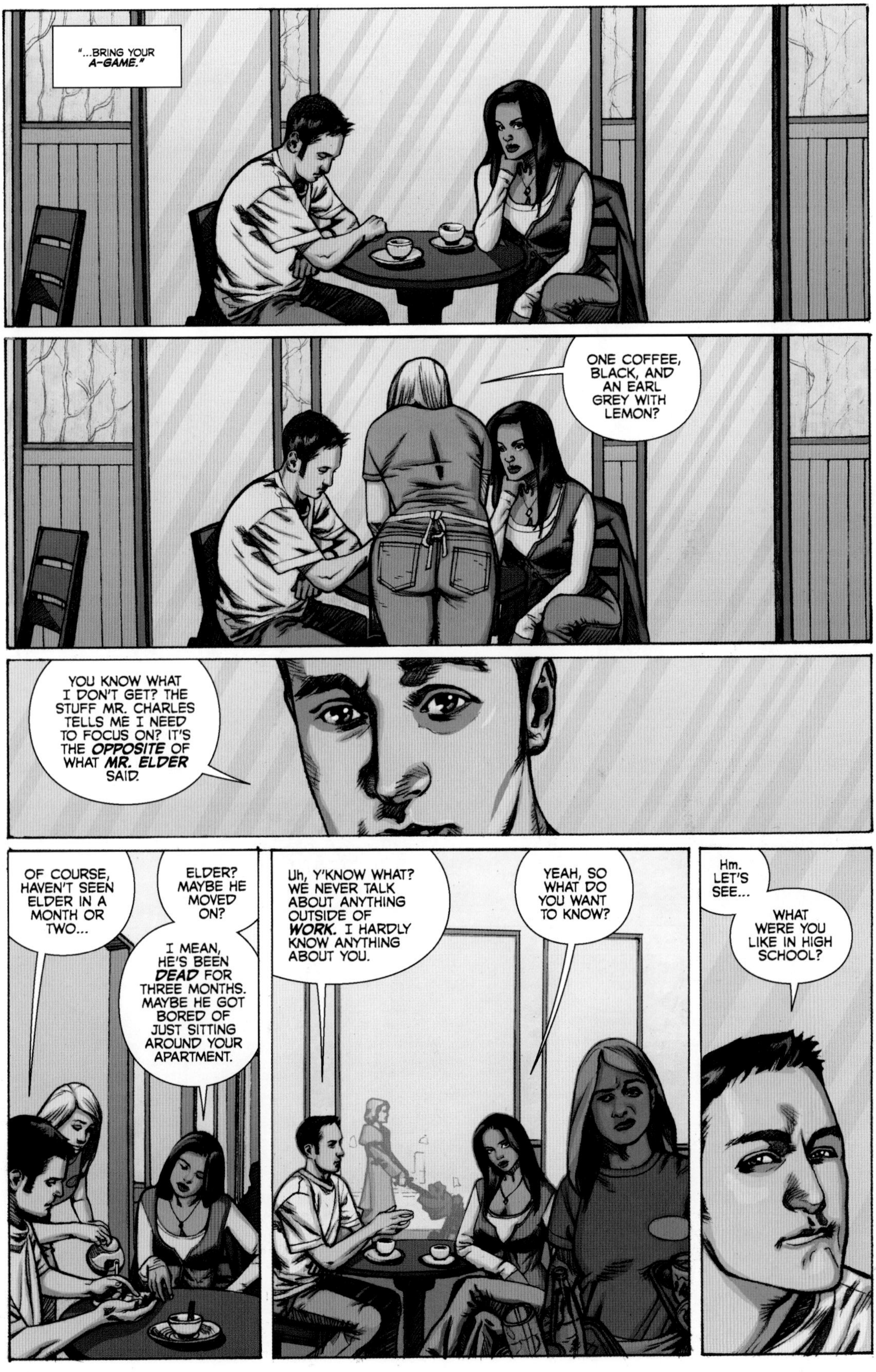
"...BRING YOUR *A-GAME.*"
ONE COFFEE, BLACK, AND AN EARL GREY WITH LEMON?
YOU KNOW WHAT I DON'T GET? THE STUFF MR. CHARLES TELLS ME I NEED TO FOCUS ON? IT'S THE *OPPOSITE* OF WHAT *MR. ELDER* SAID.
OF COURSE, HAVEN'T SEEN ELDER IN A MONTH OR TWO...
ELDER? MAYBE HE MOVED ON?
I MEAN, HE'S BEEN *DEAD* FOR THREE MONTHS. MAYBE HE GOT BORED OF JUST SITTING AROUND YOUR APARTMENT.
Uh, Y'KNOW WHAT? WE NEVER TALK ABOUT ANYTHING OUTSIDE OF *WORK.* I HARDLY KNOW ANYTHING ABOUT YOU.
YEAH, SO WHAT DO YOU WANT TO KNOW?
Hm. LET'S SEE...
WHAT WERE YOU LIKE IN HIGH SCHOOL?

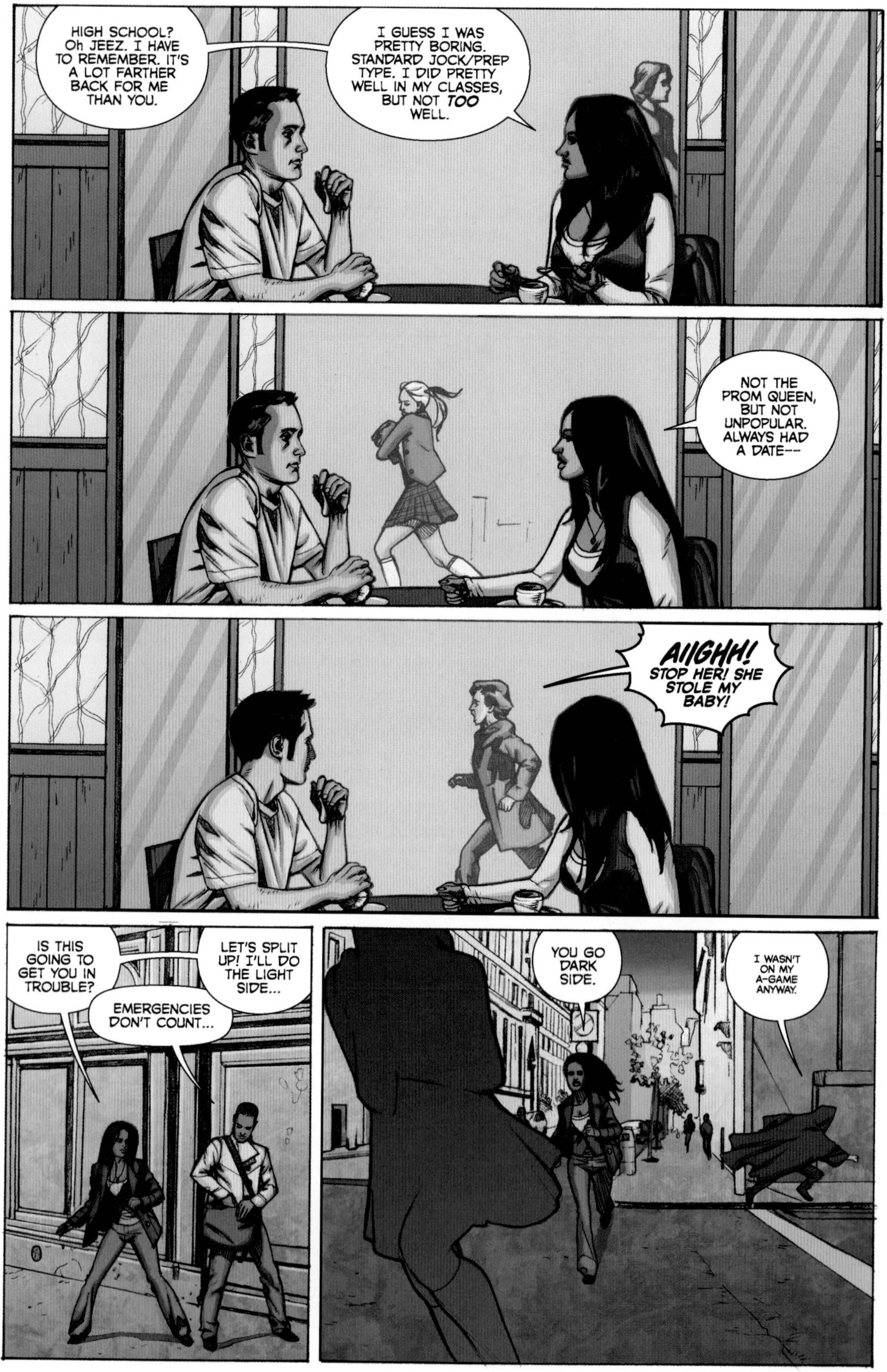
HIGH SCHOOL? Oh JEEZ. I HAVE TO REMEMBER. IT'S A LOT FARTHER BACK FOR ME THAN YOU.
I GUESS I WAS PRETTY BORING. STANDARD JOCK/PREP TYPE. I DID PRETTY WELL IN MY CLASSES, BUT NOT TOO WELL.
NOT THE PROM QUEEN, BUT NOT UNPOPULAR. ALWAYS HAD A DATE--
AIIGHH! STOP HER! SHE STOLE MY BABY!
IS THIS GOING TO GET YOU IN TROUBLE?
LET'S SPLIT UP! I'LL DO THE LIGHT SIDE...
EMERGENCIES DON'T COUNT...
YOU GO DARK SIDE.
I WASN'T ON MY A-GAME ANYWAY.

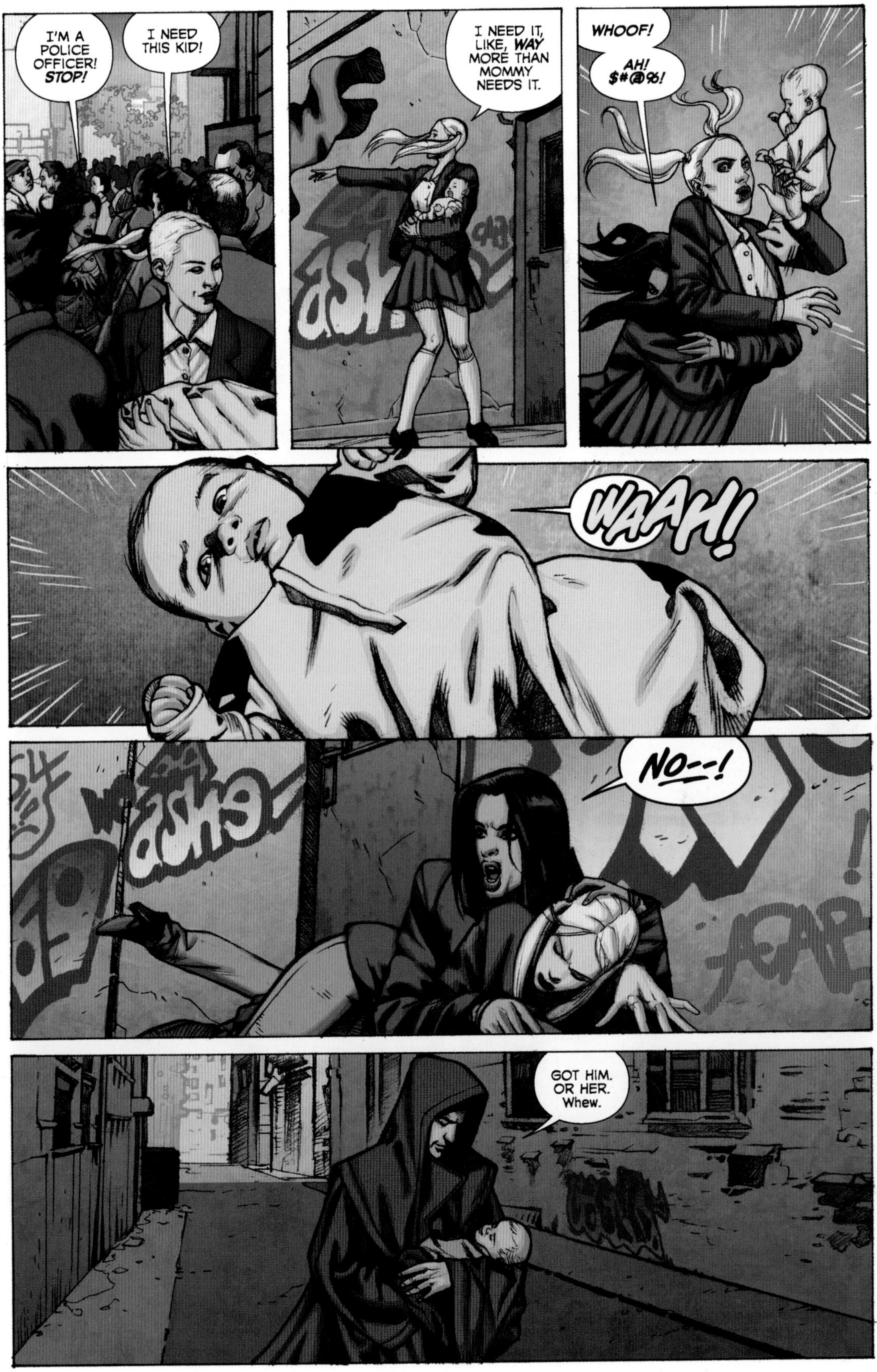
I'M A POLICE OFFICER! STOP!
I NEED THIS KID!
I NEED IT, LIKE, WAY MORE THAN MOMMY NEEDS IT.
WHOOF!
AH! $#@%!
WAAH!
NO--!
GOT HIM. OR HER. Whew.

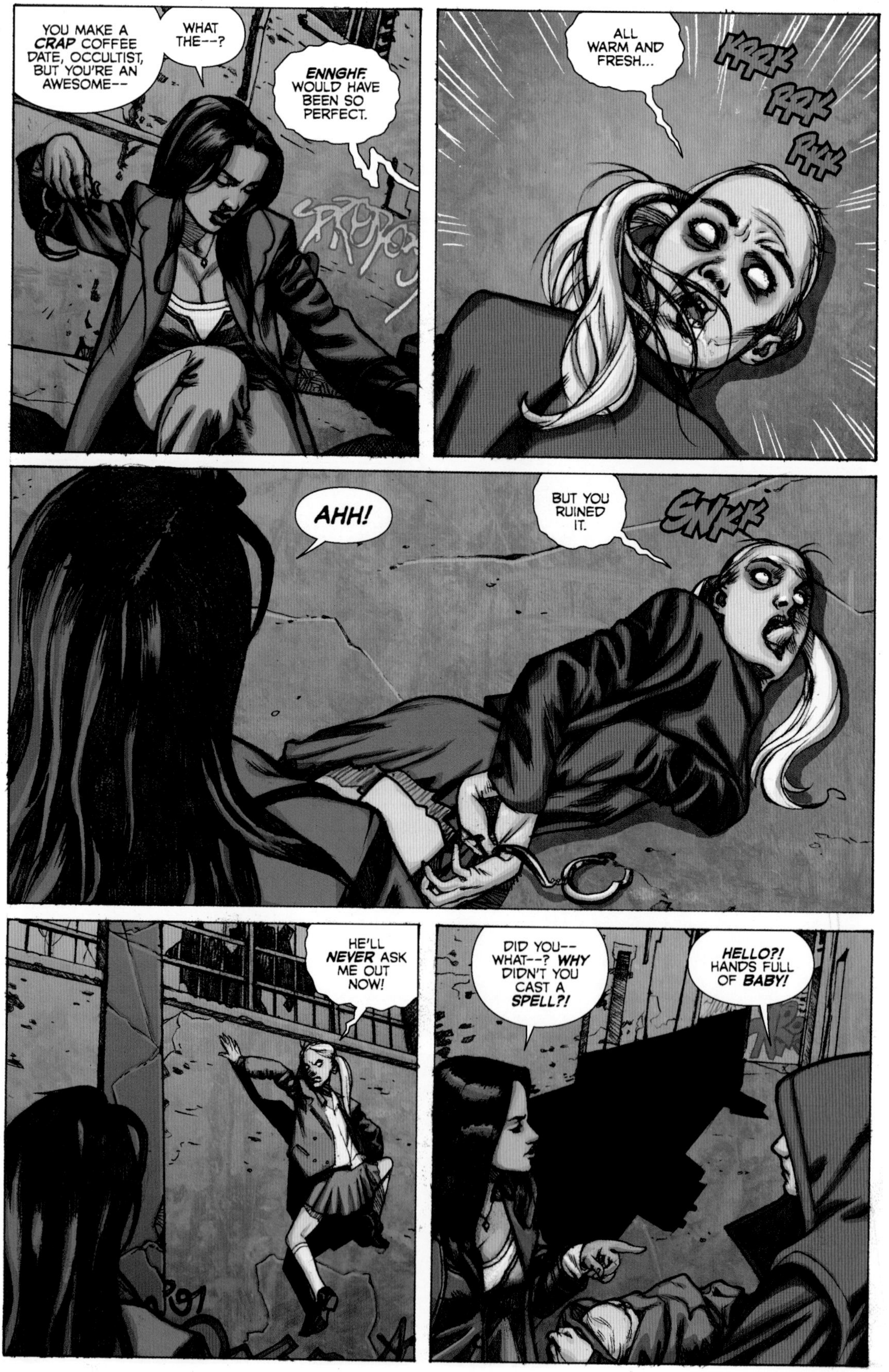
YOU MAKE A CRAP COFFEE DATE, OCCULTIST, BUT YOU'RE AN AWESOME--
WHAT THE--?
ENNGHF. WOULD HAVE BEEN SO PERFECT.
ALL WARM AND FRESH...
KRRK RRK RKK
AHH!
BUT YOU RUINED IT.
SNKK
HE'LL NEVER ASK ME OUT NOW!
DID YOU-- WHAT--? WHY DIDN'T YOU CAST A SPELL?!
HELLO?! HANDS FULL OF BABY!

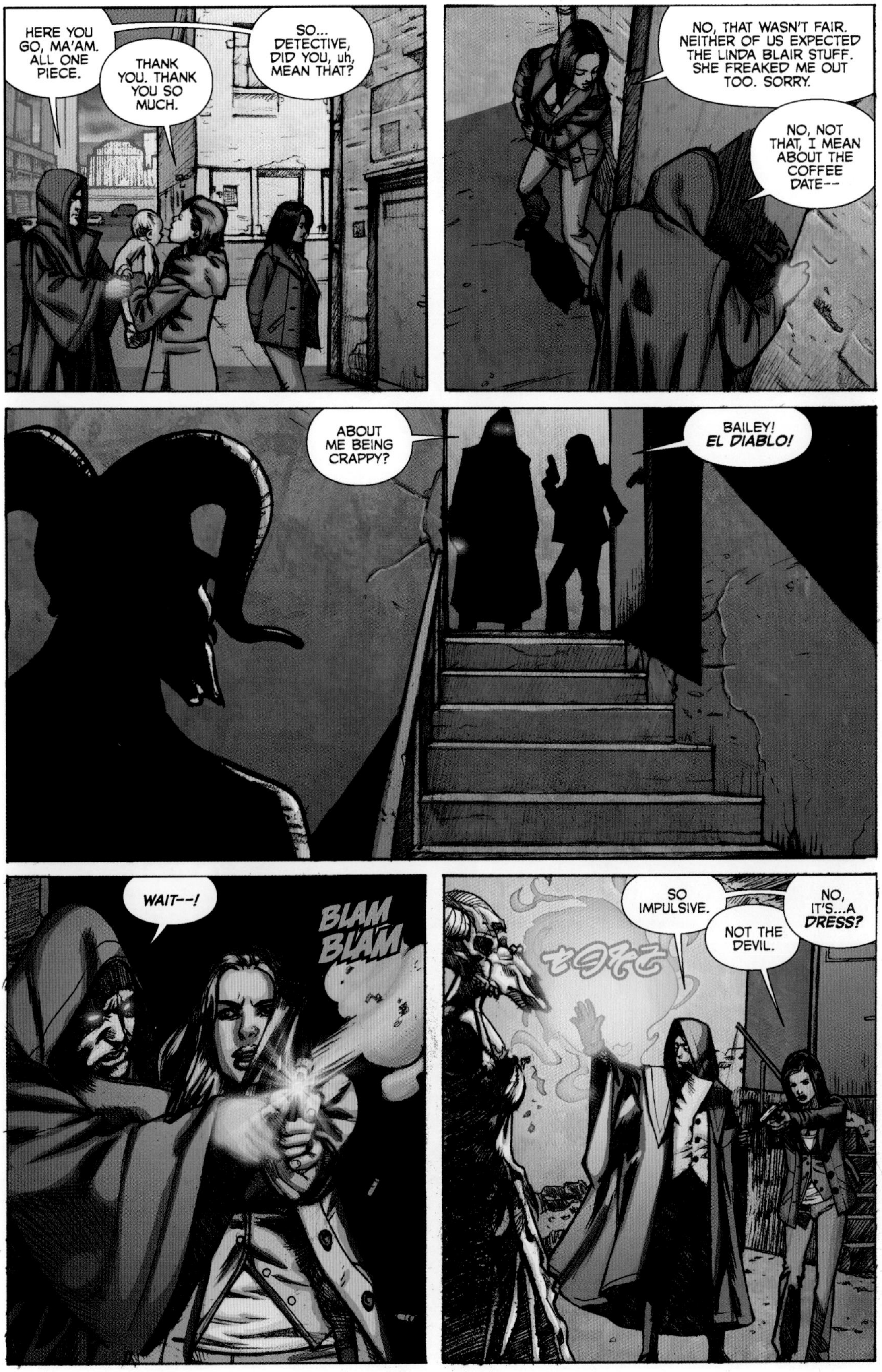
HERE YOU GO, MA'AM. ALL ONE PIECE.
THANK YOU. THANK YOU SO MUCH.
SO... DETECTIVE, DID YOU, uh, MEAN THAT?
NO, THAT WASN'T FAIR. NEITHER OF US EXPECTED THE LINDA BLAIR STUFF. SHE FREAKED ME OUT TOO. SORRY.
NO, NOT THAT, I MEAN ABOUT THE COFFEE DATE--
ABOUT ME BEING CRAPPY?
BAILEY! *EL DIABLO!*
WAIT--!
BLAM BLAM
SO IMPULSIVE.
NOT THE DEVIL.
NO, IT'S...A *DRESS?*

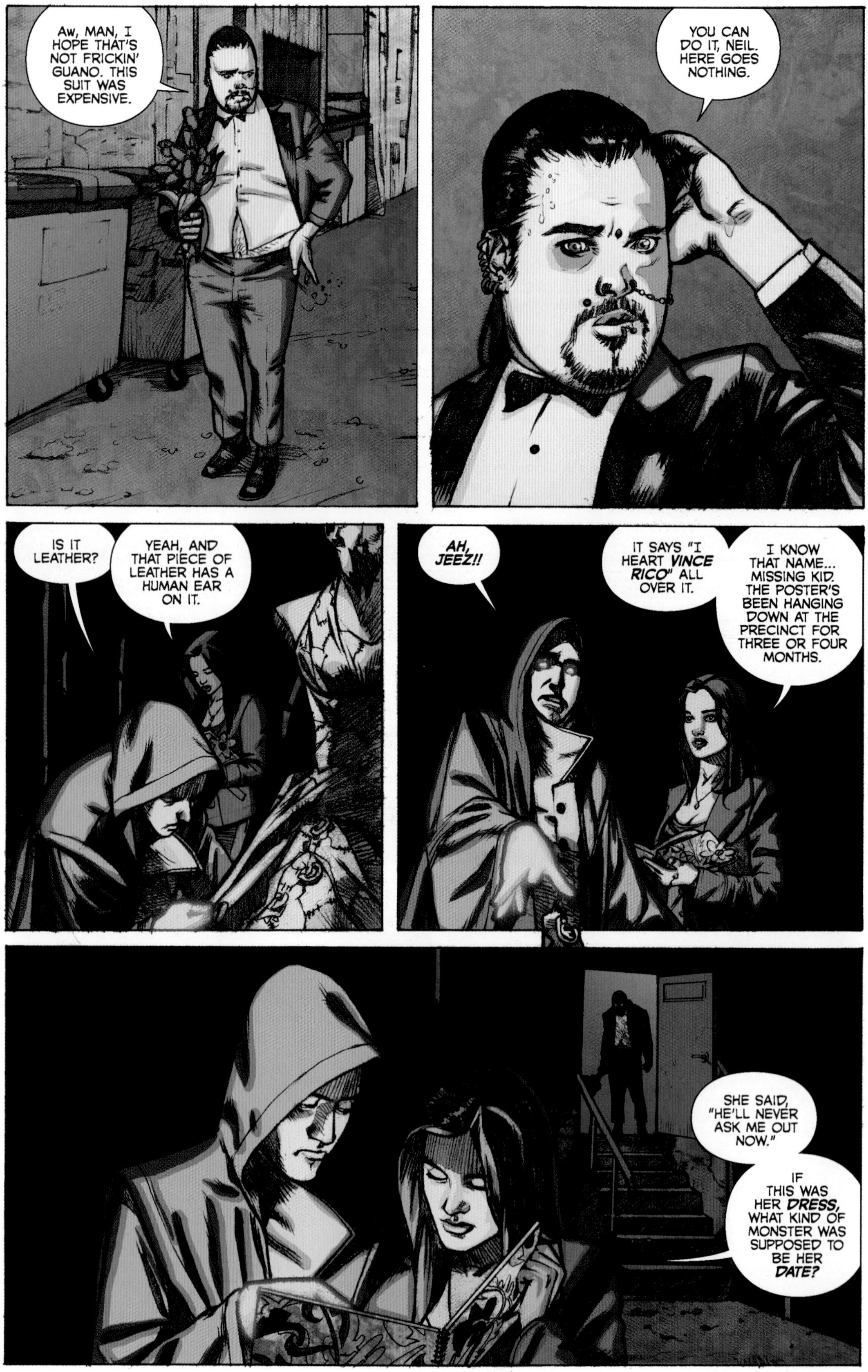
Aw, MAN, I HOPE THAT'S NOT FRICKIN' GUANO. THIS SUIT WAS EXPENSIVE.
YOU CAN DO IT, NEIL. HERE GOES NOTHING.
IS IT LEATHER?
YEAH, AND THAT PIECE OF LEATHER HAS A HUMAN EAR ON IT.
AH, JEEZ!!
IT SAYS "I HEART VINCE RICO" ALL OVER IT.
I KNOW THAT NAME... MISSING KID. THE POSTER'S BEEN HANGING DOWN AT THE PRECINCT FOR THREE OR FOUR MONTHS.
SHE SAID, "HE'LL NEVER ASK ME OUT NOW."
IF THIS WAS HER DRESS, WHAT KIND OF MONSTER WAS SUPPOSED TO BE HER DATE?

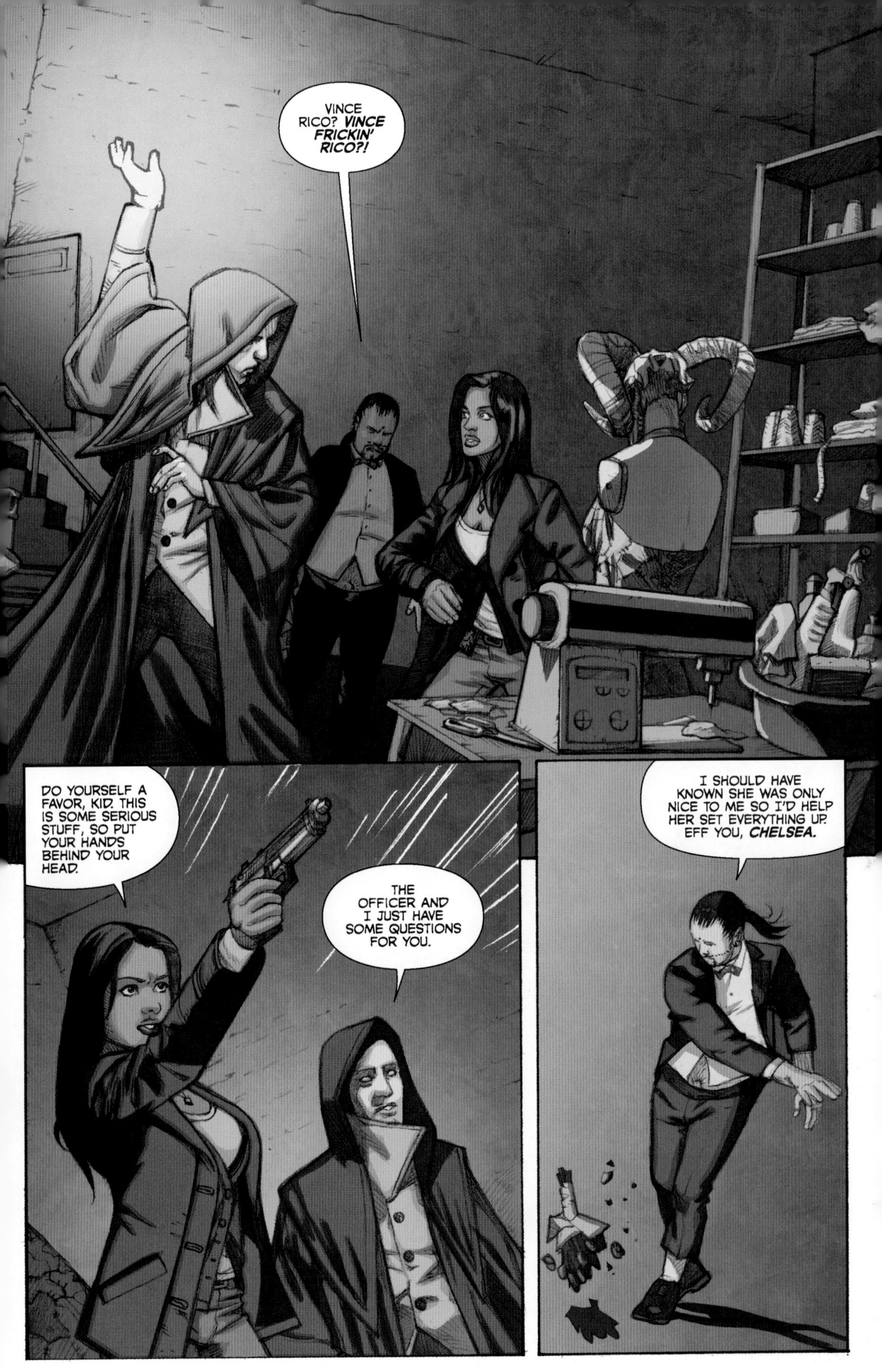
VINCE RICO? *VINCE FRICKIN' RICO?!*
DO YOURSELF A FAVOR, KID. THIS IS SOME SERIOUS STUFF, SO PUT YOUR HANDS BEHIND YOUR HEAD.
THE OFFICER AND I JUST HAVE SOME QUESTIONS FOR YOU.
I SHOULD HAVE KNOWN SHE WAS ONLY NICE TO ME SO I'D HELP HER SET EVERYTHING UP. EFF YOU, ***CHELSEA.***

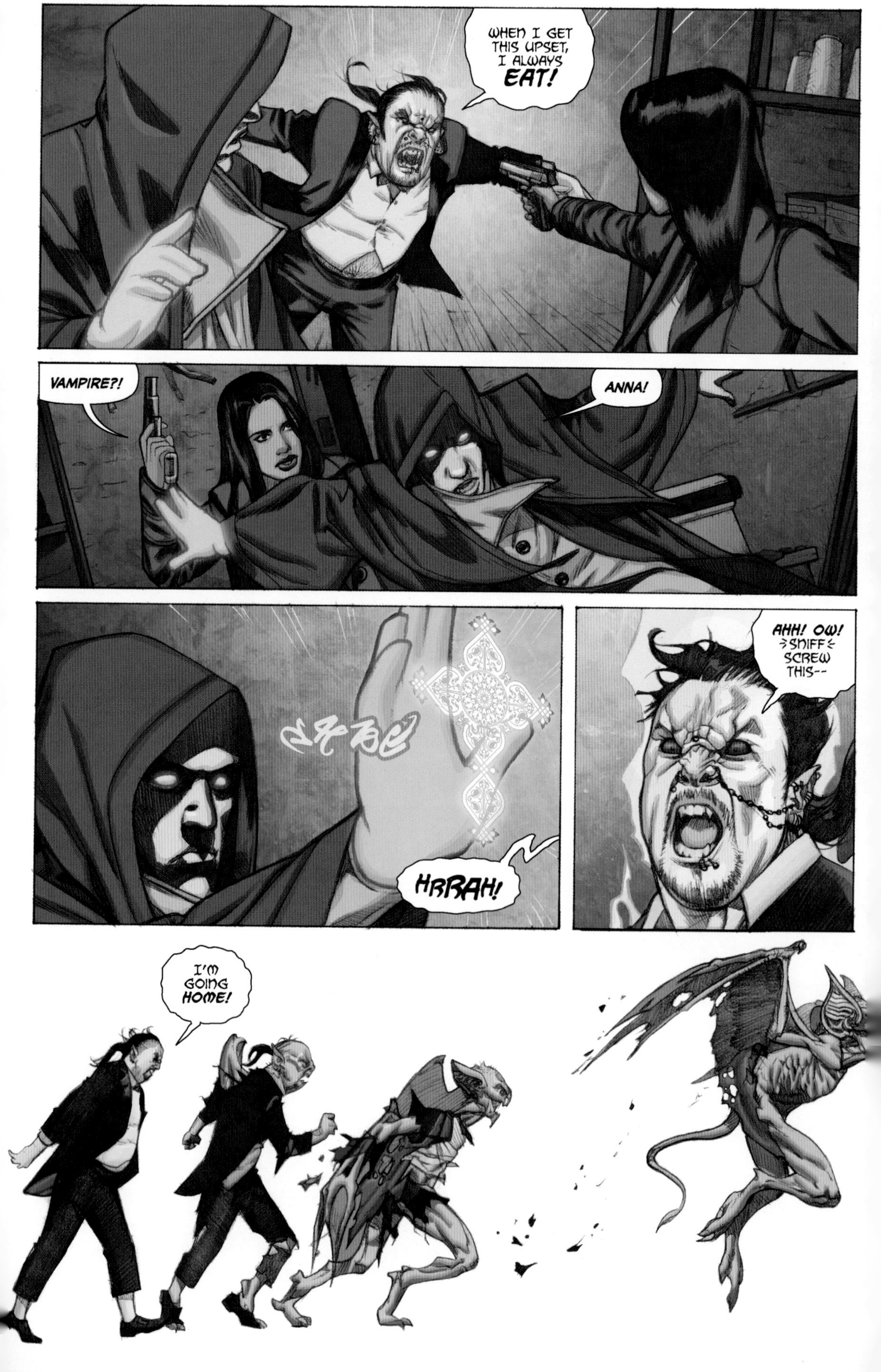
WHEN I GET THIS UPSET, I ALWAYS EAT!
VAMPIRE?!
ANNA!
HRRAH!
AHH! OW! =SNIFF= SCREW THIS--
I'M GOING HOME!

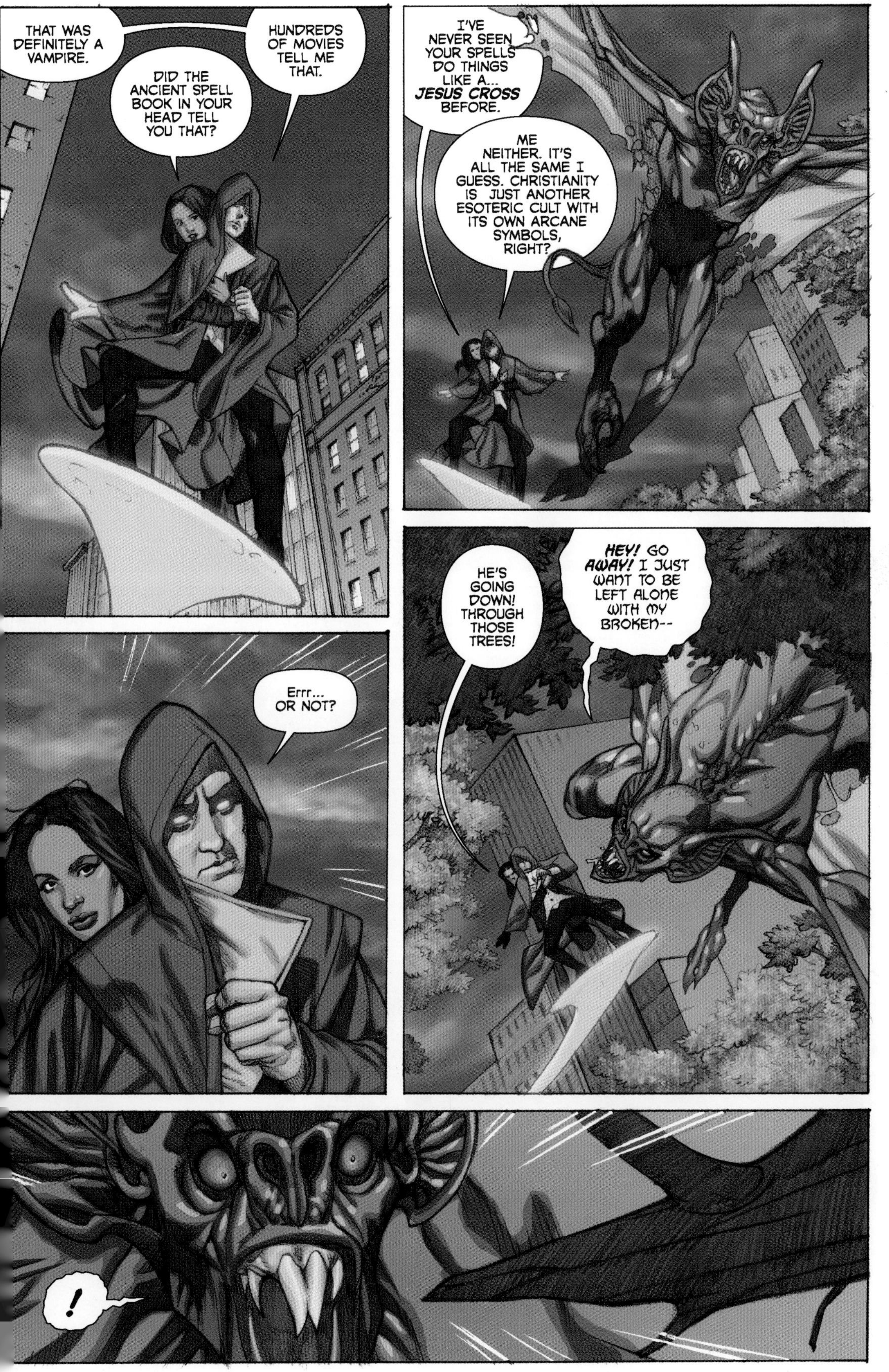
THAT WAS DEFINITELY A VAMPIRE.
DID THE ANCIENT SPELL BOOK IN YOUR HEAD TELL YOU THAT?
HUNDREDS OF MOVIES TELL ME THAT.
I'VE NEVER SEEN YOUR SPELLS DO THINGS LIKE A... JESUS CROSS BEFORE.
ME NEITHER. IT'S ALL THE SAME I GUESS. CHRISTIANITY IS JUST ANOTHER ESOTERIC CULT WITH ITS OWN ARCANE SYMBOLS, RIGHT?
Errr... OR NOT?
HEY! GO AWAY! I JUST WANT TO BE LEFT ALONE WITH MY BROKEN--
HE'S GOING DOWN! THROUGH THOSE TREES!
!

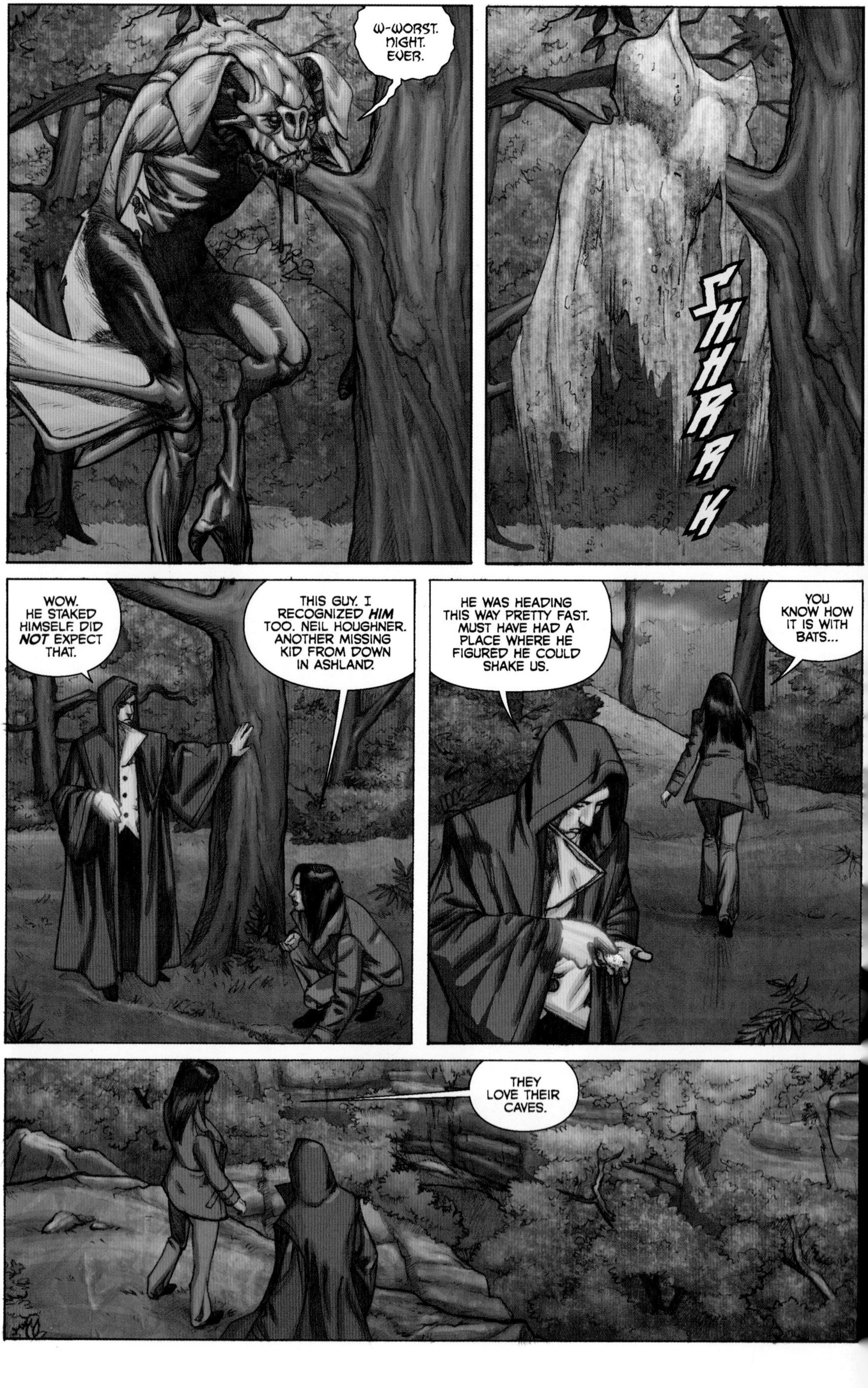
W-WORST. NIGHT. EVER.
SHHRRK
WOW. HE STAKED HIMSELF. DID *NOT* EXPECT THAT.
THIS GUY. I RECOGNIZED *HIM* TOO. NEIL HOUGHNER. ANOTHER MISSING KID FROM DOWN IN ASHLAND.
HE WAS HEADING THIS WAY PRETTY FAST. MUST HAVE HAD A PLACE WHERE HE FIGURED HE COULD SHAKE US.
YOU KNOW HOW IT IS WITH BATS...
THEY LOVE THEIR CAVES.

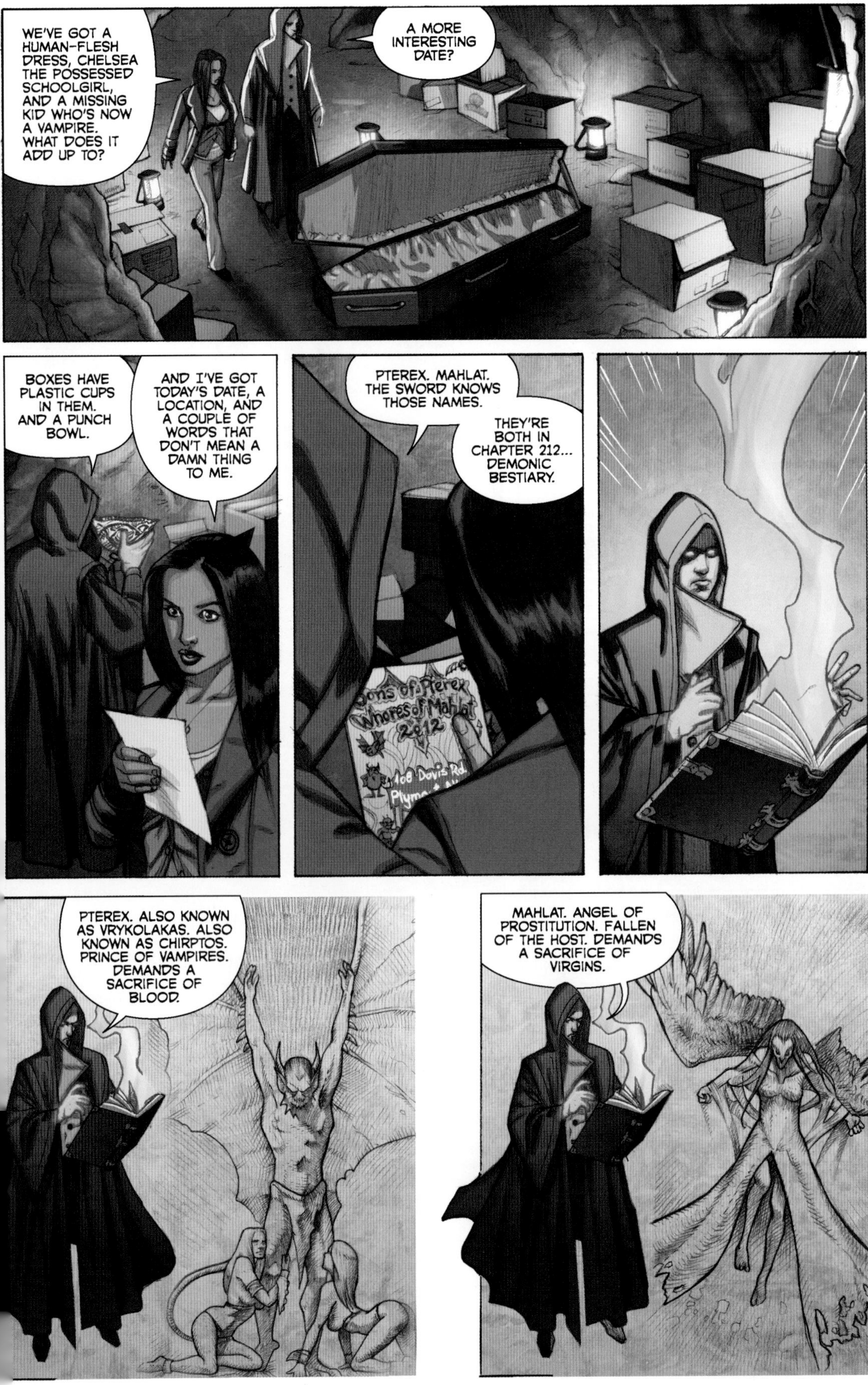
WE'VE GOT A HUMAN-FLESH DRESS, CHELSEA THE POSSESSED SCHOOLGIRL, AND A MISSING KID WHO'S NOW A VAMPIRE. WHAT DOES IT ADD UP TO?
A MORE INTERESTING DATE?
BOXES HAVE PLASTIC CUPS IN THEM. AND A PUNCH BOWL.
AND I'VE GOT TODAY'S DATE, A LOCATION, AND A COUPLE OF WORDS THAT DON'T MEAN A DAMN THING TO ME.
PTEREX. MAHLAT. THE SWORD KNOWS THOSE NAMES.
THEY'RE BOTH IN CHAPTER 212... DEMONIC BESTIARY.
Sons of Pterex
Whores of Mahlat
2012
PTEREX. ALSO KNOWN AS VRYKOLAKAS. ALSO KNOWN AS CHIRPTOS. PRINCE OF VAMPIRES. DEMANDS A SACRIFICE OF BLOOD.
MAHLAT. ANGEL OF PROSTITUTION. FALLEN OF THE HOST. DEMANDS A SACRIFICE OF VIRGINS.

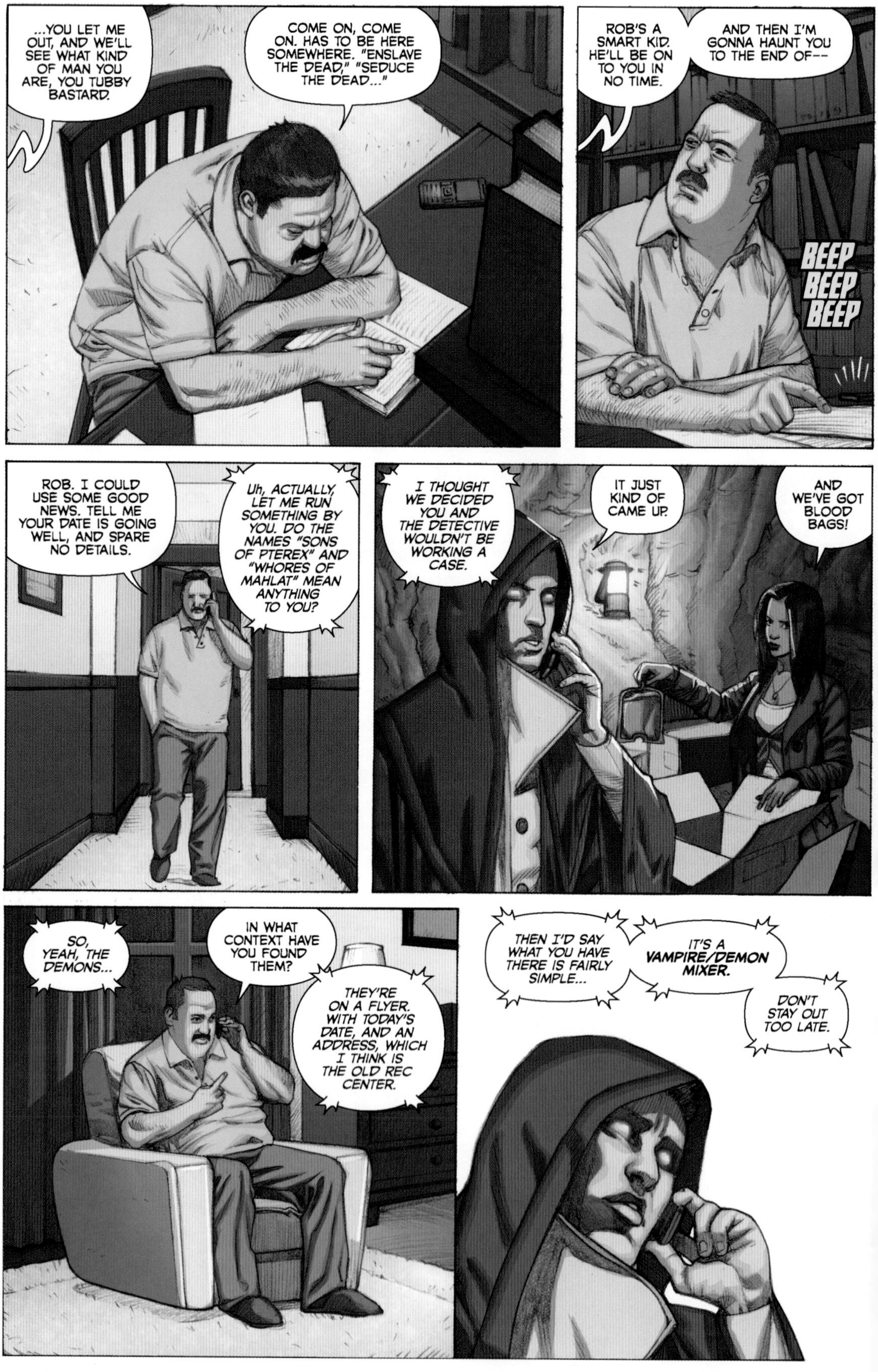
...YOU LET ME OUT, AND WE'LL SEE WHAT KIND OF MAN YOU ARE, YOU TUBBY BASTARD.
COME ON, COME ON. HAS TO BE HERE SOMEWHERE. "ENSLAVE THE DEAD," "SEDUCE THE DEAD..."
ROB'S A SMART KID. HE'LL BE ON TO YOU IN NO TIME.
AND THEN I'M GONNA HAUNT YOU TO THE END OF--
BEEP BEEP BEEP
ROB. I COULD USE SOME GOOD NEWS. TELL ME YOUR DATE IS GOING WELL, AND SPARE NO DETAILS.
Uh, ACTUALLY, LET ME RUN SOMETHING BY YOU. DO THE NAMES "SONS OF PTEREX" AND "WHORES OF MAHLAT" MEAN ANYTHING TO YOU?
I THOUGHT WE DECIDED YOU AND THE DETECTIVE WOULDN'T BE WORKING A CASE.
IT JUST KIND OF CAME UP.
AND WE'VE GOT BLOOD BAGS!
SO, YEAH, THE DEMONS...
IN WHAT CONTEXT HAVE YOU FOUND THEM?
THEY'RE ON A FLYER. WITH TODAY'S DATE, AND AN ADDRESS, WHICH I THINK IS THE OLD REC CENTER.
THEN I'D SAY WHAT YOU HAVE THERE IS FAIRLY SIMPLE...
IT'S A **VAMPIRE/DEMON MIXER.**
DON'T STAY OUT TOO LATE.

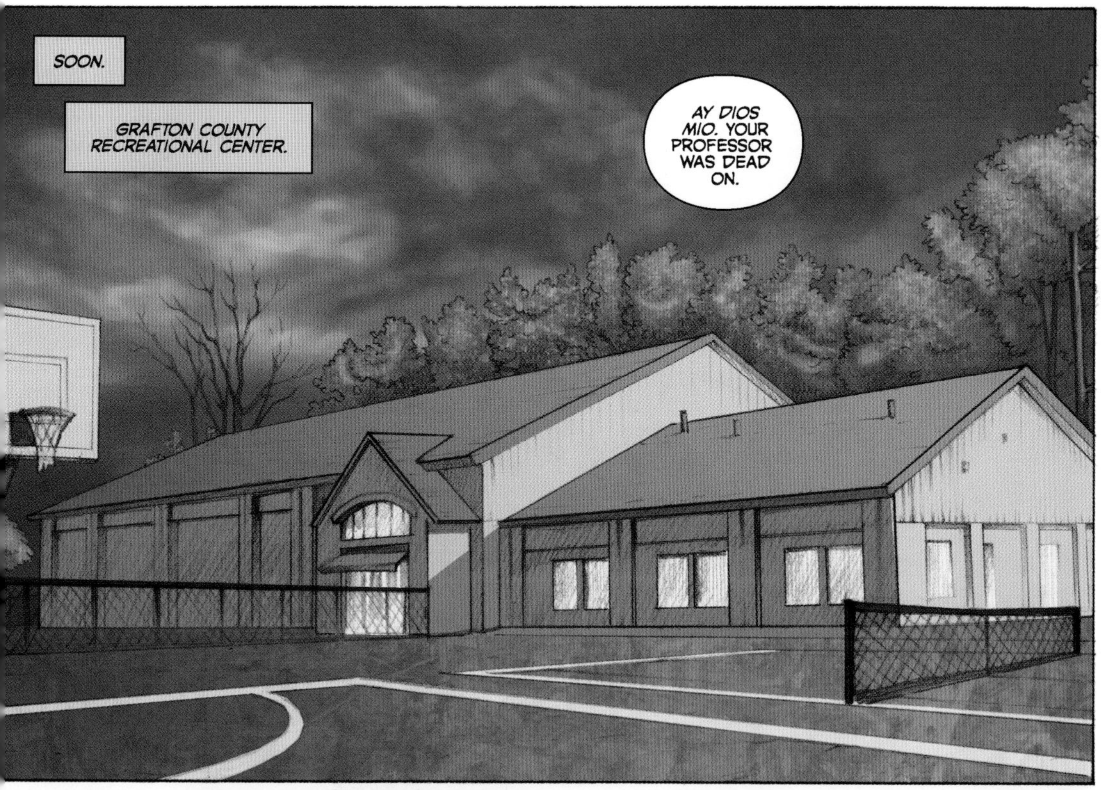
SOON.
GRAFTON COUNTY RECREATIONAL CENTER.
AY DIOS MIO. YOUR PROFESSOR WAS DEAD ON.

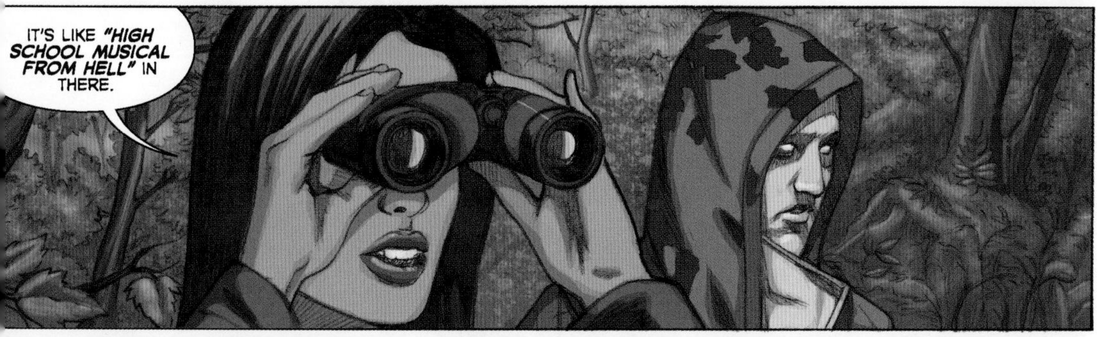
IT'S LIKE "HIGH SCHOOL MUSICAL FROM HELL" IN THERE.

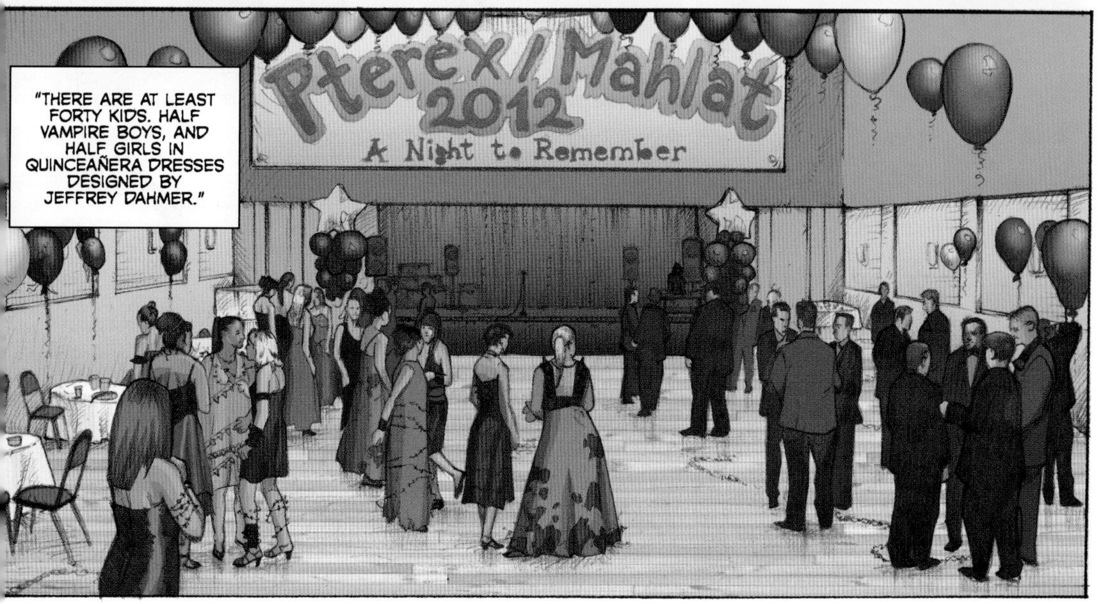
"THERE ARE AT LEAST FORTY KIDS. HALF VAMPIRE BOYS, AND HALF GIRLS IN QUINCEAÑERA DRESSES DESIGNED BY JEFFREY DAHMER."
Pterex / Mahlat 2012
A Night to Remember

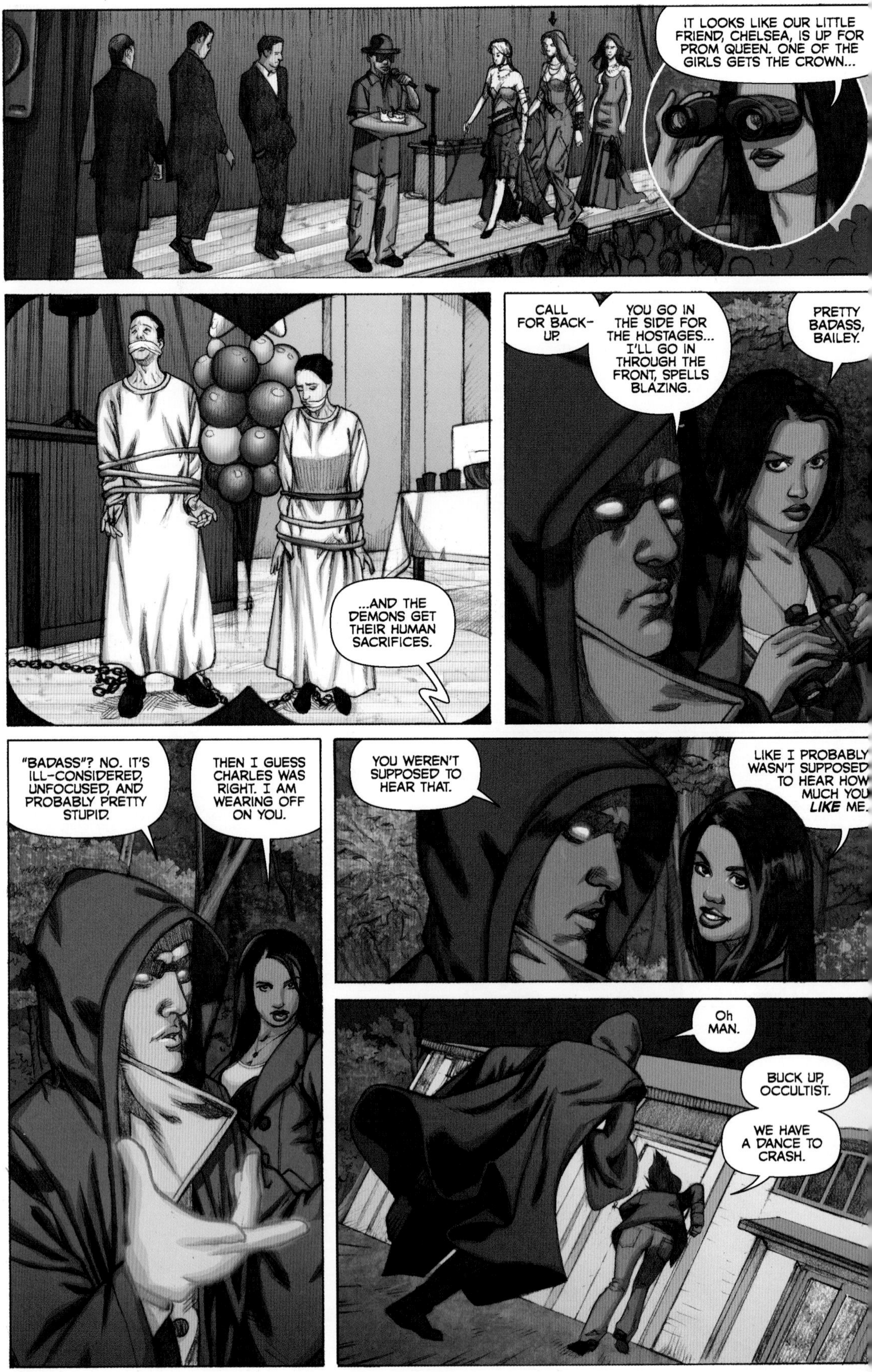
IT LOOKS LIKE OUR LITTLE FRIEND, CHELSEA, IS UP FOR PROM QUEEN. ONE OF THE GIRLS GETS THE CROWN...
...AND THE DEMONS GET THEIR HUMAN SACRIFICES.
CALL FOR BACK-UP.
YOU GO IN THE SIDE FOR THE HOSTAGES... I'LL GO IN THROUGH THE FRONT, SPELLS BLAZING.
PRETTY BADASS, BAILEY.
"BADASS"? NO. IT'S ILL-CONSIDERED, UNFOCUSED, AND PROBABLY PRETTY STUPID.
THEN I GUESS CHARLES WAS RIGHT. I AM WEARING OFF ON YOU.
YOU WEREN'T SUPPOSED TO HEAR THAT.
LIKE I PROBABLY WASN'T SUPPOSED TO HEAR HOW MUCH YOU *LIKE* ME.
Oh MAN.
BUCK UP, OCCULTIST.
WE HAVE A DANCE TO CRASH.

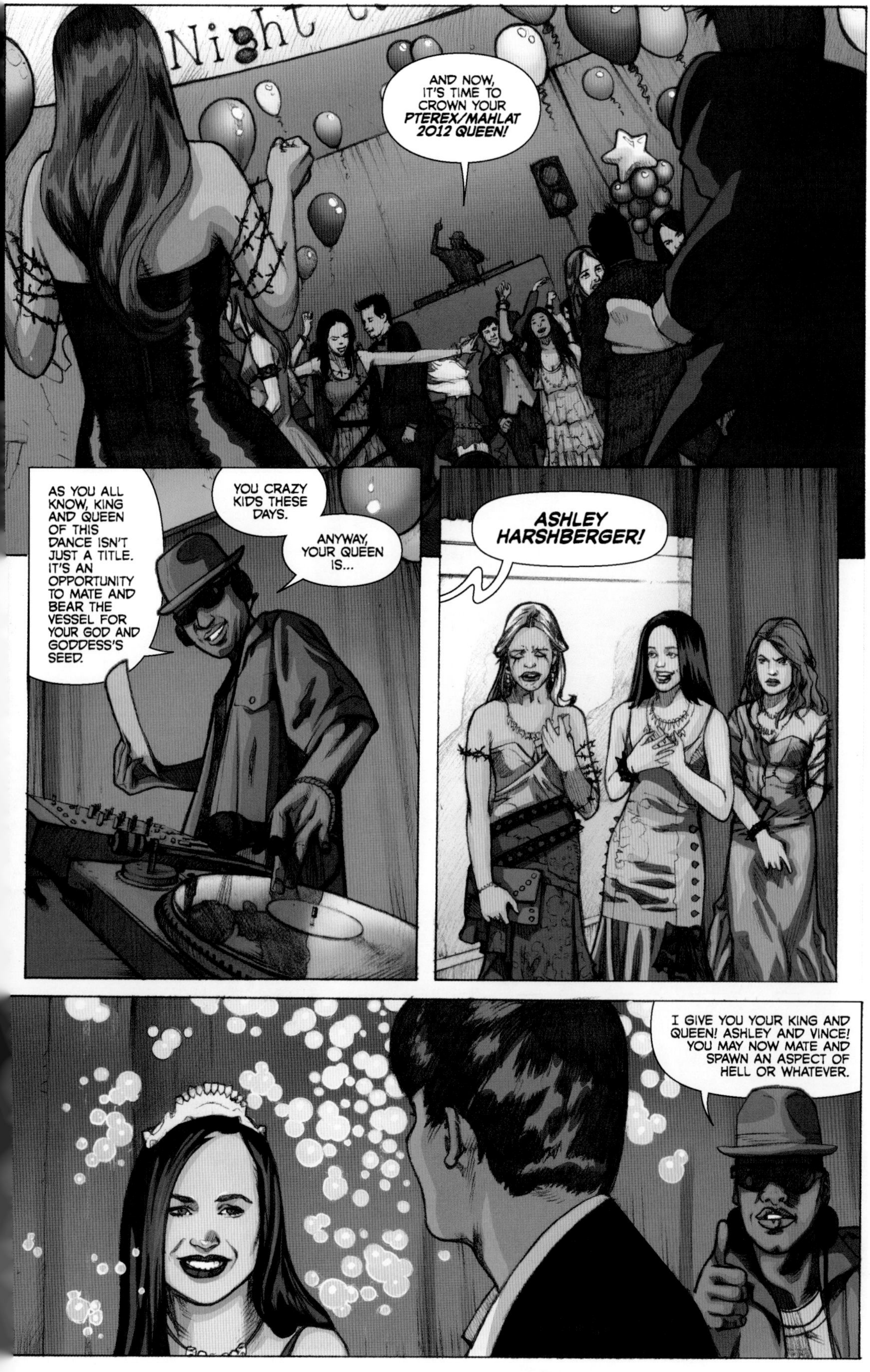
Night
AND NOW, IT'S TIME TO CROWN YOUR PTEREX/MAHLAT 2012 QUEEN!
AS YOU ALL KNOW, KING AND QUEEN OF THIS DANCE ISN'T JUST A TITLE. IT'S AN OPPORTUNITY TO MATE AND BEAR THE VESSEL FOR YOUR GOD AND GODDESS'S SEED.
YOU CRAZY KIDS THESE DAYS.
ANYWAY, YOUR QUEEN IS...
ASHLEY HARSHBERGER!
I GIVE YOU YOUR KING AND QUEEN! ASHLEY AND VINCE! YOU MAY NOW MATE AND SPAWN AN ASPECT OF HELL OR WHATEVER.

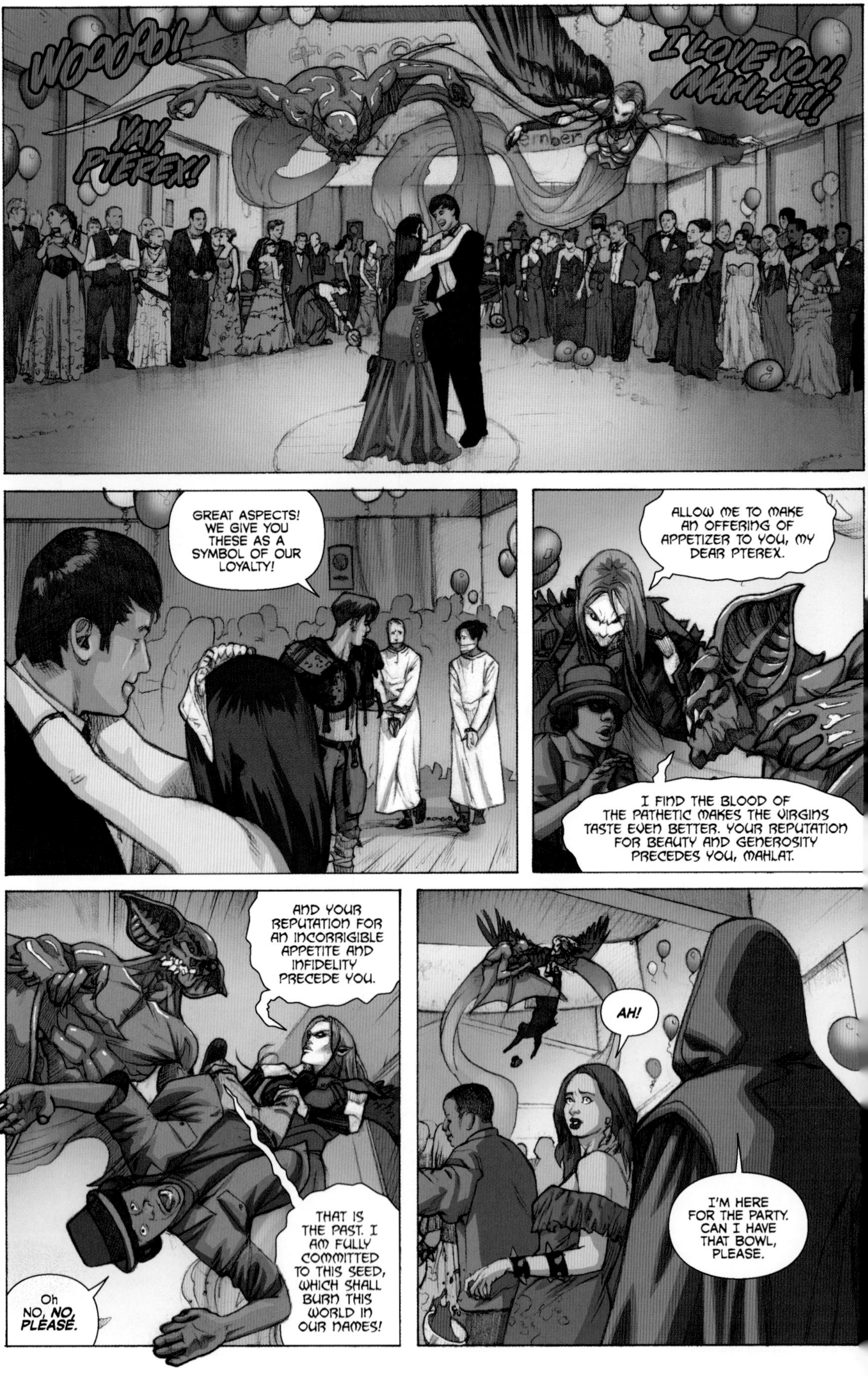
WOOOOO!
YAY, PTEREX!
I LOVE YOU, MAHLAT!!
GREAT ASPECTS! WE GIVE YOU THESE AS A SYMBOL OF OUR LOYALTY!
ALLOW ME TO MAKE AN OFFERING OF APPETIZER TO YOU, MY DEAR PTEREX.
I FIND THE BLOOD OF THE PATHETIC MAKES THE VIRGINS TASTE EVEN BETTER. YOUR REPUTATION FOR BEAUTY AND GENEROSITY PRECEDES YOU, MAHLAT.
AND YOUR REPUTATION FOR AN INCORRIGIBLE APPETITE AND INFIDELITY PRECEDE YOU.
THAT IS THE PAST. I AM FULLY COMMITTED TO THIS SEED, WHICH SHALL BURN THIS WORLD IN OUR NAMES!
Oh NO, NO, PLEASE.
AH!
I'M HERE FOR THE PARTY. CAN I HAVE THAT BOWL, PLEASE.

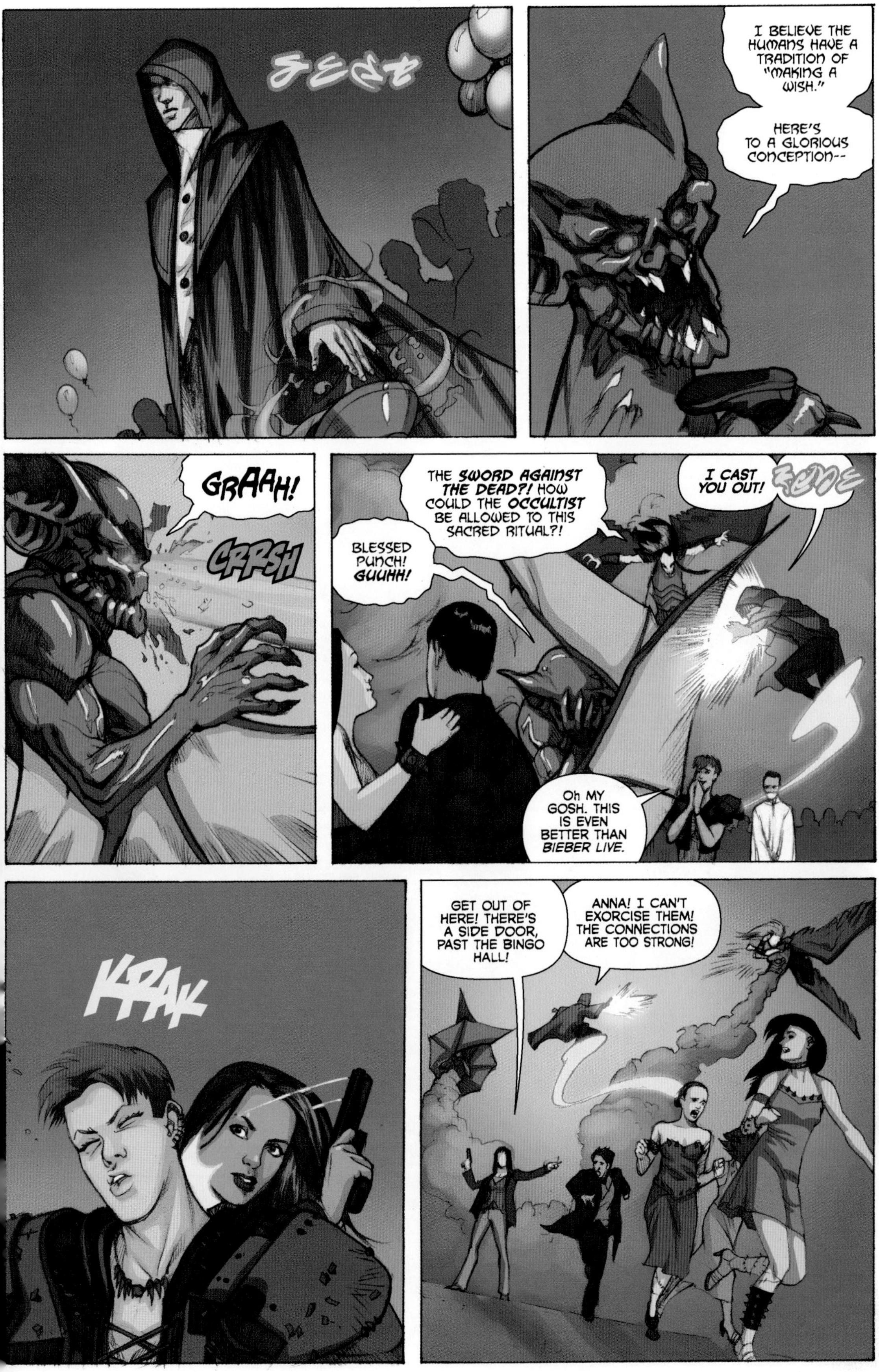
I BELIEVE THE HUMANS HAVE A TRADITION OF "MAKING A WISH."
HERE'S TO A GLORIOUS CONCEPTION--
GRAAH!
CRRSH
THE SWORD AGAINST THE DEAD?! HOW COULD THE OCCULTIST BE ALLOWED TO THIS SACRED RITUAL?!
BLESSED PUNCH! GUUHH!
I CAST YOU OUT!
Oh MY GOSH. THIS IS EVEN BETTER THAN BIEBER LIVE.
KRAK
GET OUT OF HERE! THERE'S A SIDE DOOR, PAST THE BINGO HALL!
ANNA! I CAN'T EXORCISE THEM! THE CONNECTIONS ARE TOO STRONG!

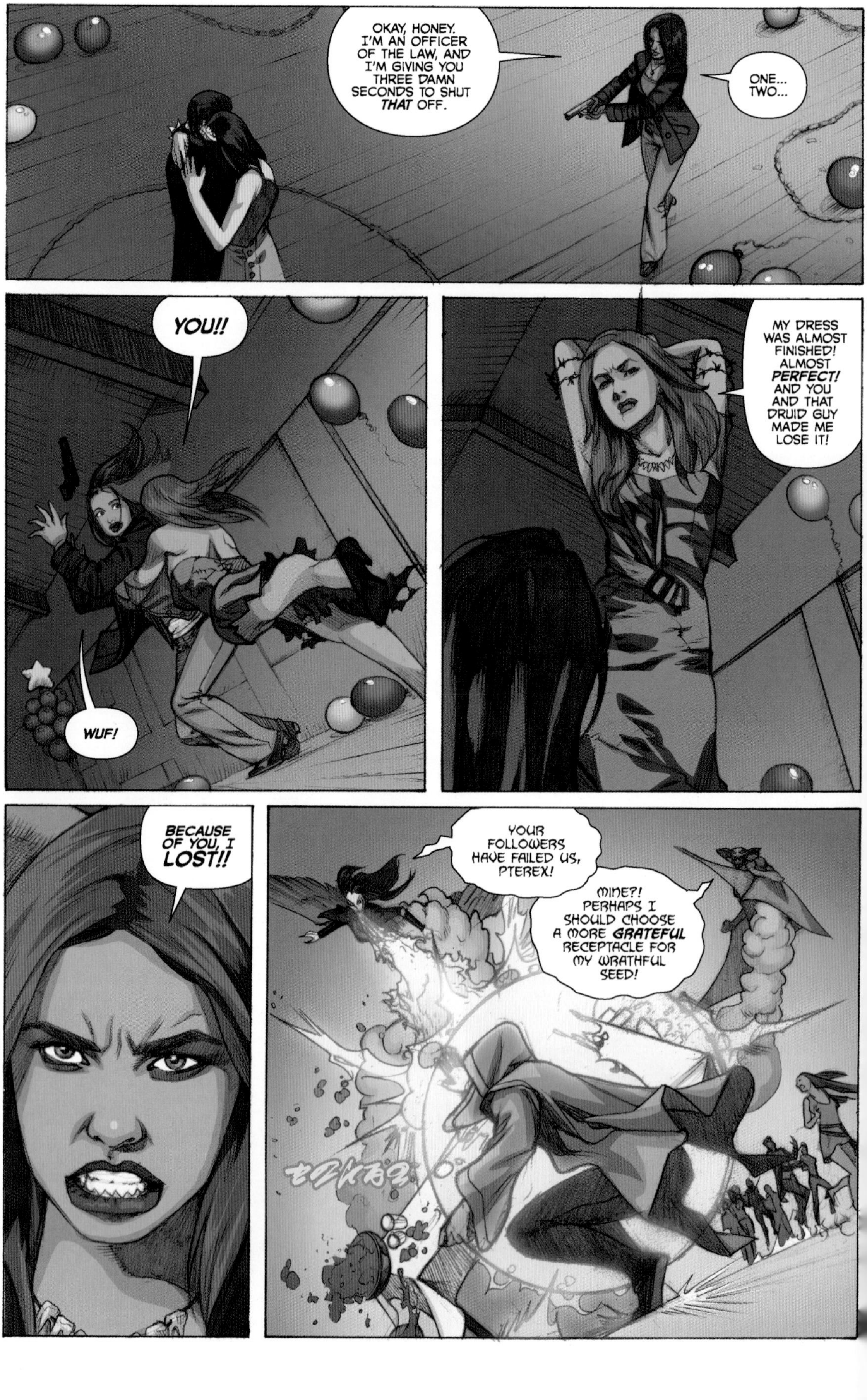
OKAY, HONEY. I'M AN OFFICER OF THE LAW, AND I'M GIVING YOU THREE DAMN SECONDS TO SHUT *THAT* OFF.
ONE... TWO...
YOU!!
WUF!
MY DRESS WAS ALMOST FINISHED! ALMOST *PERFECT!* AND YOU AND THAT DRUID GUY MADE ME LOSE IT!
BECAUSE OF YOU, I *LOST!!*
YOUR FOLLOWERS HAVE FAILED US, PTEREX!
MINE?! PERHAPS I SHOULD CHOOSE A MORE *GRATEFUL* RECEPTACLE FOR MY WRATHFUL SEED!

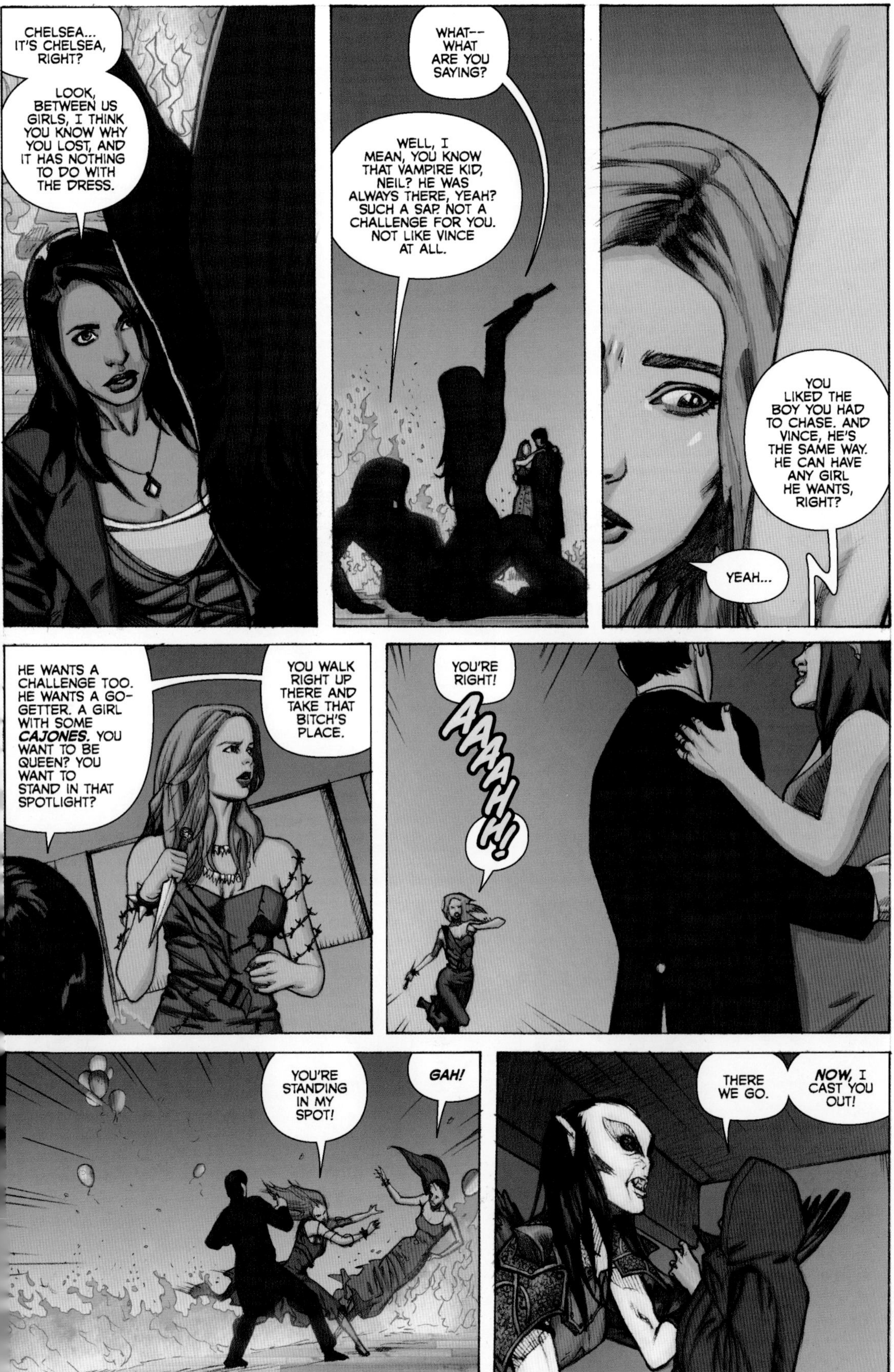
CHELSEA... IT'S CHELSEA, RIGHT?
LOOK, BETWEEN US GIRLS, I THINK YOU KNOW WHY YOU LOST, AND IT HAS NOTHING TO DO WITH THE DRESS.
WHAT-- WHAT ARE YOU SAYING?
WELL, I MEAN, YOU KNOW THAT VAMPIRE KID, NEIL? HE WAS ALWAYS THERE, YEAH? SUCH A SAP. NOT A CHALLENGE FOR YOU. NOT LIKE VINCE AT ALL.
YOU LIKED THE BOY YOU HAD TO CHASE. AND VINCE, HE'S THE SAME WAY. HE CAN HAVE ANY GIRL HE WANTS, RIGHT?
YEAH...
HE WANTS A CHALLENGE TOO. HE WANTS A GO-GETTER. A GIRL WITH SOME CAJONES. YOU WANT TO BE QUEEN? YOU WANT TO STAND IN THAT SPOTLIGHT?
YOU WALK RIGHT UP THERE AND TAKE THAT BITCH'S PLACE.
YOU'RE RIGHT!
AAAAHH!
YOU'RE STANDING IN MY SPOT!
GAH!
THERE WE GO.
NOW, I CAST YOU OUT!

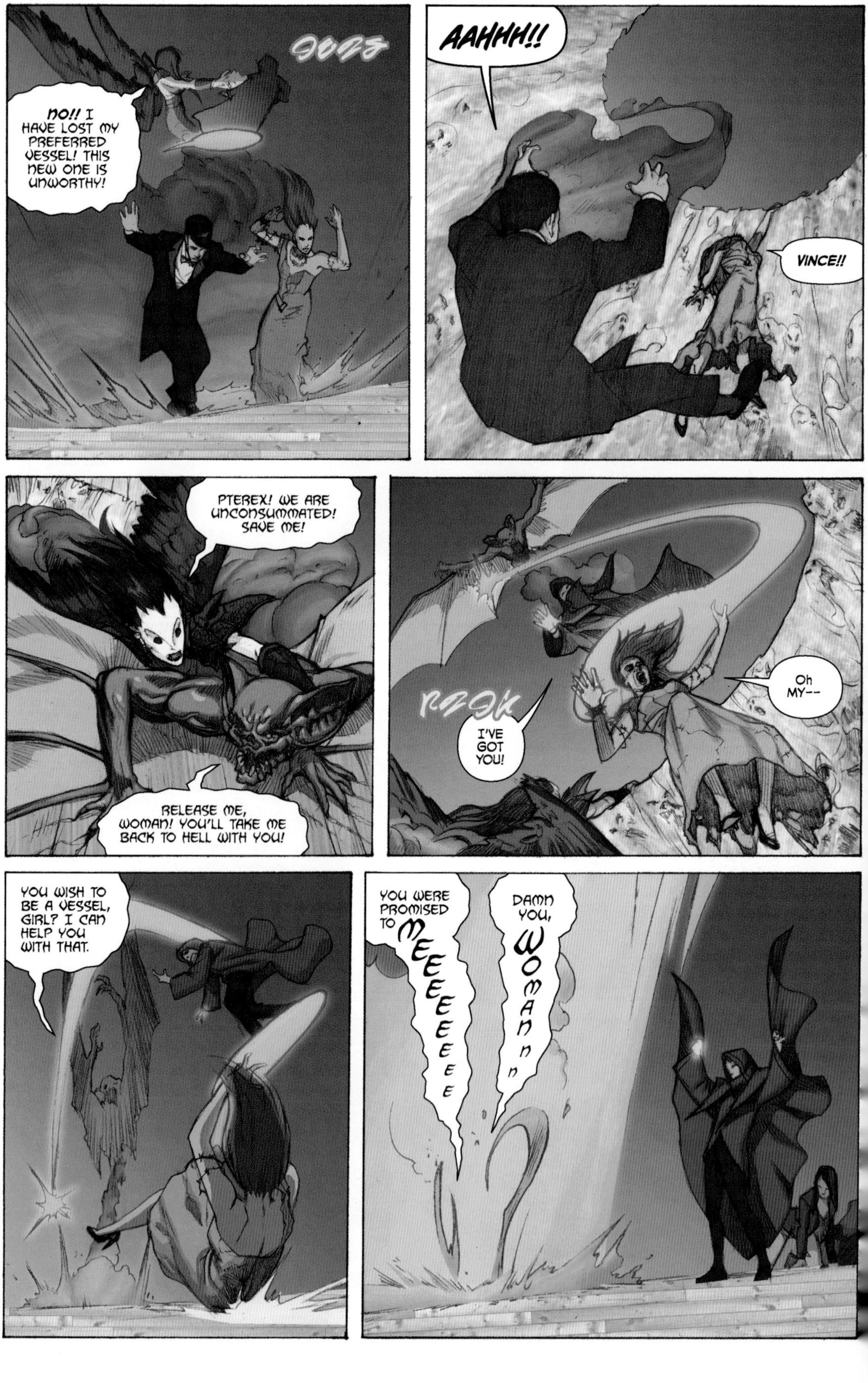
NO!! I HAVE LOST MY PREFERRED VESSEL! THIS NEW ONE IS UNWORTHY!
AAHHH!!
VINCE!!
PTEREX! WE ARE UNCONSUMMATED! SAVE ME!
RELEASE ME, WOMAN! YOU'LL TAKE ME BACK TO HELL WITH YOU!
Oh MY--
I'VE GOT YOU!
YOU WISH TO BE A VESSEL, GIRL? I CAN HELP YOU WITH THAT.
YOU WERE PROMISED TO MEEEEEEEE
DAMN YOU, WOMANnn

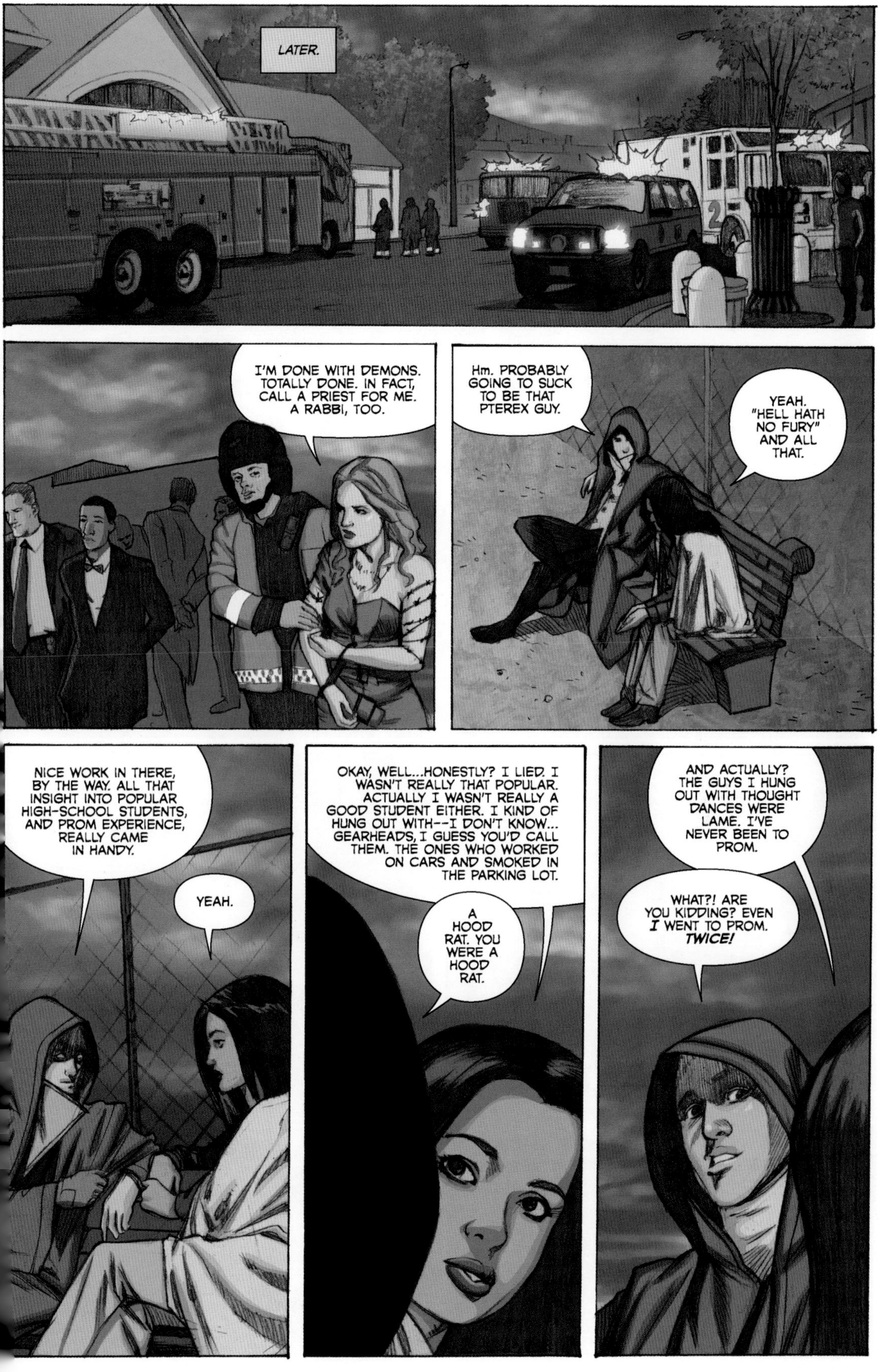
LATER.
I'M DONE WITH DEMONS. TOTALLY DONE. IN FACT, CALL A PRIEST FOR ME. A RABBI, TOO.
Hm. PROBABLY GOING TO SUCK TO BE THAT PTEREX GUY.
YEAH. "HELL HATH NO FURY" AND ALL THAT.
NICE WORK IN THERE, BY THE WAY. ALL THAT INSIGHT INTO POPULAR HIGH-SCHOOL STUDENTS, AND PROM EXPERIENCE, REALLY CAME IN HANDY.
YEAH.
OKAY, WELL...HONESTLY? I LIED. I WASN'T REALLY THAT POPULAR. ACTUALLY I WASN'T REALLY A GOOD STUDENT EITHER. I KIND OF HUNG OUT WITH--I DON'T KNOW... GEARHEADS, I GUESS YOU'D CALL THEM. THE ONES WHO WORKED ON CARS AND SMOKED IN THE PARKING LOT.
A HOOD RAT. YOU WERE A HOOD RAT.
AND ACTUALLY? THE GUYS I HUNG OUT WITH THOUGHT DANCES WERE LAME. I'VE NEVER BEEN TO PROM.
WHAT?! ARE YOU KIDDING? EVEN *I* WENT TO PROM. ***TWICE!***

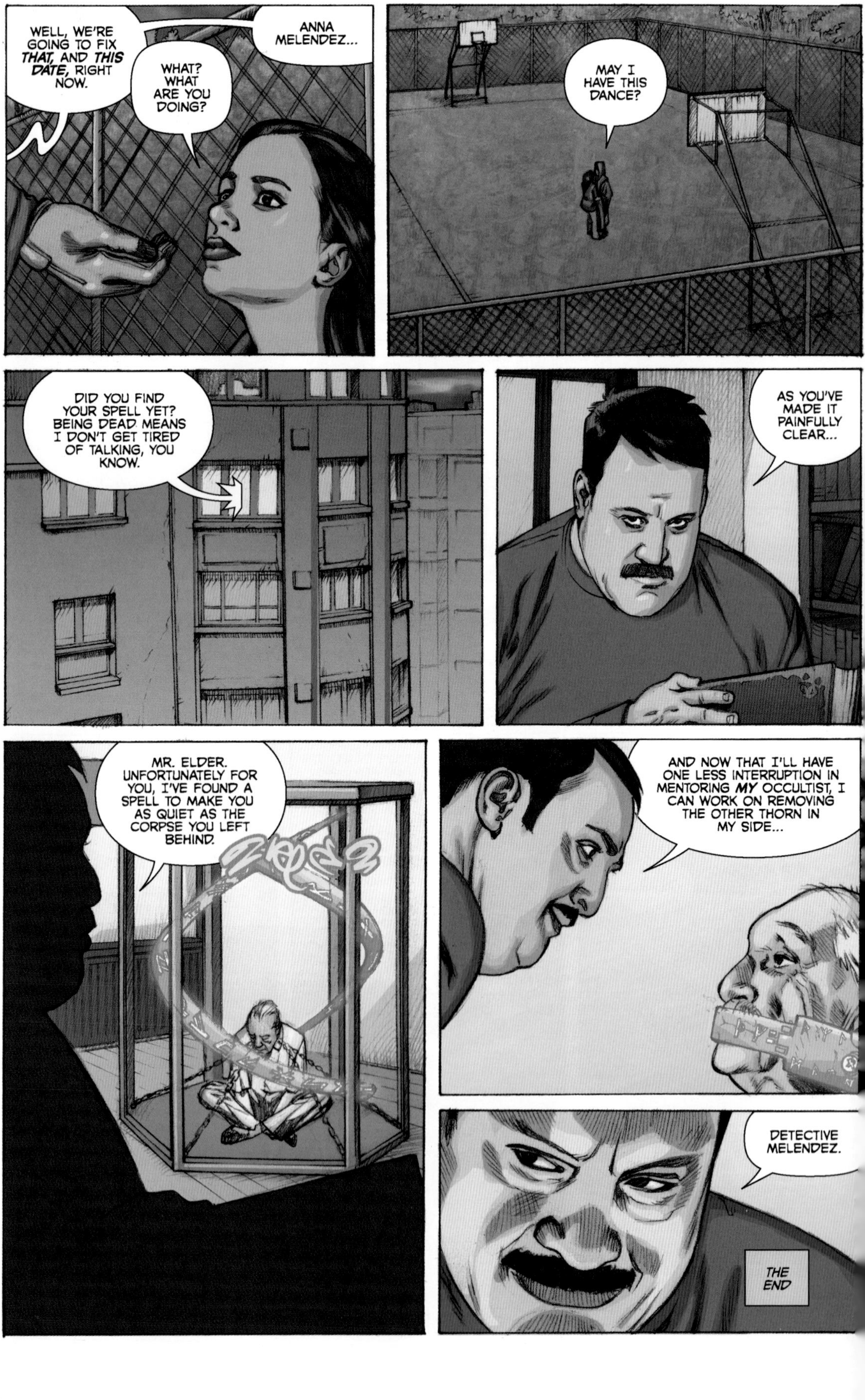
WELL, WE'RE GOING TO FIX *THAT,* AND *THIS DATE,* RIGHT NOW.
ANNA MELENDEZ...
WHAT? WHAT ARE YOU DOING?
MAY I HAVE THIS DANCE?
DID YOU FIND YOUR SPELL YET? BEING DEAD MEANS I DON'T GET TIRED OF TALKING, YOU KNOW.
AS YOU'VE MADE IT PAINFULLY CLEAR...
MR. ELDER. UNFORTUNATELY FOR YOU, I'VE FOUND A SPELL TO MAKE YOU AS QUIET AS THE CORPSE YOU LEFT BEHIND.
AND NOW THAT I'LL HAVE ONE LESS INTERRUPTION IN MENTORING *MY* OCCULTIST, I CAN WORK ON REMOVING THE OTHER THORN IN MY SIDE...
DETECTIVE MELENDEZ.
THE END

THE OCCULTIST SKETCHBOOK

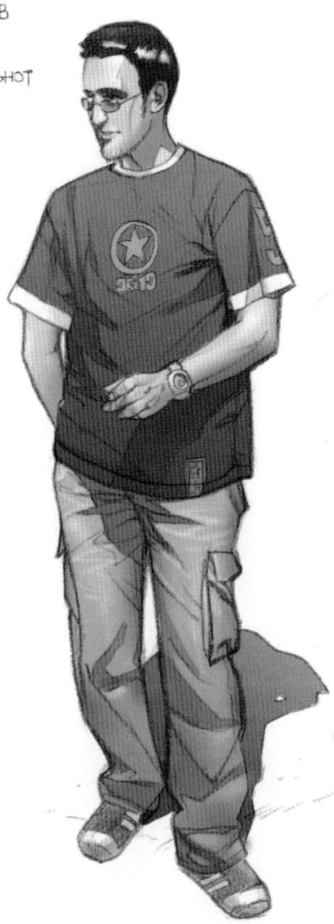
ROB
FULL SHOT

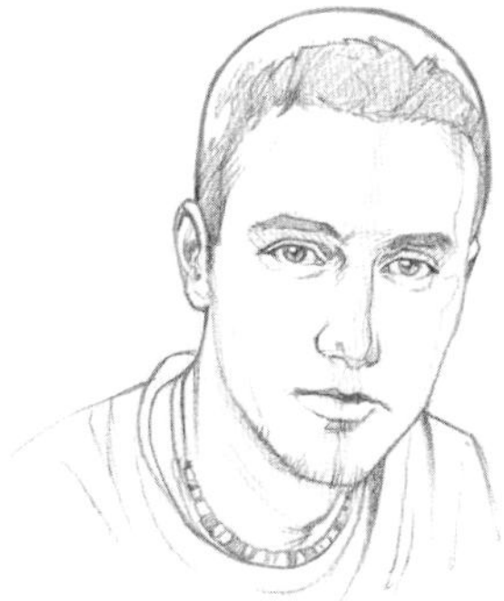
FRONTAL

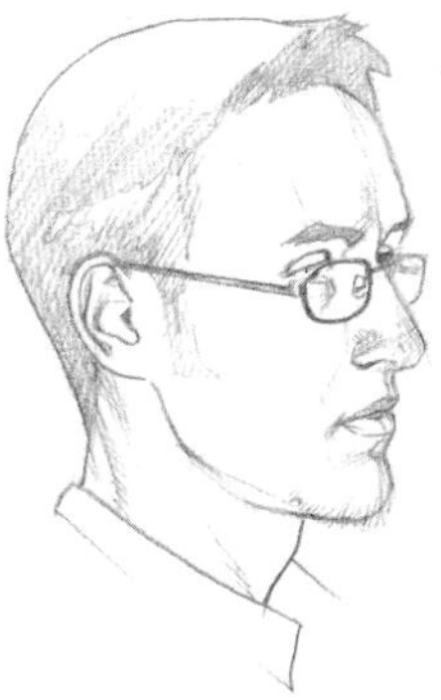
ANGLE

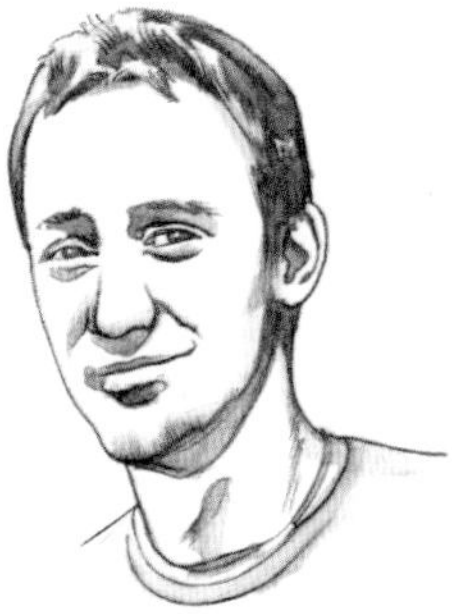

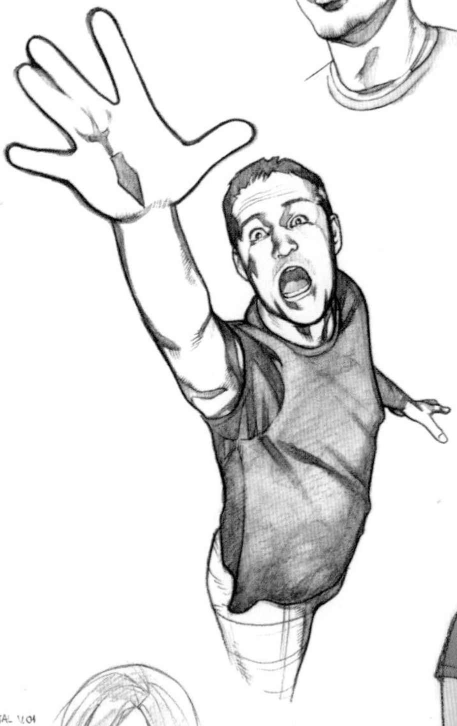

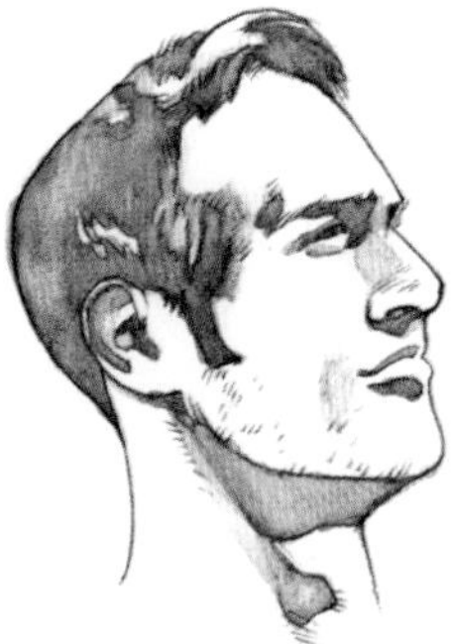

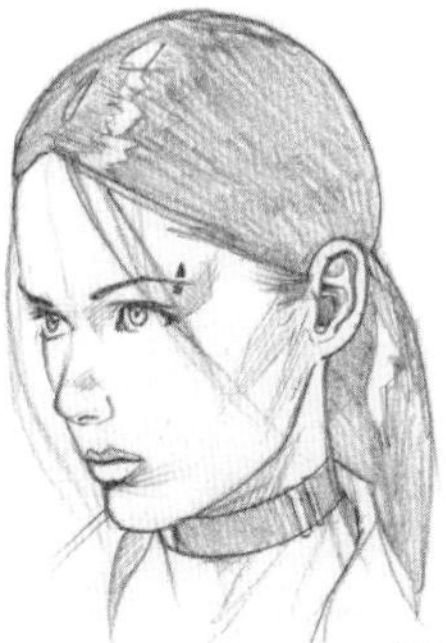
ANGLE V.01

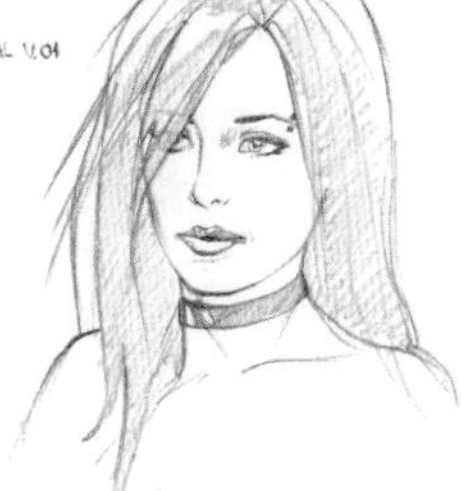
FRONTAL V.01

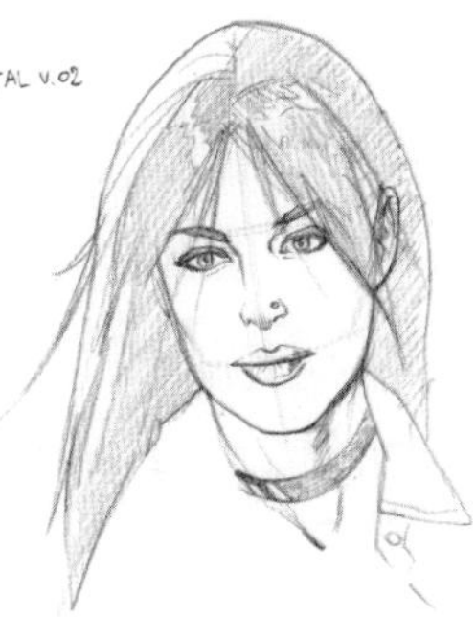
FRONTAL V.02

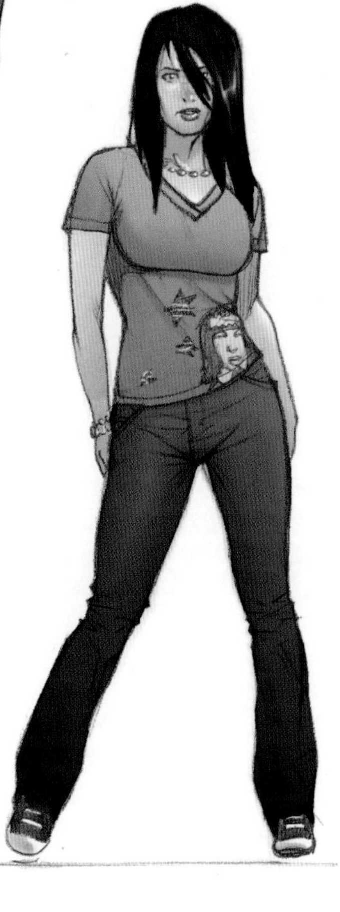

The image on page 2 of this book was the original Occultist model sheet, by Guy Davis, based on a dream Mike Richardson had. A lot of the story that Mike and Tim Seeley came up with evolved out of Guy's original drawing. Victor Drujiniu was left to design Rob (the character under the cloak), as well as his girlfriend and his many adversaries.

Victor had designed most of the villains for the last page of the first standalone issue (chapter 1 in this book), but the second time most of them were drawn was in the wraparound cover by Steve Morris for the follow-up miniseries, an image we've reused for the cover of this book. Steve tackles a cover in pieces, compositing with different colors in order to keep track of the separate bits.

Facing: A "classic" tale of the Occultist, from his fabricated silver age stint as a jungle character. Tim Seeley put the page together with regular collaborators on his excellent *Hack/Slash* series from Image Comics: artist Kyle Strahm, colorist Mark Englert, and letterer Crank!

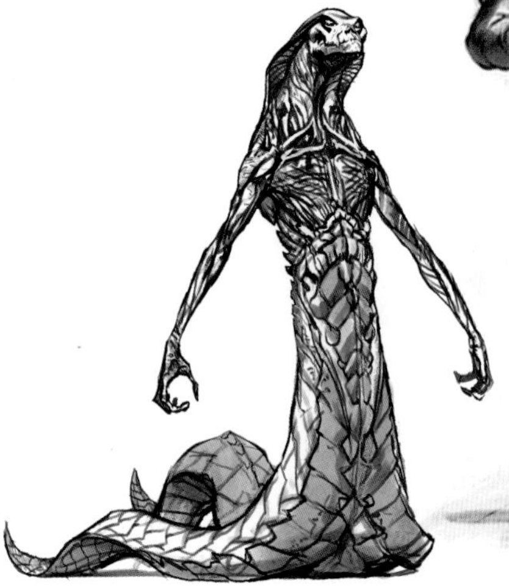

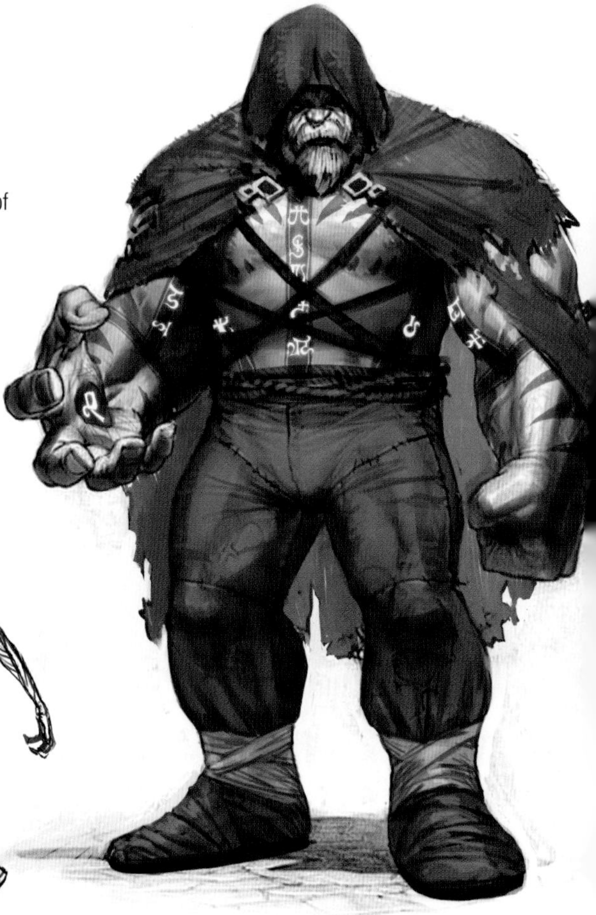

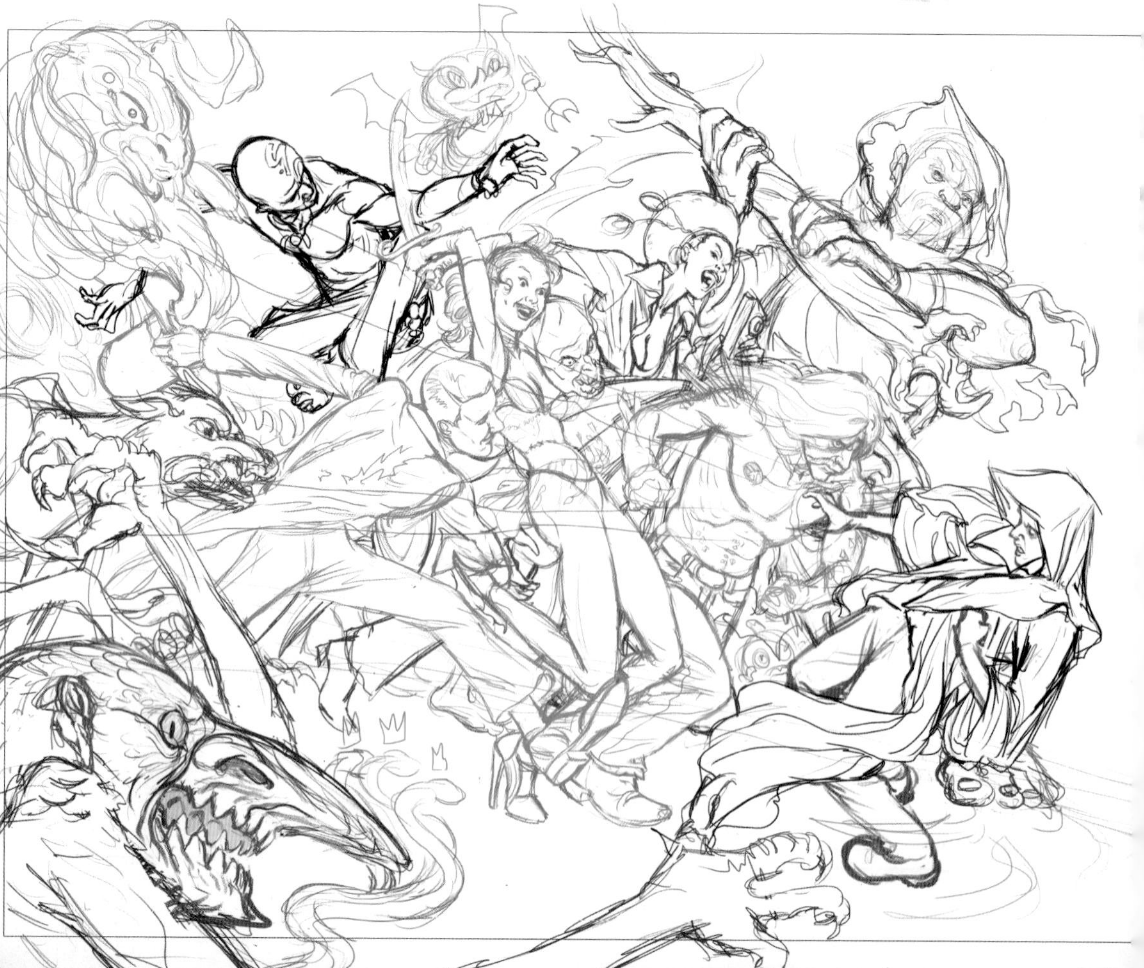

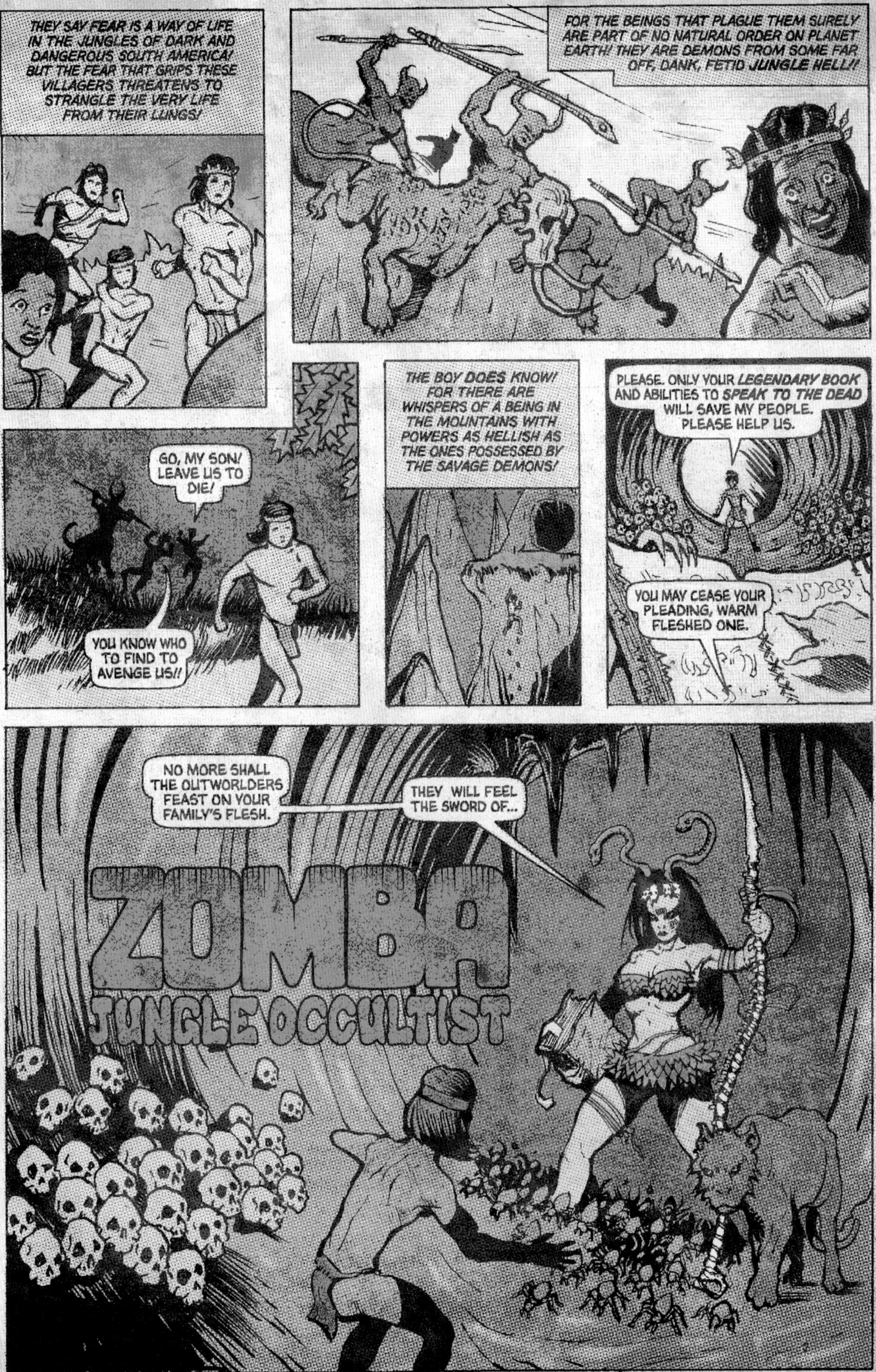

THEY SAY FEAR IS A WAY OF LIFE IN THE JUNGLES OF DARK AND DANGEROUS SOUTH AMERICA! BUT THE FEAR THAT GRIPS THESE VILLAGERS THREATENS TO STRANGLE THE VERY LIFE FROM THEIR LUNGS!
FOR THE BEINGS THAT PLAGUE THEM SURELY ARE PART OF NO NATURAL ORDER ON PLANET EARTH! THEY ARE DEMONS FROM SOME FAR OFF, DANK, FETID JUNGLE HELL!!
GO, MY SON! LEAVE US TO DIE!
YOU KNOW WHO TO FIND TO AVENGE US!!
THE BOY DOES KNOW! FOR THERE ARE WHISPERS OF A BEING IN THE MOUNTAINS WITH POWERS AS HELLISH AS THE ONES POSSESSED BY THE SAVAGE DEMONS!
PLEASE. ONLY YOUR LEGENDARY BOOK AND ABILITIES TO SPEAK TO THE DEAD WILL SAVE MY PEOPLE. PLEASE HELP US.
YOU MAY CEASE YOUR PLEADING, WARM FLESHED ONE.
NO MORE SHALL THE OUTWORLDERS FEAST ON YOUR FAMILY'S FLESH.
THEY WILL FEEL THE SWORD OF...
ZOMBA
JUNGLE OCCULTIST

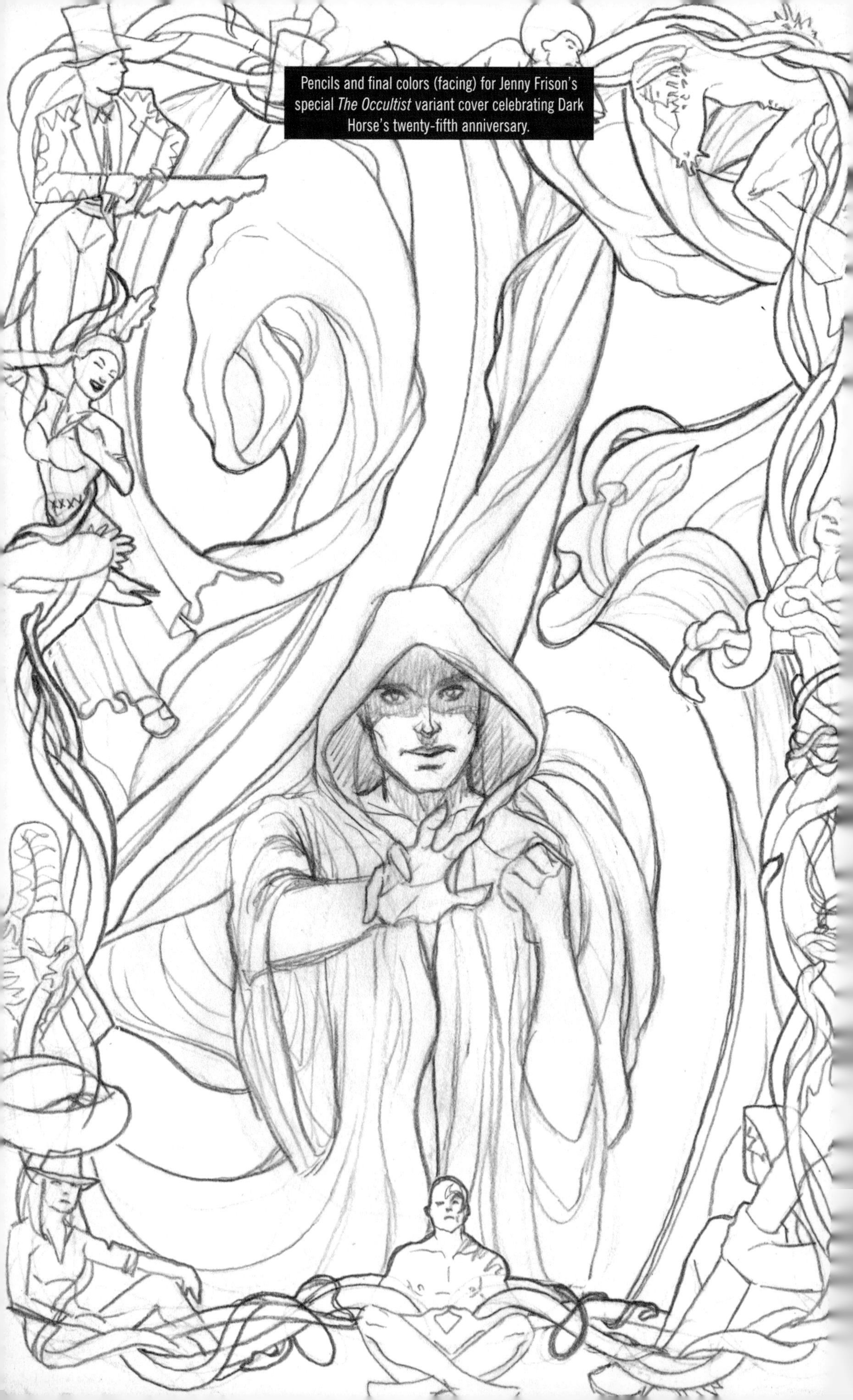

Pencils and final colors (facing) for Jenny Frison's special *The Occultist* variant cover celebrating Dark Horse's twenty-fifth anniversary.

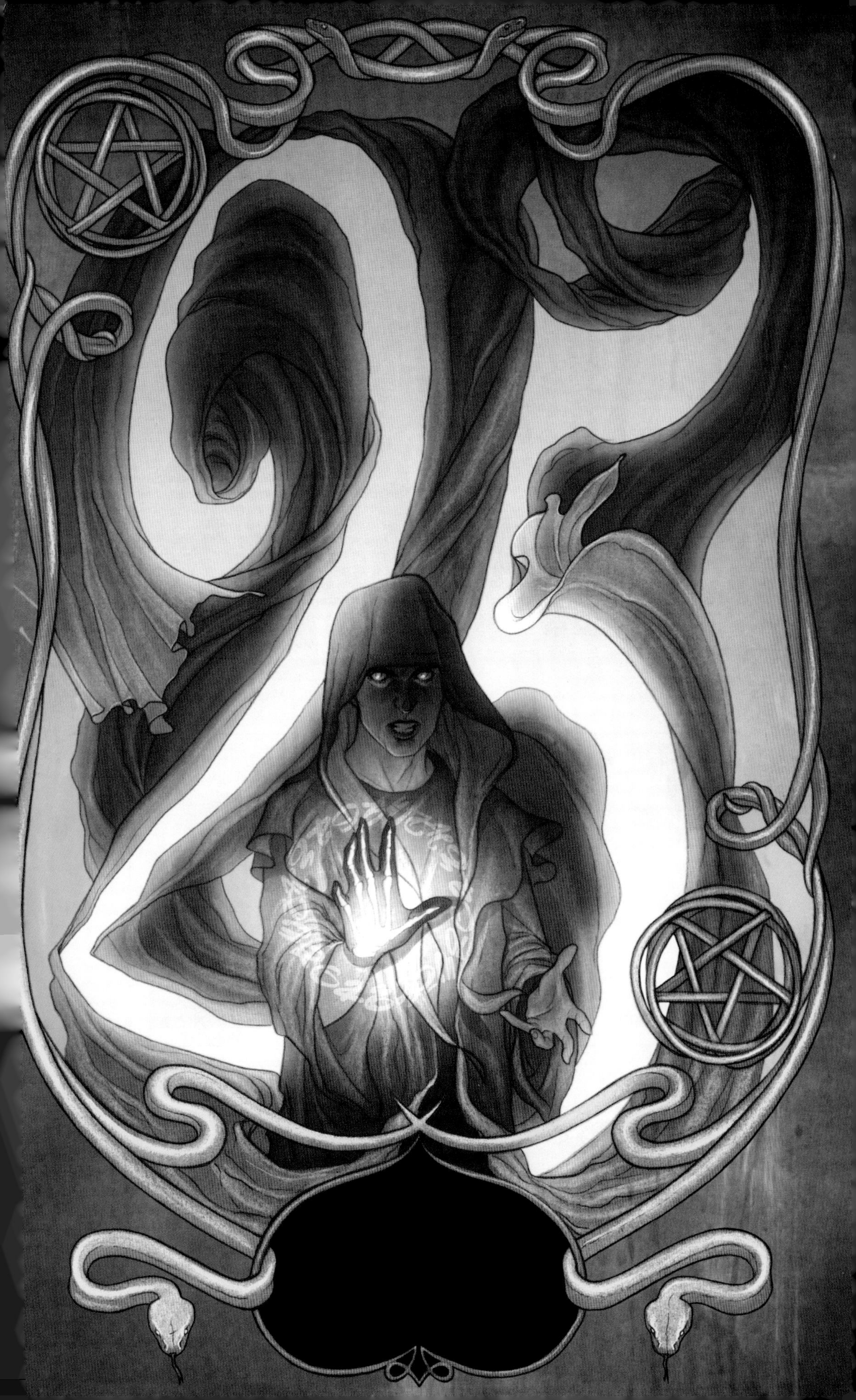

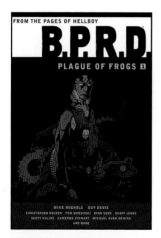